MotoGP
Season Review 2007
Julian Ryder

Published in November 2007

A catalogue record for this book is available
from the British Library

ISBN 978 1 84425 451 4

Library of Congress catalog card no 2007931177

Haynes Publishing, Sparkford, Yeovil,
Somerset BA22 7JJ, UK
Tel: +44 (0) 1963 442030
Fax: +44 (0) 1963 440001
E-mail: sales@haynes.co.uk
Website: www.haynes.co.uk

Haynes North America, Inc.,
861 Lawrence Drive, Newbury Park,
California 91320, USA

Printed and bound by J.H.Haynes & Co Ltd,
Sparkford, Yeovil, Somerset BA22 7JJ, UK

This product is officially licensed by Dorna SL,
owners of the MotoGP trademark (© Dorna 2007)

Managing Editor Louise McIntyre
Design Lee Parsons, Richard Parsons
Sub-editor Kay Edge
Special Sales & Advertising Manager
David Dew (david@motocom.co.uk)
Photography Front cover, race action and portraits by
Andrew Northcott/AJRN Sports Photography – except
the Norick Abe pictures on page 181 by Gold and Goose,
the bike-change pictures in the reports of Le Mans and
Motegi by Neil Spalding, and the giggling girls on page
175 who were photographed by Toby Moody

Author's acknowledgements

Thanks to:

Andrew Northcott , who yet again supplied more stunning
photography than designer Lee Parsons could shoehorn
into this book, Dr Martin Raines and his all-powerful
database, Neil Spalding, Mat Oxley, Andy Ibbott, Peter
Clifford, Gary McLaren, David Dew, Yoko Togashi, Bradley
Smith and his family, Danny Webb, Eugene Laverty, Chaz
Davies and Dan Linfoot, the British racers who tried so hard
with greatly varying levels of support, Mike & Irene Trimby
and the staff of IRTA, Phaedra Haramis, Mark Hughes and
Merlyn Plumlee.

Special thanks to Wayne Gardner for agreeing to write
the Foreword.

CONTENTS
MotoGP 2007

2007. THE BEGINNING

OF THE STONER AGE

Shell
ADVANCE
MOTORCYCLE OILS

FOREWORD
WAYNE GARDNER

What an unpredictable year it's been. Australia has a new World Champion and I am very proud of him. Casey Stoner's Championship has been great for Australian motorsport.

This has been a year of huge changes, first with the change in capacity to 800cc and the new tyre regulations. I've ridden a 990 (and as you can see from the picture on the right, I am about to ride Casey's winning 800) so I and understand a little bit about how they work, but I was curious to see what would happen with the 800s. What we got was higher corner speeds, shorter braking distances and lap times equal to or slightly quicker than last year. With less power on tap, the riders had to work harder in the corners and that meant the tyres and electronics had to be integrated better than ever before. It wasn't about just the tyres or just the electronics, they both had to be spot on. I predicted this year that there would be a tyre war. There was a gap, but that was as much down to the electronics as the tyres.

I thought Ducati made a huge leap forward with their bike, Casey utilised his opportunity and did an exceptional job. What a turnaround in Casey now he's surrounded by a great team. Last year I was concerned for him, this year he raced impeccably. I haven't seen any mistakes from him all year.

At the start of the season I think it's fair to say you could see Casey had a machinery advantage. The thing that really impressed me was that as the opposition improved and got faster, Casey managed to maintain his advantage – and we know that Ducati hardly changed the bike all year. Casey's going to be around for a long time, and if I was him I would be trying to keep the momentum going. Now that Casey has won his first title he'll find that next year is going to be an even bigger challenge, but I think he has a strong chance of retaining his crown.

I'll be watching with a lot of interest.

WAYNE GARDNER
WORLD CHAMPION 1987

THE SEASON
MAT OXLEY

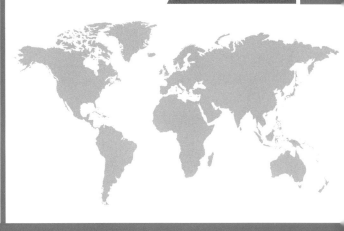

RED SUMMER

Casey Stoner and Ducati painted MotoGP red in 2007, making a little bit of history in the sport's year of transition

Valentino Rossi didn't know what had hit him. The seven-times World Champion had just sneaked inside Casey Stoner with a pass that would have made most rivals step onto the back foot for a moment. But not Stoner. The Aussie's counter-attack was immediate, his body language like that of a boxer moving in for the kill, head down, torso hunched over the handlebars, his Ducati a'wobblin' and a'shakin' as he gave it heaps and exploded back into the lead. This didn't happen once at June's Catalan GP, it happened half-a-dozen times, and it was the best glimpse we had all year of Stoner's high-explosive aggression because at that moment he was still getting up to speed. By the time he had fully crystallised with his Ducati V4 and Bridgestone tyres, no-one could really see which way he'd gone.

Stoner and his Duke were the undoubted stars of the 2007 MotoGP series – the feisty young Aussie on a fiery red motorcycle. Cool, calm and personable off the bike, Casey is full of that controlled aggression that bubbles gently beneath the surface, ready to erupt the moment he rides out of pit lane. His childhood hero, Mick Doohan, was exactly the same. Both men share that same Aussie implacability, and Troy Bayliss has it too. It's all about keeping it low key off the bike, then giving it full throttle every second you're on the racetrack. Stoner isn't the cocky type, he doesn't do the strut. Like Doohan he has an Aussie tendency towards dry-as-dust understatement, such as saying, when he was on the verge of securing the title at Estoril, 'Things seem to be going quite well for us this year.' Also like Doohan, the throttle only really works one way for Stoner – he gives it heaps from pit exit to pit entrance, he doesn't do slow laps, and his out-laps and in-laps invariably look faster

Below Casey Stoner started 2007 after signing two life-changing contracts – his marriage to Adriana and his Ducati deal

than his rivals' race laps. He is awesome to behold.

Stoner has always been mightily quick, but in 2007 he was transformed from fast yet flawed to unerringly consistent, a sure-fire winner when things went his way, a dead-cert points scorer when they didn't. He kept it rubber side down in some tricky, rain-affected races during which it would have been all too easy to let the pressure get to him, and he was the same when he encountered technical issues during races: he simply rode around the problems. Casey is already a member of an elite club – one of the five youngest premier-class winners. The other four? Freddie Spencer, Mike Hailwood, John Surtees and Valentino Rossi. He is firmly in the pantheon, at 21 years old.

Rossi knew what was coming after Qatar – and not Qatar 2007, when Stoner beat the former champ for his first MotoGP win, but 2006, when the young Aussie battled for the lead on his Honda in only his second MotoGP race. 'Casey was racing like he's been in this class for ten years,' said Rossi at the time. Fourteen months later he had reason to revise his opinion. 'Stoner is riding like a god,' he said after the youngster had defeated him at Catalunya.

Rossi has huge respect for Stoner – probably more so than for any of the others with whom he has disputed tarmac over the years – and he was gracious in defeat, just like he'd been when Nicky Hayden took the title from him in 2006. And if he thought 2006 was bad, 2007 was much worse, MotoGP's former golden boy battered on all sides by the icy winds of misfortune: horsepower woes, tyre issues, a genius rival and the taxman hammering at his door – '112 million Euros please, Mr Rossi.'

Of course, there was no doubt that Stoner enjoyed a performance advantage all season, prompting Rossi to joke (probably not to the amusement of his team sponsors, Fiat) that 'I seem to have the Fiat and Casey has the Ferrari.' But Loris Capirossi, Alex Barros and Alex Hofmann all had Ferraris too, and yet between the three of them they couldn't amass as many points as did Stoner over the 18 races.

Nevertheless, Ducati worked a miracle in 2007, its Desmosedici GP7 undoubtedly the best machine on the grid, and the factory fully deserved to make history, the first non-Japanese marque to win the premier crown in more than three decades. No-one had expected that. Most of the paddock had presumed that Honda would build the fastest 800, but at the start of the season some learned pit-laners estimated that the Ducati had 20–30 horsepower on its rivals. Stoner's GP7 hit 324.7 km/h (201.8mph) at Losail in March 2007, which just so happens to be exactly the same speed that Yamaha's 990 M1 managed at the Qatari track the previous spring.

And the big red Duke wasn't just fast in a straight line. Stoner knew how to make it go around corners, wobbles and all, and its electronics were clear class leaders, something that Casey noticed the moment he stepped off his LCR RC211V and onto the GP7 at Valencia in November 2006. 'The traction control is really great, you can do what you want with it, it's always there to back you up, it's so nice. And the engine braking is great too, the bike never wants to step sideways into the turns.'

Ducati's secret is straightforward – plenty of hard work, lots of Bologna University ingenuity, and total

mastery of MotoGP's new-age electronics that are currently spiralling through a hyper period of development. The boys from Borgo-Paginale were so exact in their science that Stoner won September's San Marino GP and then ran out of fuel 50 yards before he got back to his pit. The GP7's architect, Filipo Preziosi (or 'precious' as some Ducatisti like to call him), got the GP7 so right that some of Ducati's rivals declared that their only hope for the immediate future was that the bike was already close to its full potential. As Rossi's crew chief, Jeremy Burgess, said mid-season: 'I hope Ducati have hit all their targets first time out, so they've no room to improve.'

Of course, whenever there's a change in motorsport technical rules it's normal procedure for one constructor to get it right, or very nearly right, while the rest are off the mark and have to play catch-up. Honda got it right in 2002 with its RC211V; this time it was Ducati who immediately got the most out of the new formula.

Honda did close the gap somewhat, but it took until July's German GP before the RC212V won its first race. Honda was red-faced – this was the company's worst start to a premier-class championship in almost three decades, since the oval-piston NR500 four-stroke's quixotic battle with the two-strokes. The RCV needed more power, more handling, more everything really. Of course everyone knew that HRC would get there in the end. At August's Czech GP some proper Honda horsepower arrived to put the RC212V top of the speed charts for the first time.

Did HRC get it badly wrong by preferring to ignore pneumatic-valve technology? Possibly, because by the end of the season they were the only factory competing with conventional valve actuation. Nicky Hayden, for one, doesn't expect Honda to get it wrong two years running. 'I just can't believe that Honda will bring anything other than a weapon next year,' said the 2006 champ. 'I mean, I'll sleep in the streets if they come with anything less than a straight weapon.'

Meanwhile Suzuki and Kawasaki were rejuvenated by their decision to build pneumatic-valve 800s. The GSV-R looked and sounded spectacular in the hands of John Hopkins, the American never backward in coming forward when commitment's required, his scuffed elbows more than adequate testimony to that. But it was the team's slow-burn talent, Chris Vermeulen – the yin to Hopper's yang at Rizla Suzuki – who won the bike's first GP at a soaking Le Mans, before the duo went on to become podium regulars. It was all very different from Suzuki's early efforts in four-stroke MotoGP, which Kenny Roberts Junior once famously described thus: 'It's like bringing a knife to a gunfight.'

Kawasaki's 2007 Ninja ZX-RR was without doubt the factory's best MotoGP bike so far, and certainly the biggest improver of the year. The Ninja was quick and easy to handle; it just needed a rider. Since they entered MotoGP in late 2002 with their first prototype race bike in two decades, Kawasaki have claimed that they've been building 'defensive bikes', gradually developing 'true and robust racing technology inside Kawasaki' before producing an 'offensive' machine. During 2007 the Ninja began to look like a bike ready to compete at the very front, so it was no surprise when Kawasaki went on the offensive in hiring the very best riders. It will be great to see John Hopkins in green in 2008.

The 18,000rpm (and counting) 800s were amazing

machines – perhaps 15–20 per cent less powerful than the 990s but just as fast around many tracks and actually faster around some. Over the full season the fastest laps of the 800s were on average just 0.062 seconds slower than those of the 990s (race by race, it looked like this: Losail –0.8 seconds, Jerez +0.3, Istanbul +1.1, Shanghai +0.6, Mugello +0.24, Catalunya +0.2, Assen +0.3, Sachsenring –0.27, Laguna –0.79, Brno +0.14, Estoril –0.42, Phillip Island +0.47, Sepang –0.02, Valencia –0.18.

The 2007 bikes were the inverse of the racing maxim that 'an extra 10 horsepower is the best way to ruin your handling'. With less power, nimbler handling (thanks in part to the smaller engines that allowed shorter wheelbase dimensions), better tyres and general year-on-year developments, the 800s were fast enough through the corners to sometimes more than compensate for their slower straight-line speed (the top-speed difference between the 990s and the 800s was not inconsiderable – 12.9km/h (8mph) at Catalunya, 10.7km/h (6.6mph) at Mugello).

Corner speed was the new deal. There was no other way to ride the bikes because they lacked the deep-down grunt of the 990s that had allowed men like Hayden and Loris Capirossi to sling their bikes sideways into turns and then bolt away from the apex with a monster handful of throttle. The 800s needed to maintain momentum through the corners for a rapid exit speed to compensate for their lack of torque.

At least that was the theory, but Preziosi believes that Stoner's approach owes less to smooth, arcing 250-style lines than to the good old-fashioned flick-it-in, fire-it-out

Above The best riders of 2006 and 2007 – Nicky Hayden swaps with Casey Stoner

Below Ex-Yamaha man Ichiro Yoda's team built a seriously quick Ninja

Top Dani Pedrosa, here with brolly boy Alberto Puig, scored the largest victory margin of the year in Germany

Above Ducati boss Livio Suppo guided the Italian brand to an historic first MotoGP title

Below Yamaha's Masao Furusawa – necessary more horsepower. At Qatar, Ducati's 800 was as fast as Yamaha's 990

technique employed to such devastating effect by fellow former dirt-trackers King Kenny Roberts, Wayne Rainey and Mick Doohan. 'Casey makes very sharp corners so he doesn't stay at full lean angle for very long,' reveals Preziosi. 'Then he picks up the bike as soon as possible, so he can use all the power.'

Of course, all things are relative. The real secret to Stoner's success is that he has used his genius and Ducati technology to morph the two styles – the rapier cut of the 250 and the bludgeoning punch of the dirt-tracker – to leave his rivals baffled, bewildered and badly beaten. It's what the greats do, creating their own riding style by blending different elements of different techniques, as Doohan did in the early 1990s when he combined his tyre-smoking exits with dazzling corner speed, thanks to Michelin's latest radial front tyre. Stoner was simply the only man who could tame the Ducati, using massive aggression to get the bike steered through turns and riding through the wobbles, while the other Duke riders struggled.

Nowadays the trick is for riders to harness the rapidly developing electronics technology and use it to allow them to get more out of the engine, the chassis and the tyres. Electronics are now fundamental in MotoGP, just like they've been for years in F1 cars, demanding as much of a crew's time as suspension set-up and tyre choice. They are inevitable because they allow riders to ride faster and more safely, but not everyone is convinced they are good news. FIM president Vito Ippolito was one of these. 'More and more, electronic technological devices are levelling things out towards the lowest level of rider talent,' he lamented.'This may diminish the attraction generated by battles between the riders, which would be a great loss for the sport.'

Many MotoGP riders aren't sure that ultra-sophisticated electronics are good for the sport, but they have a love/hate relationship with the technology. They appreciate traction control, engine-braking control and all the other on-board control systems because without them they'd be in trouble, but they resent the technology because it takes some of the fun out of the motorcycles and allows lesser riders to get on the pace.

Stoner is aware of this paradox. 'To race four-strokes with this much power you need electronics to keep the engines smooth without risk,' he said. 'If the power was turned down they would be easy to ride, but without electronics they would not be smooth and actually pretty lethal.' But, at the same time, the World Champion mourns the fact that technology has taken

some of the wildness out of racing, and he has regrets not so much for the passing of the 990s but for the wildest bikes ever known to GP racing – the rip-snorting 500 two-strokes – which he used to watch on TV as a child. 'I miss the 500s,' he said. 'Right now I'd be happier if we were riding 1500s instead of 800s – they'd be real beasts!'

But electronics are here to stay – no rider is unilaterally going to discard the technology and there is no way that electronics are going to be banned. The genie is out of the bottle and it can't be put back, because progress cannot be denied; it simply isn't possible, whatever the rights or wrongs. And there is no doubt whatsoever that they've made premier-class racing much safer. Toni Elias proved that it's still possible to get hurt badly on a rider-friendly MotoGP bike when he lost the front at Assen and broke his left femur, but traction control has mostly banished the highside, once the biggest cause of broken bones. As Colin Edwards said: 'These days we start a lot of GPs with full and healthy grids. In years past I don't know how many times guys like Schwantz, Rainey and Doohan rode with broken arms and legs. The technology definitely makes it safer, so you don't have so much of that ass pucker going on.'

Certainly, the people who run MotoGP will be watching the 2008 F1 series closely to gauge how their move to control ECUs, with zero traction control, works. But could you apply such a system to bikes? Motorcycle performance is much more complex, much more nebulous than car performance, and the safety factor also looms larger.

Concerns over the sport's technological future were not the biggest paddock talking point during 2007. There were much graver, more immediate worries which followed a run of processional races. Dorna knows full well that the sport lives and breathes by its TV audience figures, and if fans are turning off their tellies because they're not getting excited by the racing, that's bad news for everyone.

The pack did get a lot more strung out during 2007, with few of the dogfights that we'd come to expect week in, week out during the 990 era. Generally it was Stoner way out in front, but not always. Pedrosa's German GP win boasted the biggest victory margin of the season – and, in fact, the biggest margin of the four-stroke MotoGP era. Understandably Casey got fed up with all the talk of boring races and might have echoed Doohan's wise words when Mighty Mick was accused of making racing boring in the mid-1990s: 'What do you want me to do, slow down?'

The 800s weren't as much to blame – though their lower top speed and faster corner entry shrinks the braking zone and thus makes overtaking more difficult – as the new tyre rules. Well, the tyre rules themselves weren't at fault, but MotoGP's first-ever tyre restrictions did upset the status quo, and they tended to exacerbate the differences between the tyre brands at each racetrack. As Hayden said: 'Now it just seems like so much of your race is decided on Thursday afternoon, when you choose your tyres. If you choose the wrong batch it's hard to dig yourself out of that hole. I think it's hurt the racing, whereas before, come Sunday, everyone was pretty close because during practice you'd eventually try a tyre that worked.'

While Bridgestone's investment and commitment

were richly rewarded with its first MotoGP title, Michelin took time to adapt to the new rules, perhaps because the French company had previously been able to produce overnight tyres at many events; or maybe it was the new testing restrictions that hurt them. Michelin worked very hard during the season to get back on the pace but, due to testing restrictions, were unable to test with their MotoGP riders between the Catalan and Brno GPs – that's a gap of two months, much too much in a seven-month season.

Bridgestone dominated more often than not, supposedly because their tyres worked well over a broader range of operating temperatures, a very desirable performance factor when limited to a set number of tyres.

Dorna, shocked into action by a handful of not-so-exciting races, came close to introducing a single-tyre rule for 2008, but some wise counsel from up and down pit lane persuaded them otherwise. Motorcycle GP racing has always been about pure speed – it shouldn't be about contrivances, so Stoner was bang on the money when he said: 'This class is about prototypes, it's not about everyone going out on street bikes, so tyres should be prototypes as well. If everything is one tyre or one bike then we might as well go and ride in the R6 Cup.'

Control tyres dumb technology down, hinder development and thus spoil the R&D kickback that ultimately benefits street riders, a crucial element in motorcycling since race machines and street machines are much more closely allied than in the car world. Remember when Colin Edwards rode his M1 on Michelin's Pilot 2CT street tyres in early 2006? That would never happen with an F1 car on street tyres.

And you have to wonder where MotoGP tyre development might be if there had been a single-tyre rule since the advent of the four-strokes. Tyres have come a long way since Rossi found that Honda's RC211V would destroy a 500 tyre in just five laps during the winter of 2001–2. Indeed, MotoGP rubber technology has developed so well that tyres have played their part – along with fancy electronics – in sucking the sideways action out of MotoGP. The trigonal rear slicks developed by Michelin and Bridgestone over the past half-decade or so have also reduced wheelspin by putting much more rubber on the ground. Ducati Corse boss Claudio Domenicali believes it is fast-improving tyre performance that is at the heart of the 800s' impressive lap times. 'The improvement in tyres is greater than the loss of 20–25 horsepower,' he said.

MotoGP in 2007 was a year of transformation – new bikes and new tyres – so it was hardly surprising that everything wasn't perfect. Let true competition take its course and watch the vanquished forces of 2007 come out fighting in 2008. It's going to be great seeing HRC and Yamaha stung into action and there's plenty more to look forward to: Jorge Lorenzo, James Toseland, Andrea Dovizioso and Alex de Angelis stepping up, Elias, Marco Melandri and Sylvain Guintoli on Ducatis, Hopper on the Ninja and Capirossi on the Suzuki...

Above Rizla Suzuki boss Paul Denning fired up the factory to produce its first competitive MotoGP bike

Below Lorenzo and Rossi – we will watch with interest as their relationship develops in 2008

1 2007
MotoGP
CAMPIONI DEL MONDO

Champions!

Ducati Stores & Dealerships

Avon
DUCATI BRISTOL
Bristol
Tel: 0117 9588777

Buckinghamshire
DUCATI AYLESBURY
Westcott
Tel: 01296 655759

Cambridgeshire
St Neots Motorcycles
St Neots
Tel: 01480 212024

Cheshire
DUCATI MANCHESTER
Knutsford
Tel: 01925 753958

Derbyshire
Clay Cross Powersports
Chesterfield
Tel: 01246 250128

Dorset
Three Cross Motorcycles
Wimborne
Tel: 01202 824531

Essex
Parkinson Motorcycles
Colchester
Tel: 01206 368500

Hyside Motorcycles
Romford
Tel: 01708-763360

Greater Manchester
Italsport
Bury
Tel: 0161 797 6124

Hampshire
W.M. Snell
Alton
Tel: 01420 84480

Moto Rapido
Winnall, Winchester
Tel: 01962 877998

Hertfordshire
Red Dog UK Ltd
Potters Bar
Tel : 01707-663344

Kent
Motorline Ducati
Ashford
Tel: 01233 648686

Lincolnshire
Italia Moto
Lincoln
Tel: 01522 511851

London - Central
Metropolis
London
Tel: 0207 793 9313

Middlesex
Daytona Motorcycles
Ruislip Manor
Tel: 01895 675511

Norfolk
Seastar Superbikes
Newton Flotman
Tel: 01508 471919

Somerset
Riders of Bridgwater
Somerset
Tel: 01278 457652

Surrey
Pro Twins
South Godstone
Tel: 01342 892888

West Sussex
CMW Motorcycles
Chichester
Tel: 01243 782544

P&H Motorcycles
Crawley
Tel: 01293 413300

Tyne & Wear
M&S Motorcycles
Newcastle upon Tyne
Tel: 0191 261 0121

Warwickshire
DUCATI COVENTRY
Coventry
Tel: 02476 335300

West Midlands
DUCATI WOLVERHAMPTON
Kingswinford
Tel: 01384 400234

Yorkshire - West
DUCATI LEEDS
Shipley
Tel: 01274 591620

Wales - North
Woods of Abergele
Conwy
Tel: 01745 822922

Scotland - Strathclyde
DUCATI GLASGOW
Glasgow
Tel: 0141 3334998

Ireland - Northern
Millsport Motorcycles
Ballymoney
Tel: 028 276 67776

Ireland - Southern
DUCATI DUBLIN
Dublin 12
Tel: 00 353 1 4603168

Channel Islands
Church Road Motorcycles
Guernsey
Tel: 01481 243281

Bikers
Georgetown Garage
Jersey
Tel: 01534 736531

Isle of Man
Jason Griffiths Motorcycles
Castletown
Tel:01624-825940

Ducati Service Centres

Berkshire
Pegasus
Reading
Tel: 01189 571977

Leicestershire
G-TEC Performance
Market Harborough
Tel: 01858 535411

London
Daytona Motorcycles
London
Tel: 0207 833 5866

Nottinghamshire
Cornerspeed
Nottingham
Tel: 01623 758877

Wales - South
Garlands Motorcycles
Haverfordwest
Tel: 01437 768434

Scotland
ERS Racing
Dunfermline
Tel: 01383 841752

Shirlaws
Aberdeen
Tel: 01224 584855

Ireland - Northern
Charles Hurst Motorcycles
Belfast
Tel: 02890 381721

Casey Stoner, on his Ducati Desmosedici GP07, has won the MotoGP World Championship. The entire Ducati world congratulates Casey, Ducati Corse and all of the engineers, designers, mechanics and team members, as well as all sponsors, who made this wonderful dream a reality. Another world title, another day for all Ducati fans to remember.

ADVANCE is used by **DUCATI**

www.ducatiuk.com

VOTED FOR BY

Kousuke Akiyoshi	Toni Elias	Marco Melandri	Valentino Rossi
Alex Barros	Sylvain Guintoli	Shinya Nakano	Casey Stoner
Loris Capirossi	Nicky Hayden	Dani Pedrosa	Makoto Tamada
Carlos Checa	Alex Hofmann	Randy de Puniet	Chris Vermeulen
Chaz Davies	John Hopkins	Kenny Roberts Jnr	Anthony West
Colin Edwards	Olivier Jacque	Kurtis Roberts	

RIDERS' RIDER OF THE YEAR

The man who wins the championship isn't always the one his opponents think is the best. To find out who the MotoGP riders think is the fastest of them all, for the fourth year running the Official MotoGP Review polled every rider who has taken part in more than one race. They named their top six men, we counted the votes. Here are the results

1st
CASEY STONER
124 POINTS

2nd
VALENTINO ROSSI
103 POINTS

3rd
DANI PEDROSA
63 POINTS

5th
CHRIS VERMEULEN
38 POINTS

6th
NICKY HAYDEN
27 POINTS

8th
SYLVAIN GUINTOLI
11 POINTS

9th
LORIS CAPIROSSI
7 POINTS

4th
JOHN HOPKINS
60 POINTS

7th
MARCO MELANDRI
23 POINTS

10th
RANDY DE PUNIET
6 POINTS

There was precious little disagreement this year: Casey Stoner won the vote for the Riders' Rider of the Year (RROTY) with Valentino Rossi as the runner-up. No fewer than 20 of Casey's 22 rivals voted him their top man and 14 of them put Valentino in second place.

Of the two voters who didn't put Casey top, one rated him fourth and the other didn't vote for him at all – as this is a secret ballot we obviously can't reveal who that was! These two voters gave their first-place nominations to Rossi and John Hopkins.

Riders aren't allowed to vote for themselves (a rule that both Team Gresini men tried their best to ignore). Six points are awarded for a first place, five points for a second place, and so on down to one point for a sixth place. Casey had a substantial winning margin – 21 points – over Valentino, who himself had an even bigger margin – 40 points – over third-placed Dani Pedrosa. No riders placed Rossi lower than fourth.

The candidate with the widest spread of votes was Hopkins: voters had him everywhere from first to sixth, and only five didn't vote for him at all. In previous years John has regularly been the man who finished with a higher position in our vote than in the Championship points table; this time he was fourth in both, and only three points behind Pedrosa.

In 2007 the man who was held in more regard by his peers than the Championship table would suggest is Sylvain Guintoli. The Rookie of the Year may only have been 16th in the overall classification but in our poll he ended up an impressive eighth. Rossi, Chris Vermeulen, Nicky Hayden and Randy de Puniet were also placed higher in the vote than in the Championship table.

Looking back to the 2006 top ten, eight of the same riders were present in the 2007 rankings. Carlos Checa and Kenny Roberts Jnr slipped out of the charts, to be replaced by the Frenchmen – de Puniet and Guintoli.

The shock in this year's vote mirrors the Championship itself. Twelve months ago Loris Capirossi won the Riders' Rider of the Year by the narrowest possible margin from Rossi. This year he slumped to ninth, even lower than his Championship finish. Maybe it's like a shark sensing blood in the water; once a racer senses a weakness in an opponent he can't help but exploit it. This might explain why only nine riders voted for Marco Melandri. This phenomenon was very noticeable at the end of the 2006 season when Rossi, who had finally been shown to be fallible, lost the top spot even though in the two previous years he had won by massive margins. Conversely, Hayden was only voted fourth-best rider by the rest of the field in his Championship year, but this year, despite dropping to eighth in the Championship, he has only slipped two places in our poll, to sixth. Vermeulen's stealthy progress this season is mirrored by his rise from tenth to fifth in our poll.

In previous years, votes have been spread right down the field. This season it was very clear who the riders regarded as the top men. See how the number of voting points plummets once you get below fourth place. The 2007 season may have been one of massive changes, with 800cc bikes and new tyre regulations, but the riders haven't had their minds changed too much about who are the fastest racers out there.

TECHNICAL REVIEW

NEIL SPALDING

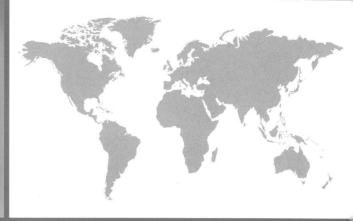

THE POWER & THE GLORY

The bike was right, the fuel strategy was right, the tyres were right – and in Stoner Ducati found a man who could ride the bike as it was designed to be ridden; very, very hard

Ducati spent four long years painstakingly developing their 990cc Desmosedici MotoGP bikes. Many hard lessons were learned and mistakes were made, but ultimately the wins started to come. In the entire 990cc era only three factories won races and towards the end of the formula, in 2006, Ducati were very competitive.

For 2007 the game was to change, with a new 800cc engine capacity and a 21-litre fuel limit which was seen by all as the real performance limiter. Ducati had fought against the new 800cc limit within the MSMA (the racing manufacturers' organisation) and had extracted a promise from Honda that they would not suddenly turn up with all their Formula 1 technology. Ducati, however, had clearly decided that if the rules were changing they were going to use everything they had learned to date and come out fighting.

The new machine is the product of evolution not revolution. Nevertheless, the only parts unchanged are the wheels. From the outside some aspects seem quite familiar: the Alan Jenkins-developed fairing is only slightly modified, the engine is still a V4 using desmodromic valve gear, and the chassis is still unique in using a latticework of steel tubes. But look more closely and it is clear that everything has moved on. This was not the fiddling round the edges that one sometimes felt occurred on the 990; this was a root and branch rethink.

THE ENGINE
Now 800cc, the 90-degree V4 keeps its unique desmodromic valve gear. Always the highest revving of the four-strokes, the new motor uses an even more radical bore-to-stroke ratio than the old 990, and that was the most extreme motor in motorcycling at 2.02.

Above Capirossi's bike in testing at Jerez. Note the separately mounted carbon-fibre rear subframe

Below Stoner's bike in the process of being stripped for an engine change; the abbreviated steel-tube chassis and 2-into-1 pipes for the screamer engine are clearly visible

system to work at these stratospheric revs should not be underestimated. It will have taken a lot of modelling to get a valve-closing rocker (which incorporates a 90-degree bend) to flex in a way that enhances the performance of the engine rather than simply breaking as the revs rise.

Desmo appears to have a key advantage, too. It appears that the Desmo system uses less energy than a valve-spring system, especially at lower revs, thus improving efficiency. All other valve-control systems use some form of spring, and when the valve is pushed open by the cam the spring has to be compressed, which takes energy. That energy is recovered when the valve comes back to its seat, but the valve gear soaks up some power in dealing with the energy fluctuations. On the racing Desmo there are no springs, just a pair of levers moved by the cam to open and close the valves, so it is lighter and more efficient. In addition, the lack of a spring means the valve opening and closing accelerations ('jerk' is the usual term) can be very violent, aiding top-end and mid-range power.

The later 990s used a crankshaft design called 'Softpulse' which fired all four cylinders during one revolution of the crank. This seemed to aid grip and make the rider feel more in control. For the 800, Ducati reverted to the screamer design of their first 990, reasoning that with the 800's much lower torque output, grip was not so much of an issue – and neither was there the need, now the electronic controls had evolved, to help the rider so much. The reasoning is simple. All the various irregular or big-bang firing sequences cost power, so airbox design and exhaust-pipe configurations all had to be imprecise in order to

Initial 800cc tests were done with an engine that was merely a shorter stroke version of the 990, which would have required a stroke of around 34.5 mm and a bore of 86mm, implying a bore-to-stroke ratio of approximately 2.5, well into the zone occupied by the most extreme Formula 1 engines.

Ducati had decided to go for full power – no low revving engines simply to save fuel, they were going to make as much power as possible and then work out how to finish the race. They have probably come back a little from their initial radical figures and a bore and stroke of 82 x 37.9mm giving a bore-to-stroke ratio of 2.165 seems more likely. Desmodromic valve gear was retained, this being a smaller version of the 'testastretta evolution' design used on Ducati's latest street engines. Ducati's achievement in getting this unique springless

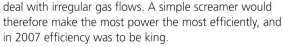

deal with irregular gas flows. A simple screamer would therefore make the most power the most efficiently, and in 2007 efficiency was to be king.

With a challenging but technically achievable BMEP of around 14 bar this could produce around 250bhp at the crank or 215bhp at the rear wheel at just over 20,000rpm. We know the engine can go to 20,500rpm, but it is very unlikely that the bike could finish the race on 21 litres of fuel if it did. Reliability would also suffer at these levels. In racing use 19,500 seems to have been the limit for most of the year, which would equate to 243bhp at the crank and about 210bhp at the rear wheel, again only with 'full fuel'.

Ninety degrees is the best V angle for a combination of power and smoothness, but it creates some packaging issues. On the original 990 bikes Ducati were always moving weight around and setting up the bike to try to compensate for the rearward weight bias that having a pair of cylinders pointing straight at the front wheel gave them. In designing the 800, therefore, the opportunity was taken to make the cylinder heads more compact and also to roll the whole 90-degree V backwards to obtain a little more clearance between the front cylinder head and the front wheel. Add these to the change in stroke and it is likely that the engine is between 10 and 12mm shorter than before.

ELECTRONIC CONTROLS

An engine does not make power in isolation, however. The 990 Ducati was always somewhat unruly and Ducati led the way in sophisticated electronics to try to calm down the way it delivered its power. The electronics

team at the factory consists of more than ten people, and while Magneti Marelli provide excellent hardware, it is software developed in-house that has given Ducati the ability to use the motor they have built.

The new 21-litre fuel limit is so restrictive that it fundamentally affects the nature of the competition. As a constructor there are two choices: build a slow bike and work it very hard on the track, or build a fast bike and find ways to cut back its fuel consumption. This latter strategy is the one that Ducati embraced.

Ducati seem to have decided that they could use 'sector fuelling', a strategy that allows them not only to set fuel maps for each gear but also for where the bike is on the track. It is not known how they decide where the bike is: the easiest and most reliable indicator would be distance, corrected three to four times per lap by the signal from the sector timing transponders. If they could save fuel in the twists they could use more where it really counted – onto and down the main straights. The snag was that running the bike very lean while leaned over would not give the 'feel' that riders need to open the throttle and accelerate off corners.

Historically Ducati have used three different traction control strategies: radically reducing ignition advance; closing throttle butterflies electronically; and deliberately misfiring different cylinders. All are used to reduce power and all do so in different ways. It is possible to change the ignition advance within one revolution of the engine, but the overall effect isn't that dramatic. Shutting the throttle butterfly is by far the most effective but it takes just a little bit too long, while deliberately misfiring different cylinders is fine as long as there is fuel

Top left The original catch tank was built into the carbon radiator surround, and its opaque construction led to insinuations that it was being used to carry additional fuel

Above left The clear plastic catch tank was added at Le Mans to underline that the only fuel on board was that in the tank

Above right The 2007 800 engine looks very similar to the older 990 but is more compact and the 90-degree vee angle has been rolled 'back' for better packaging in the chassis

AMBUSH!

Ducati's first public tests at Brno and Motegi in mid-2006 were stunning, with many engineers from opposing factories convinced they were watching a 990cc prototype. Then, suddenly, at the Valencia test, the bike was slow, revs were down and the whole point of the factory's testing appeared to be to improve fuel economy. Ducati never let the bike run fast during the whole of winter testing, leaving many observers asking why build a high rpm rocketship if they were unable to use it.

The answer came at the first GP, in Qatar. The Ducati ran the twisty sections of the track relatively slowly, just as everyone had got used to seeing. Then, on the main straight, the rocketship was back. No-one outside Ducati had expected it. The opposition never recovered, Ducati had seized the performance high ground and they never gave it up.

Opposite The Ducati garage was a very busy place at the Italian GP at Mugello

Below Casey catches up on his e-mails during a break in testing at Jerez

to waste. It is noticeable that in MotoGP this year there has been a lot less of the machine-gun noise that goes with a cylinder being deliberately misfired. With all these different ways of controlling traction – and the attitude to date has been to use them as little as possible because they all slow the motorcycle down – the next big hurdle is to be able to use them at full lean. This year's Ducati carries sufficiently sophisticated gyroscopes and accelerometers, and sufficient on-board computing power, to enable the traction control to be used at full lean.

Why concentrate so much on traction control? It is simply because Ducati's big leap forward was to provide a throttle system where the rider is not expected to try to feel for grip with a difficult-to-control, overly lean motorcycle engine. Instead, the rider is required to bang the throttle open and let the motorcycle's electronics deal with it. This is a major conceptual leap. Most riders have spent years not banging open the throttle at full lean; they would fully, and usually perfectly correctly, expect to fly straight over the top and towards an ambulance if they do. This year, however, Ducati have built a bike that requires the rider to do just that, so the rider simply has to trust the ability of the electronics to get him out of trouble, and his team's ability to set the bike up to let the electronics do it properly.

This is also why, in this Technical Feature, Casey Stoner has to be mentioned. Stoner has spent years developing the correct level of aggression and skill to deal with the world's best riders on the racetrack. His historic weakness has been a need for an ultra-sticky front end to deal with his assertive riding and to control the side-effects of his aggressive throttle use. What Ducati have done is put Stoner on a bike with the best front tyre in motorcycling – Bridgestone's slick – and find a way for the electronics to provide the throttle subtlety to allow the machine to be taken to the limit.

A side-effect of this, when looking at the other Ducati riders, is that their success is balanced by their ability to delegate one of MotoGP's most carefully learned skills: opening the throttle. Capirossi found the 'lean set-up' almost impossible to deal with, but if the bike was fuelled rich he could ride it very well. Ducati even built a one-off, fuelled-rich engine for him for Mugello; it was rev limited quite low and Loris promptly set much faster times in the more twisty sections of the circuit, but he lost speed on the straights where the engine could be clearly heard hitting the rev limiter. His win at Motegi was in a race where he swapped bikes, and where the fuel limit was therefore irrelevant.

SO WHAT ELSE CHANGED?

The chassis on the 990 was revised in 2006 using a more complex 'birdcage' construction latticework. More tubes but lighter and of smaller diameter were used to stiffen the chassis and to give the required rigidity under braking, yet still allow some flexibility for the best possible grip at high angles of lean. The 800 chassis for 2007 takes this a step further. Most of the tubes seem to be in the same places, but now the chassis stops where it bolts to the rear cylinder head. Where the previous version had extensions further back to support the seat unit, the new bike has a

separate carbon-fibre sub-frame supporting the rider, his feet and the tail bolted to the back of the rear cylinder head and the swingarm pivots. This seat unit is far more rigid than the older design, which took criticism for flexing when the rider tried to control the bike by weighting a footpeg.

The fairing also had a new undertray, but to all intents the main fairing was identical to the older bike's, just painted a little differently. The screamer firing order of the new motor meant that each bank of cylinders only needed one two-into-one pipe rather than the pair of tapering megaphones used for the last three years, and that meant the size of the undertray could be reduced. To reduce side-wind sensitivity a new, shorter top fairing was also tested at Brno and used at the notoriously blustery Phillip Island circuit. There is a price to pay in increased high-speed drag with this fairing, but increased stability on windy days more than makes up for that.

WHERE DOES THAT LEAVE US?

For 2007 Ducati built a new 800 using the most fuel- and power-efficient layout and design they could, a 90-degree V4 with a screamer crankshaft and desmodromic valve gear: no power-sapping balancers or long-bang firing arrangements here. MotoGP's best high-speed aerodynamic package was further fine-tuned. Then they added a world leading electronic throttle system to further manage their fuel use and a rider who could use it. Ducati have raised the technical bar a long way and it's going to take a while for the rest to catch up.■

RULE INTERPRETATION

Racing can be bitchy, and when someone grabs an advantage the size of Ducati's, all sorts of accusations fester just beneath the surface. Two came to the fore quite quickly in 2007.

All fuel tanks are required to vent into a catch tank, minimum capacity 250cc, but with no specified maximum. Ducati built a tidy carbon tank into the side of their radiator surround. Team Roberts used a similar idea, while most other teams used clear plastic containers located somewhere on the front of their bikes. As soon as the Qatar race was over the rumblings started, with Ducati effectively being accused of filling their catch tank with fuel and allowing the in-tank vacuum to pull that fuel into the tank as the first few laps went by. Ducati were so annoyed that, by Le Mans, they had fitted their own, highly transparent plastic catch tanks in the front of the fairing to prove they were not starting the race with them topped up – and it didn't stop them going fast or winning races!

The second accusation was more of a spoiler. The tail section of a race bike cannot be more than 150mm higher than its seat. That, of course, depends where the seat is measured from, and tellingly the rule book is not as specific on such points as might be expected once all the alternative ways of measuring the height of the hump have been worked through. Ducati decided not to risk any sort of protest and built new flatter-topped tail sections from Catalunya onwards.

opinionleader.i

my BEST **music**

THE BIKES
2007 MotoGP MACHINERY

DUCATI
DESMOSEDICI GP7

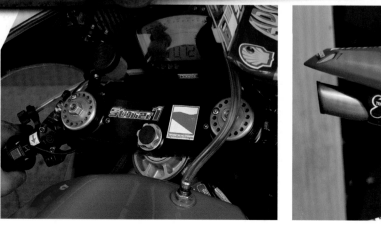

Right Casey seemed to prefer a bike with a longer set-up at the front, signalling a bike that responded well to a more aggressive style

Far right Prior to the Turkish race, a seat with a slightly higher top section was used, leading to complaints from other teams

Ducati spent four years campaigning the 900cc Desmosedici, their first new GP bike for a quarter of a century. It was fast but needed painstaking development, and the factory learnt an awful lot about Grand Prix motorcycling while getting their bike and their strategies fully competitive. The new 800cc formula was the first real opportunity to build a completely new motorcycle incorporating all those lessons. Issues that were something they just had to work around could finally be resolved, and with the 800cc category's new 21-litre fuel limit they had a chance to leapfrog their opposition.

The resulting motorcycle is the peach of the 800cc class. The engine is slightly shorter, with more compact cylinder heads, a rolled-back V angle and a slightly shorter stroke. This allows the engine to be placed ever so slightly closer to the front wheel, just enough to resolve some historic handling issues. The chassis tubes are shorter and the seat unit and tail are finally rigid enough for the rider's weight transfer to have a significant and consistent effect on handling. After four years of high-revving 990s, the 800 was in another league: it is capable of 20,500rpm. To let the bike run at these revs the mechanically opened and closed valves of Ducati's desmodromic system were accurate, reliable and – critically – very fuel efficient. And Ducati's electronics finally came of age. Spending four years learning to control the unruly 990cc engine meant they could apply the finesse that would allow an 800 to perform at its best on the minimum possible fuel.

Ducati also kept their strategy secret, managing to complete an entire winter's public testing without disclosing the bike's true performance. At the first race in Qatar opposing teams were left so dumbfounded by the Ducati's combination of speed and fuel efficiency that they could hardly believe it was legal. We are going to have to wait until the first race of 2008 to find out whether they have managed to catch up, because they certainly didn't in 2007.

Left Ducati remained faithful to their 'top of shock mounted to the bottom of swingarm' system, which allows them room to roll back the vee and still route their rear exhausts out

Far left To bleed all water through the radiator system, the mechanics would roll the bike from side to side to help release any trapped air

HONDA
RC212V

Right Honda used upwards of nine different exhaust pipe designs over the course of the year. This is the one used at the start; the main picture shows the final version

Far right Pedrosa used the original 'Unit Pro Link' chassis only once in the season, at Jerez. In this system the top of the shock mounts to a bracket on the top of the swingarm

Everyone expected the Honda to be among the most competitive of the new 800cc motorcycles: how wrong they were. The bike that rolled to the line at Qatar at the start of the year wasn't that much changed from the test bike first seen at Motegi in mid-2006; it was still slow and the front end still didn't give the rider any confidence.

The Honda is believed to be a 75-degree V, with a four-cylinder engine that has a balance shaft at the front of the crankcase. The cams are gear driven off the right-hand end of the crankshaft, with the gear train travelling up the side of the engine block to the double overhead cams situated in each cylinder head. The engine itself is an evolution of the 'Nicky Hayden special' RC211V (see 'The Ghost Bike', *MotoGP Official Season Review 2006*), with the longest possible swingarm, the shortest possible engine and, seemingly in an attempt to help the lighter riders, quite a high centre of gravity. The new chassis was constructed entirely of aluminium sections created by CNC machining – a major change to the stampings used on all previous Honda designs. A completely new ECU and 'ride by wire' system was also debuted.

It was the high centre of gravity design feature that proved so difficult to change once the engines had been cast. The bike suffered badly from excessive forward pitch under braking. Rather than the front suspension being progressively compressed, loading the front tyre and improving front-end grip as the rider hit the brakes, this bike pitched forward, dramatically overloading the tyre and making it push, giving the front a vague and uncertain feel. The works bikes quickly started evolving, with at least nine different designs of exhaust pipe being used by the Repsol team riders. Some were there to try to produce a quieter pipe for Dani Pedrosa who, like Rossi, uses the sound of opponents' bikes to judge precisely where they are, but all were also supposed to extract more power. It would appear that the basic laws of physics say it is impossible to extract enough power out of an 800cc GP engine with all the pipes coiled underneath the engine.

While the works bikes were being developed, the customer teams were hung out to dry. By Brno they had some cause to celebrate, with new chassis and pipes being available, but these were small improvements, and they were expensive. The works bikes received regular engine and chassis upgrades. At the start of the year the engines were revving to 17,000rpm; by the end they were in the 19,000rpm region. Hayden and Pedrosa tried at least three basic designs of chassis, and undoubtedly several others with different flexibilities that were much more difficult to spot.

Left The Repsol works bikes quickly swapped over to a new frame design with 'Pro Link' rear suspension that mounted the top of the shock to the frame. 'Rider feel' improved dramatically

Far left To try and reduce the Honda's excessive desire to pitch forward, Gresini moved the steering head as far forward as possible and dropped the bike about 6mm

YAMAHA
YZR-M1

Right To maintain stability when trying to outbrake Stoner's Ducati, Rossi fitted bigger-diameter 48mm forks, and to allow the forks to flex for grip at full lean they were held by this flexible-top triple clamp

Far right For the high-speed straights at Mugello, Yamaha fitted the old fairing with these hand extensions. By Brno the Yamaha had a whole new fairing designed for better high-speed aerodynamics, as seen in the main picture

Yamahas have always been famous for their agility into corners and their ability to accelerate out of them. Yamaha prefers to win by using its advantages on a lot of small sections of the racetrack rather than merely concentrating on ultimate top speed. It was no different this year. Yamaha kept their trademark across-the-frame irregular-firing-order four-cylinder engine with its reverse rotating crank and merely re-engineered it as an 800. Believing that the fuel limit would cause everybody to build a slower motorcycle Yamaha chose, along with Honda, to stay with steel valve-springs and the calmer cam timing that this necessitated.

The chassis was a minor step forward compared to the one used by Rossi in the final version of the 990, his bike now having a non-adjustable headstock, with the seat unit and its mounts resembling the chatter-prone chassis of early 2006. Swingarm pivot position was also clearly quite similar to the 990, but it rapidly became apparent that the bike handled best with the swingarm pivot very close to its lowest possible position. Rossi and Edwards did move the swingarm pivot position a couple of times during the year, but they always ended up back at the extreme bottom end of its adjustment range, with the swingarm angle as flat as possible.

After unnecessarily restricting the red line on Rossi's engine at Qatar, fuel-consumption calculations rapidly improved. In Turkey, a higher revving engine arrived with a new exhaust system using shorter primary pipes and a revised sump casting to make room for them. There was a further upgrade for Mugello, or at least an exhaust system with even shorter primary system pipes. Yamaha debuted their long-awaited pneumatic-valve-spring motor at Misano, unfortunately suffering some form of bottom-end failure. Curiously, the new engine did not seem to rev any higher than the last version with steel valve-springs. What it could do was hang on to the peak power slightly longer, helping top speed and high rpm acceleration, and quite possibly improving fuel consumption by using valve accelerations that would not have been achievable with steel valve-springs. Yamaha started the year revving to about 18,000, reduced occasionally to improve fuel consumption, but by the end of the year the bikes were clearly capable of nearer 19,000rpm.

Many criticised Yamaha during the course of the year for not having a fast enough bike but, given the way that Yamaha designs its bikes to work, what hurt them far more was Michelin's grip crisis. Having to use tyres that, in the first half of the season at least, seemed to have lost their edge grip robbed the Yamaha of its ability to pick up the throttle accurately and quickly, and burst out of corners using its mechanical traction and very smooth engine to gain an early advantage on the straights.

Left Yamaha built a higher-revving engine for Valentino which required shorter exhaust pipes – and a new sump design to allow them to fit

Far left By Mugello Yamaha tried an exhaust system with an even shorter primary pipe length for better power at high rpm. This one was so short it could go around the old sump. A similar system was later used on the pneumatic valve spring bike

SUZUKI
GSV-R

Right The Suzuki's left handlebar has the customary clutch lever, front brake span adjuster and kill switch. Now launch control and pit lane speed limiter are added

Far right The right side has the normal twistgrip and front brake lever, now with a switch to change fuel maps and programmable up and down buttons that allow the rider to select anything from additional maps to different tickover levels for corner entry feel

Suzuki developed their new 800 in the 2006 season, so the bike that rolled out in 2007 was clearly a development of 2006's 990 machine, with the engine redesigned as an 800. The bodywork had been tidied up, with a cover over the 21-litre fuel tank replacing the exo-skeleton-style 22-litre tank used on the 990. Subtly different welds and shapes on the swingarm and headstock showed that different flexibilities had been designed to cope with the different chassis requirements of the 800. All 800s except the Ducati seem to spend substantially longer on their sides in the corners and this means that the flexibility designed to provide some suspension movement at full lean has to be both very carefully measured and very carefully controlled.

One area where the Suzuki has historically been extremely weak is in its mid-range grunt. The new design comprehensively solved that problem with quite a low revving engine but with a significant level of mid-range power. This was most evident on twisty circuits and in the wet, where the particular combination of Vermeulen's wet-weather riding skills and the Suzuki's drive and handling gave the team their first victory of the four-stroke era (and, coincidentally, the first-ever victory by a pneumatic-valve-spring engine in GP motorcycle racing).

Suzuki have continued to develop their own electronic throttle system with Mitsubishi, giving them a significant level of independence in this critical area. The extra year of research and development meant that the throttle systems as well as the engine were developed to better suit the new fuel limit. At the start of 2006 Suzuki's fuel pressure was similar to the rest of the bikes in pit lane at a – fairly low by automotive standards – 3.5 bar. However, by the end of the season it was at 10 bar, improving atomisation and quite possibly fuel consumption as well. This brings its own problems, however, with the higher fuel pressure apparently making it more difficult to control the way the power comes in at very small throttle openings.

Left Suzuki carried over much of the design of their last 990 to the new 800, the slightly smaller fuel tank capacity allowing a cover over the tank rather than continuing with the old 'exo-skeleton' style.

Far left Hopkins' slipper clutch uses two types of coil spring to get the desired overall rate and to adjust the 'feel' to his liking

KAWASAKI
ZX-RR

Right Kawasaki's new 800 keeps it simple with a 4-into-2-into-1 pipe, gear-driven cams and a coil spring slipper clutch

Far right In keeping with the rest of the bikes, the Kawasaki's gearbox uses a six-speed cluster in an easy-to-access cassette design

Last year's 990cc bike was Kawasaki's first fully made in Japan project for two years and the new 800 was a further development of that bike. The Kawasaki uses a fairly conventional across-the-frame four-cylinder engine with revised cam drive, pneumatic valve springs, and an irregular-firing-order crankshaft very similar to that used for the last three years by Yamaha. Like the Yamaha, the bike only needs to use a single balancer shaft to cope with engine vibration but, unlike the Yamaha, the Kawasaki's crank turns forwards.

Kawasaki quickly got to grips with PVRS, the Pneumatic Valve Recovery System. The first versions of the cylinder head had some reliability issues in testing towards the end of 2006, but Kawasaki's engineers managed to correct all the problems over the short Christmas break. The system comprises a regulated feed to the spring system running at between 14 and 16 bar, with a gas cylinder, pressurised at approximately 200 bar, sitting behind the cylinders to act as a 'top up'. The gas pressure is trapped in a sealed canister occupying the same space around the valve stem as the old steel spring. The gas inside the canister is compressed as the valve is lifted and returns the valves to their seats as soon as the cam moves away.

Kawasaki managed to improve performance without any increase in fuel consumption over the course of the year. Clearly some of this was down to the rushed initial design being perfected during the course of the year, but credit should also go to Kawasaki's rapidly evolving technical abilities.

The chassis was again a development of the last of the 990s; at least two different designs were used during the course of the year in the search for maximum grip. Without a doubt Kawasaki's initial choice of riders meant that crashing was a fairly frequent occurrence but, by the end of the year, results were better and the previous Kawasaki specialty of losing the front end going into a corner was not seen as often. This may simply be due to an improvement in overall competitiveness and bike set-up, or it may be that some fundamental chassis design issue was resolved.

Left Once the clutch is off, removing a single plate gives access to the gearbox

Far left Kawasaki kept the reservoir for their pneumatic valve spring system fully topped up with nitrogen at somewhere around 200 bar

Right Team Roberts used the knowledge they gained in late 2006 to build a chassis that wouldn't twist under any circumstances

Far right The shorter engine required a shorter main chassis and a longer swingarm. Team KR built new ones later in the year but started with extended 2006 ones

Kenny Roberts finally got a good engine for his team in 2006, with Honda's iconic 990cc V5 bringing power and reliability. A year's development and several top-six finishes later and Kenny Junior very nearly won the Portuguese GP. After years in the doldrums hopes were high for the new 800. Certain they had made major advances in design during 2006, the new-for-2007 chassis incorporating everything they knew. The team invested in the latest Ohlins suspension and even built new fairings. They kept their central air intake and straight exhaust pipes with the exhaust exiting through the seat hump (refusing to follow Honda's house style).

In racing many things are needed in order to finish well, but the four most critical are a good rider, a quick engine, a responsive chassis and reliable tyres on which to race. In 2006 Team Roberts had the tyres and the power they'd craved – they already had the other two requirements – and then in 2007 both suppliers dropped the ball. The Honda motor wouldn't pull on the straights, it simply would not rev out, and their Michelins had no grip. Sliding around at the back of the field, the team tried everything they knew, even re-engineering their chassis and rotating the engine for a better weight distribution, but to no avail.

By mid-season Kenny Junior had had enough and effectively retired, leaving Team Roberts with a good chassis. Honda sold engine and chassis revisions for its private teams after Brno, but these made no difference to Team Roberts, who needed an engine supplier that could make competitive, usable power. It is difficult to believe that next year's Honda won't be a lot better than this year's, but the company will only provide enough engines for one rider and the way the sport is funded means it is only commercially viable to run a two-rider team. Team Roberts will therefore have to find a new engine or bike supplier, and only Ducati fits that bill. In a perfect world they would be able to lease competitive Ilmor engines.

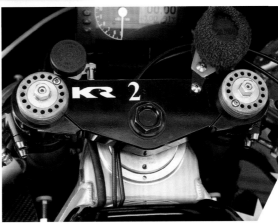

Left All Team KR chassis have fully adjustable steering heads; this one is marked up as giving 5mm more wheelbase

Far left Although he didn't return to riding, Kenny Junior recommended a new engine position; it wasn't really the problem but the team built new chassis anyway

ILMOR
X3

Ilmor's season only lasted one race. Mario Illien's brave attempt to build a private MotoGP contender fell at the first hurdle: lack of adequate sponsorship was the reason. The 800cc pneumatic-valve V4 was still three seconds a lap slower than the major contenders after a winter of testing, and although fast on long straights it seemed to have major throttle-control issues. The bike hopped going into corners and looked very snatchy coming out. Higher-inertia engine internals were fitted for the last test at Jerez to try to smooth things out, but these did not solve their problems.

It is difficult to believe an engineer of Illien's reputation would not get it right in the end, but it is apparent that it is going to require a lot of financial backing to make the bike competitive. Although the race team has been disbanded testing is continuing, latterly at Estoril with Andrew Pitt back in the saddle. It is to be hoped that a good sponsor will step forward.

Right Andrew Pitt departs for his first and only 800cc MotoGP. After one day's testing Ilmor MotoGP pulled out, citing lack of sponsorship as the reason

Far right Mario Illien's team have just built two additional bikes overnight. McWilliams cannot ride. And right now it just isn't ready to race

MotoGP on DVD

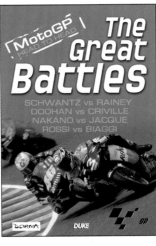

www.dukevideo.com/bikes

THE SEASON IN FOCUS

Thirty-three riders took part in MotoGP races this year. The next twelve pages detail what happened to them over the eighteen races, the longest season in Grand Prix history

1	Casey Stoner	367
2	Dani Pedrosa	242
3	Valentino Rossi	241
4	John Hopkins	189
5	Marco Melandri	187
6	Chris Vermeulen	179
7	Loris Capirossi	166
8	Nicky Hayden	127
9	Colin Edwards	124
10	Alex Barros	115
11	Randy De Puniet	108
12	Toni Elias	104
13	Alex Hofmann	65
14	Carlos Checa	65
15	Anthony West	59
16	Sylvain Guintoli	50
17	Shinya Nakano	47
18	Makoto Tamada	38
19	Kurtis Roberts	10
20	Roger Lee Hayden	6
21	Michel Fabrizio	6
22	Fonsi Nieto	5
23	Olivier Jacque	4
24	Kenny Roberts Jr.	4
25	Nobuatsu Aoki	3
26	Shinichi Ito	1

1 CASEY STONER
DUCATI MARLBORO

NATIONALITY Australia
DATE OF BIRTH 16 October 1985
2007 SEASON 10 wins,
5 pole positions, 6 fastest laps
TOTAL POINTS 367

The phrase most used in describing Casey's races this year is 'he didn't make a mistake.' He was only off the rostrum four times and scored points in every round. He could run away from the field turning metronomic lap times, as in Istanbul and Laguna Seca, or he could withstand race-long pressure from Rossi, as in Qatar, or could even win one of the best duels anyone could remember – Catalunya.

There is no doubt that Ducati interpreted the new regulations better than any of the Japanese companies and with tyre supplier Bridgestone gave Casey the tools he needed, but to see just how much Casey contributed to the mix, take him out of the Ducati/Bridgestone/Stoner equation. Where are the rest of the Bridgestone users? Where are the other Ducatis?

Only Stoner, says Ducati Corse technical director Fillipo Preziosi, used the Desmosedici motor as he intended: with the rev counter needle permanently round near the 19,000 mark. Casey could also use harder tyres for better stability than the other Ducati riders yet still find grip where they couldn't. There simply wasn't a weak spot for the opposition to exploit.

He also conducted himself well off track with just the right amount of over-reaction to anything he thought might be criticism: he frequently says how much he enjoyed proving the doubters wrong. His opinions on such issues as track safety and the proposed one-tyre rule were delivered thoughtfully and cogently. He sounded like a World Champion and he rode like one too, a great one.

2 DANI PEDROSA
REPSOL HONDA

NATIONALITY Spanish
DATE OF BIRTH 29 September 1985
2007 SEASON 2 wins,
5 pole positions, 3 fastest laps
TOTAL POINTS 242

Right up until the last race of the year, it looked as if Dani was having a bad season. The pre-season favourite in many pundits' opinion, Pedrosa suffered from a slow motor and tyres that wouldn't grip. He seethed with righteous indignation and was rumoured to have threatened to leave Honda. It certainly took a long time to announce his decision to re-sign with the Repsol team.

He did have a runaway win in Germany to console himself, but the first half of the season was pretty bleak. Dani was not concerned with the occasional second or third place – he thought he should have been a contender.

It wasn't just his machinery. Dani was twice the victim of first-lap accidents that weren't of his making, and he

would surely have won in Japan had the weather not changed.

When HRC started to deliver some power and Michelin recovered their form, Dani put in a storming finish to the season that included four consecutive pole positions in the last four races as well as victory in Valencia. It was his first win on home soil in the top class and, thanks to Valentino Rossi's misfortune, gave him second place in the Championship by the narrowest of margins. Rossi had twice as many wins as Dani, which shows how hard the Spaniard worked to pick up points when things weren't going well.

Second place when you have a bad season? Look out for Dani in 2008 when Honda and Michelin will surely give him something that works for the whole year.

2007 MOTO GP WORLD CHAMPIONS

Congratulations to
Casey Stoner and the Ducati Team
23/09/2007 - Montegi, Japan

The grip to win.

3 VALENTINO ROSSI
FIAT YAMAHA

NATIONALITY Italian
DATE OF BIRTH 16 February 1979
2007 SEASON 4 wins,
4 pole positions, 3 fastest laps
TOTAL POINTS 241

This season, according to Valentino, he found himself with the biggest machinery disadvantage he had ever had to contend with – including when he moved to Yamaha in 2003. He blamed both Michelin and Yamaha, urging both to work as hard as he and his team were doing.

Unfortunately for the Doctor, it was soon apparent that the new 800s won't let rider skill make up for any machinery deficiency in the way the old 990s would. On those monsters, Rossi was able to lap faster on worn tyres than anyone but the 800s don't offer those opportunities. Rider, tyres and engine must be perfect, you cannot mask a problem in one of those areas.

As well as his machinery woes, there was also the small matter of his run-in with the Italian tax man. There were a couple of races after mid-season when it seemed his mind wasn't really on the job in hand. Along with the government investigation came a new phenomenon for Rossi to deal with, criticism from the Italian media. Most of it bemoaned the loss of innocence in finding your idol has feet of clay rather than outright character assassination, but it was still a new experience for Valentino. Watching him battle against the odds, as in China, was nearly as entertaining as watching him win, and there were still moments of pure genius to enjoy, but it's just that they were fewer and further between than we have become accustomed to.

Valentino was agitating for Bridgestone tyres well before the end of the season and will start 2008 as the sole Yamaha rider on the Japanese rubber. It is a high-risk strategy.

4 JOHN HOPKINS
RIZLA SUZUKI MotoGP

NATIONALITY American
DATE OF BIRTH 22 May 1983
2007 SEASON 4 rostrums, 1 fastest lap
TOTAL POINTS 189

By far Hopper's best season since he arrived in Grand Prix in 2002. He stood on the rostrum for the first time in China, did so again in the Czech Republic, San Marino and Valencia, finished the year six places higher than his previous best and scored 73 points more than he's ever done in a season. Aided by the reliability of the Suzuki (the only factory not to suffer a mechanical breakdown in a race all year), John was always competitive in qualifying and the race and made a habit of being involved with the leaders. In the early part of the season, he seemed to make a habit of tangling with Rossi in the early laps.

It was this reliability that saw him win the tense fight for fourth place in the Championship with Melandri and team-mate Vermeulen. It was common knowledge early in the year that John had been lured away from Suzuki and would be a Kawasaki rider in 2008, yet he kept his head down and was never seen to give less than his maximum. Typically, he said goodbye to Suzuki with a rostrum in the last race of the year at Valencia. There was also a new maturity about John as a person, maybe not unconnected to his mid-season engagement. He could still enjoy the flash stuff, like getting his elbow down, and allow himself to make mistakes when overriding, as at Jerez. However, that was the only time he failed to score points all season. This was the year Hopper added consistency to his undoubted speed. It took John a long time to get his first rostrum but more followed quickly. The first win will come soon, and you know more will arrive right behind it.

5 MARCO MELANDRI

HONDA GRESINI

Like all the other Honda satellite team riders, Marco had a tough time with his bike's handling. Chatter under hard braking and lack of feel from the front end were the perennial problems. As he has an HRC contract, Marco expected more help from Japan and was not happy when very little materialised. Missing out on fourth in the Championship by just two points didn't help his temper.

As usual, his year was punctuated by enormous crashes that would have put most people out for weeks. Not Marco. The day after a crunching fall at Laguna he rode to a rostrum finish. His trainer had to carry him to the post-race press conference. He had been riding with a broken ankle. Two races later at Misano he crashed on one of the fastest corners in the calendar during practice

and subsequently finished fourth in the race. He only missed one race, Brno in between Laguna and Misano, and that was due to a herniated disc.

Fifth is Marco's lowest finish since he became a Honda rider in 2002, and next year he will be moving on to partner the new World Champion on a factory Ducati. It is a continuation of an old relationship. Livio Suppo, now Ducati Marlboro Team Manager, was Marco's manager back in the late 1990s when he nearly won the 125cc title on a Benetton-sponsored Honda and has wanted to get him on a Desmosedici for a long time.

This season must go down as a serious disappointment for Marco, but there has been no sign of his enthusiasm or commitment diminishing. He will be well worth watching in '08.

NATIONALITY Italian
DATE OF BIRTH 7 August 1982
2007 SEASON 3 rostrums
TOTAL POINTS 187

6 CHRIS VERMEULEN

RIZLA SUZUKI MotoGP

Suzuki's first race win, two second places and a third in your second year in MotoGP cannot be considered anything other than very impressive. On more than one occasion Chris outshone his team-mate, notably when he finished second and John Hopkins third in San Marino for the Rizla Suzuki Team's first double podium.

Chris's win in France saddled him with the reputation of being a wet-weather specialist, but in fact he hates riding in the rain. He just happens to be very good at it. Last year, this review reported that his team was sure that there was a lot more to come from the talented and intelligent Australian. The good news is that there still is. He can still find qualifying a problem and he has a tendency to talk himself out of contention at some tracks, such as

Mugello. When Chris was happy with the bike and his track knowledge, as at Laguna Seca and Misano, it took Casey Stoner at his best to keep him back in second place. This year he finished five places higher in the Championship than he did in his first year with Suzuki. That is an impressive rate of progress. Of course Chris has been helped by the pace and total reliability of the Suzuki, but he has again improved as a rider. A measure of that is his fifth place in the 2007 Riders' Rider of the Year poll. Last year he was tenth.

In 2008 Vermeulen will have a new team-mate in the shape of Loris Capirossi. It will be interesting to see how they interact. You just know that there really is more to come from a man who always seems in control, on and off the bike.

NATIONALITY Australian
DATE OF BIRTH 19 June 1982
2007 SEASON 1 win,
1 pole position, 1 fastest lap
TOTAL POINTS 179

7 LORIS CAPIROSSI
DUCATI MARLBORO

NATIONALITY
Italian

DATE OF BIRTH
4 April 1973

2007 SEASON
1 win, 1 fastest lap

TOTAL POINTS
166

Loris has ridden for Ducati for all five years of their MotoGP project, and it is fair to say they would not have got where they are without him. He gave them their first rostrum, first pole and first win. In all he won seven times on the Desmosedici. However, this was not a happy year for Loris. He did not come to terms with the new 800cc design and struggled even when Ducati Corse built him a special motor for Mugello. As a result Loris will be a Suzuki rider next year and his job at Ducati will be taken by Marco Melandri. The good news was the birth of his and Ingrid's first child, even if the approaching event did take Loris's mind off the job at the Spanish GP.

8 NICKY HAYDEN
REPSOL HONDA

NATIONALITY
American

DATE OF BIRTH
30 July 1981

2007 SEASON
3 rostrums, 1 pole position, 1 fastest lap

TOTAL POINTS
127

The defending World Champion had a nightmare start to his title defence with a bike that just would not work the way he wanted it to. Things started to come good following a test after the Catalan GP and from Donington onwards Nicky was much more competitive. Three rostrums followed in four races. His best chances of a win carrying the number-one plate were at home in the USA and in Australia. The first disappeared in a first-corner collision, the second when his engine dropped a valve as he was shadowing Casey Stoner. Nicky bore all these travails with the good grace we have come to expect from him. The whole paddock hopes his luck improves in '08.

9 COLIN EDWARDS
FIAT YAMAHA

NATIONALITY
American

DATE OF BIRTH
30 July 1981

2007 SEASON
2 rostrums, 2 pole positions

TOTAL POINTS
124

It was another season of the sort we have come to expect from Colin, typified by his French Grand Prix. He set pole position for the first time in his career at Le Mans but managed to reverse through the field on the first lap. It has always been difficult to know how difficult Colin's job has been because of cuspicions that he has been frequently used as a guinea pig. For instance, the experimental 16-inch tyres in his allocation for Catalunya and Mugello didn't work. When he was allowed to do what he wanted at the next race, Donington Park, he set pole and finished second. This was his final season as a works Yamaha rider, in 2008 he moves to the satellite Tech 3 team.

10 ALEX BARROS
PRAMAC D'ANTIN

NATIONALITY
Brazilian

DATE OF BIRTH
18 October 1970

2007 SEASON
1 rostrum

TOTAL POINTS
115

After 276 Grands Prix, 245 in the premier class, Alex ends his career with a record of seven wins, five poles and 14 fastest laps. His final season was not stellar but he was one of only three men to put a satellite bike on the rostrum. His efforts were not helped by the fact his team did not have a suspension technician or by mechanical failures at Misano and Estoril. Typically, he does not mention his wins when asked for his best moments but 1997 at Donington when he put an over-the-counter Honda V-twin on the rostrum and his ride on a 500 at Assen in '02 which winner Rossi described as the best he'd ever seen a two-stroke ridden. He'll be missed.

ROCHET®

Innovative Jewellery

SINCE 1904

OFFICIAL LICENSED PRODUCTS

11 RANDY DE PUNIET
KAWASAKI RACING

NATIONALITY
French

DATE OF BIRTH
14 February 1981

2007 SEASON
1 rostrum

TOTAL POINTS
108

The highlight of Randy's year was his first rostrum in MotoGP at Motegi. The low point the crash he instigated on the first lap at Misano. In between, he was always brave and usually fast. His fifth place in Catalunya while suffering from high-speed crashes in the previous two races was little short of heroic. His crash while leading his home race wasn't quite so clever, but it was noticeable that his crew were always very supportive. Asking a rider with only one season of MotoGP under his belt to lead a factory effort was always going to be a tall order but Randy responded and scored 71 more points than he did in 2006. He is unlucky not to have secured a factory ride for 2008.

12 TONI ELIAS
HONDA GRESINI

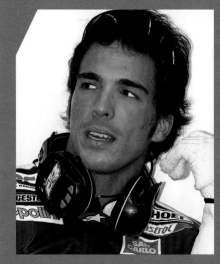

NATIONALITY
Spanish

DATE OF BIRTH
26 March 1983

2007 SEASON
2 rostrums, 2 fastest laps

TOTAL POINTS
104

Thankfully there aren't enough electronics in the world to stop Toni Elias getting a motorbike sideways. His year started well with a charge to fourth in Jerez and a splendid second at Istanbul on the way to which he upset Valentino Rossi and was entertainingly unrepentant afterwards. There were also a couple of races in which you had to look to find him – he's still frustratingly inconsistent. However, the Assen practice accident which broke his femur was the pivotal point of his year. Toni only missed two races but was obviously still convalescing when he returned. His second rostrum of the year, in Japan, was just reward for his bravery. And he's still the most entertaining rider to watch.

13 ALEX HOFMANN
PRAMAC D'ANTIN

NATIONALITY
German

DATE OF BIRTH
25 May 1980

TOTAL POINTS
65

Alex scored the best result of his Grand Prix career – fifth – in the wet French GP, but found himself unemployed after he pulled in at Estoril after a succession of mechanical problems. Team manager Luis d'Antin didn't think lack of motivation was a good reason to retire. After that, Alex and the team communicated through their lawyers. Thankfully the dreadful hand injury he suffered in first practice at Laguna Seca has responded to treatment and there should be little lasting damage. As for Alex's prospects, he will not be back in MotoGP in 2008 but is thought to be involved with the test programme for a new superbike racer.

14 CARLOS CHECA
HONDA LCR

NATIONALITY
Spanish

DATE OF BIRTH
15 October 1972

TOTAL POINTS
65

Another Grand Prix veteran moving on to other things, after 220 GP races, 192 of them in the top class, two victories, three poles and five fastest laps in a career spanning 14 years. This final year in GPs, says Carlos, was his most difficult. Like the other Honda privateers, he struggled with lack of power and grip. His best year, he thinks, was 2005 on the Ducati, specifically the end of the season when he was very competitive. After a successful forray to the Suzuka 8 Hours during the summer, he will lead Honda's World Superbike effort in 2008 riding a FireBlade for the Ten Kate team.

15 ANTHONY WEST
KAWASAKI RACING

NATIONALITY
Australian

DATE OF BIRTH
14 February 1981

TOTAL POINTS
59

The Aussie started the year on an under-funded 250 Aprilia, skipped to the World Supersport Championship to ride a Yamaha and won a couple of races, then turned up back in the MotoGP paddock as a factory Kawasaki rider after Olivier Jacque retired. Ant's first race was Donington where he ran with the leaders on a wet track. He's the best in the world when conditions are truly soaking. He secured the ride for next year against some stiff competition after scoring points in every race he rode except the last. If he hadn't jumped the start in Motegi, the final result could have been even better. Ant did have problems working out some tracks, so he knows it won't be easy.

16 SYLVAIN GUINTOLI
DUNLOP YAMAHA TECH 3

NATIONALITY
French

DATE OF BIRTH
26 March 1983

TOTAL POINTS
50

The discovery of the year, as well as Rookie of the Year (actually he was the only rookie in the class), Sylvain out-performed his much more experienced team-mate as he continued the Dunlop development work started by Carlos Checa in '06. His highlights were leading his home GP (he fell but got back on to score points) and a fighting fourth place in Japan (Dunlop's best result since the very first MotoGP race). He was also fastest in two practice sessions through judicious use of qualifying tyres when they weren't available to the Michelin and Bridgestone runners. Sylvain gets a satellite team Ducati for 2008.

17 SHINYA NAKANO
KONICA MINOLTA HONDA

NATIONALITY
Japanese

DATE OF BIRTH
10 October 1977

TOTAL POINTS
47

Shinya hasn't finished lower down the table since he came to the top class in 2001. After three years' development with Kawasaki, he must have thought that a Honda on Michelins was the answer to his prayers. But he suffered, like all the satellite Honda riders, from chatter and a lack of feedback from the front end, which is what his style depends on. It was a thoroughly dispiriting year: a rider of Shinya's pedigree does not expect his best results to be a trio of tenth places, and two of them came in the first two races of the year. However, Honda feel that he has not been given a fair chance, so he will be back in 2008 on another satellite Honda, this time with Team Gresini.

18 MAKOTO TAMADA
DUNLOP YAMAHA TECH 3

NATIONALITY
Japanese

DATE OF BIRTH
4 November 1976

TOTAL POINTS
38

The two-time winner leaves MotoGP after a slightly disappointing year. It was his first season on a Yamaha and his first in GPs on Dunlop. Makoto has always needed things to be just right to be able to give of his best and when you're developing a tyre that isn't always possible. There were times when he infuriated his team and there were times when he looked like his old self, notably in Portugal, although that adventure was ended by a crash only a few laps from the flag. He's unlikely to return to GPs, but the paddock has always enjoyed having him around. Makoto is one of several ex-GP riders investigating riding in the USA in 2008.

19 KURTIS ROBERTS
TEAM ROBERTS

NATIONALITY
American

DATE OF BIRTH
17 November 1978

TOTAL POINTS
10

The younger son of three-times champion King Kenny Roberts took over his dad's bike when older brother Kenny Jnr decided enough was enough and disappeared back home to the States after the Catalan GP. Kurtis soldiered on to five points-scoring finishes but the bike was never remotely competitive. He was usually the slowest qualifier and had to rely on the misfortune of others to get in the points. Development of the bike was hamstrung by only having one machine and by the new tyre regulations. Then there was Rossi's dismissive reference to him as 'someone who finishes thirteenth in Superstock'. It is to be hoped that this wasn't the last we saw of the Roberts dynasty in MotoGP.

20 ROGER LEE HAYDEN
KAWASAKI RACING

NATIONALITY
American

DATE OF BIRTH
30 May 1983

TOTAL POINTS
6

The younger brother of 2006 Champion Nicky Hayden was given a one-off ride at Laguna Seca as reward for his efforts in the American Superbike and Supersport Championships. He repaid American Kawasaki's faith in him handsomely, finishing tenth and only losing out on ninth at the very last corner. Surprisingly, he was the first American rider home. It was a great effort, especially as he only had a single day of testing beforehand, and there was immediate speculation about further wild-card rides. That didn't happen, but Roger Lee went on to win the AMA Supersport title – which should ensure he rides at Laguna and Indianapolis in '08.

21 MICHEL FABRIZIO
HONDA GRESINI

NATIONALITY
Italian

DATE OF BIRTH
17 September 1984

TOTAL POINTS
6

The Italian took over Toni Elias's Honda for the German GP after the Team Gresini rider broke his leg at Assen. Fabrizio had replaced Elias once before, but broke his collarbone in the first session at Donington '06. He fitted in the GP around his World Superbike ride with the support of Honda Europe and did a solid job. Michel, who has had a lot of fans in the Italian media since his MotoGP season with the WCM team in 2004, secured a deal to ride a factory Ducati in the World Superbike Championship in 2008, despite sporadic form first in Supersport and then in Superbike, on Hondas.

22 FONSI NIETO
KAWASAKI RACING

NATIONALITY
Spanish

DATE OF BIRTH
2 December 1978

TOTAL POINTS
5

Kawasaki called up their World Superbike rider to replace the injured Olivier Jacque for the French GP. Fonsi had never ridden a MotoGP bike before he went out for practice on Friday morning – and promptly ran across the the gravel trap at the first corner on his first flying lap. From there on he did a thoroughly professional job and under the most difficult of circumstances brought the bike home in 11th place. The team was mightily impressed with his application and his professionalism. It was Fonsi's 100th race in Grands Prix.

23 OLIVIER JACQUE
KAWASAKI RACING TEAM

NATIONALITY
French

DATE OF BIRTH
29 August 1973

TOTAL POINTS
4

The 250cc World Champion of 2000 brought down the curtain on his racing career after heavy crashes in Turkey and China followed by a seemingly insignificant get-off in Catalunya that left him with pain in his neck. That was the final straw. In truth, Olivier had never wanted to continue racing full-time this season but was made an offer he couldn't refuse. Olivier's decision to retire was influenced by his wife and the imminent arrival of their first child. He won seven 250cc GPs but only got on the rostrum once in the top class – when he gave Kawasaki what was then their best result in MotoGP. He continues with the Kawasaki team as an advisor and development rider.

24 KENNY ROBERTS Jnr
TEAM ROBERTS

NATIONALITY
American

DATE OF BIRTH
25 July 1973

TOTAL POINTS
4

The 500cc World Champion of 2000 was one of several veterans to retire from competition during or at the end of the 2007 season. Being a Roberts, Kenny didn't exit the sport in a conventional manner. He simply didn't tell anyone. When it became obvious that the Team KR bike couldn't be made competitive, Kenny stayed at home in the States and his younger brother Kurtis took over. After the 2006 season, when he regularly got the bike on the rostrum and the front row, Kenny couldn't summon up the motivation to ride round at the back of the field hoping to score a point if someone else had a problem. Not many people blamed him.

25 NOBUATSU AOKI
RIZLA SUZUKI MotoGP

NATIONALITY
Japanese

DATE OF BIRTH
31 August 1971

TOTAL POINTS
3

The Rizla Suzuki team had a very successful season, and that is due in no small part to their test riders Akiyoshi and Aoki. When parts arrive from Japan, the GP team know that they will work because the testers are fast enough and experienced enough to understand the level of competition in MotoGP. Nobu Aoki won a 250 GP back in 1993 and then rode in over 100 500cc races, getting on the rostrum four times. When he turned up at Sepang with what was essentially a prototype of the 2008 Suzuki, it was already fast and reliable – Nobu scored points in a race that nobody dropped out of.

26 SHINICHI ITO
PRAMAC D'ANTIN

NATIONALITY
Japanese

DATE OF BIRTH
7 December 1966

TOTAL POINTS
1

The 40-year-old veteran was called up to ride the d'Antin Ducati at Motegi after the first-choice replacement, Chaz Davies, suffered from an infection to an arm injury following a testing crash at Mugello. Ito hadn't ridden at the top level regularly for several seasons and, despite being an official Bridgestone test rider in recent few years, had never ridden the Ducati Desmosedici at the Twin Ring. He took time to adapt but as befits a man who has been on pole and the podium in 500cc GPs he got it home to become the oldest man to score a point since the introduction of the MotoGP formula in 2002.

KOUSUKE AKIYOSHI
RIZLA SUZUKI MotoGP

Suzuki's veteran test rider got to race in two GPs this year, and as he won the Suzuka 8 Hours with Yukio Kagayama, breaking Honda's ten-year winning streak, it's safe to assume we'll see him again in the near future. Like his fellow test rider Nobu Aoki, Akiyoshi-san has played an important part in making the Suzuki GSV the most improved motorcycle of the year. He didn't score points in either of his rides, Jerez and Motegi, although he was desperately unlucky at home in Japan. He was running in seventh place, well ahead of both of his team-mates, when the bike stopped on him. Ironically, it was the Suzuki's only failure all season.

CHAZ DAVIES
PRAMAC D'ANTIN

Chaz was preparing to practise for the American Supersport Championship event at Laguna Seca when he was asked to replace the injured Alex Hofmann on the d'Antin Ducati. His performance in the race was enough to secure him a two-day test on the factory bike at Mugello and get him the offer of a full-time testing job for 2008. His other replacement rides, in the last three races of the year, didn't go so well. He finished out of the points in Australia and Malaysia, and two crashes prevented him racing at Valencia. Over winter he has to decide whether to take up Ducati's offer or return to racing in the AMA Championship.

IVAN SILVA
PRAMAC D'ANTIN

The Spaniard acted as replacement rider for the d'Antin team at three races in the 2006 season, and did so once again at the Czech Republic Grand Prix in 2007. When regular rider Alex Hofmann was hurt in the very first practice session of the American GP, there obviously wasn't time to fly Silva in from Europe, so Chaz Davies got his chance. When Hofmann was sacked by the team after the Portuguese GP, the British rider was preferred to finish the season and Silva went back to domestic racing. Unfortunately, he suffered a serious injury while racing in the Spanish Championship.

AKIRA YANAGAWA
KAWASAKI RACING

Five years after he debuted the 990cc Kawasaki ZX-RR Ninja at the Pacific Grand Prix of 2002 at Motegi, Akira Yanagawa finished the 2007 race in 17th place, his best finish in the four GPs he has contested after a long and successful career in the World and All-Japan Superbike Championships. That first race had resulted in a crash due to mechanical failure and injury, but Yanagawa continued as development rider for the MotoGP project. He came back to ride Motegi this year after the regular tester, Naoki Matsudo, who was Kawasaki's wild card in Japan in 2006, suffered a badly broken leg early in the season.

MIGUEL DUHAMEL
HONDA GRESINI

Fifteen years after he last rode in a Grand Prix, the legendary French-Canadian got to ride at Laguna Seca as replacement for the injured Toni Elias. American Honda had pressed for 39-year-old Miguel to get the ride as a 'thank you' for the AMA Superbike Championship and Daytona 200 wins he racked up for them. However, it was the first time Miguel had ridden a MotoGP bike – no testing – and the first time he'd ridden on Bridgestone tyres. He also had to ride in the AMA race on the same day as the GP. Not surprisingly, he decided to pull in early, saying that he hadn't got his head in the race, and concentrate on the AMA event.

JEREMY McWILLIAMS
ILMOR GP

The Ulsterman never got to race this season. A massive crash in qualifying for the Qatari GP, the first race of the year and the only one the Ilmor team contested, aggravated the still-healing femur he broke in winter testing. When McWilliams can't race because of an injury you know it must hurt, and hurt a lot. Don't think we've seen the last of Jeremy, he's still keen to get back on the grid.

ANDREW PITT
ILMOR GP

The most improved rider of the 2006 World Superbike season came back to MotoGP after a two-year gap. His reputation as a more than useful development rider got the Aussie a seat with the Ilmor squad, but the plug was pulled after the first race, leaving Pitt and team-mate McWilliams unemployed. However, rumours that the team resumed testing towards the end of the year refused to go away.

CASEY.　　ALPINESTARS.
ONE GOAL.　　ONE VISION.

alpinestars.com

THE RACES
MotoGP 2007

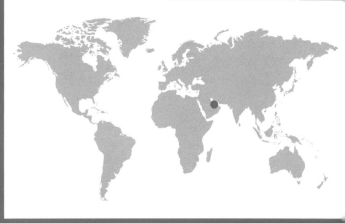

RED SHIFT

The first race under the new 800cc engine capacity regulations saw Casey Stoner, Bridgestone and Ducati rack up their own list of firsts

Anyone who saw Casey Stoner when he first appeared in the UK to ride in the 2000 Aprilia Challenge knew immediately they were looking at a kid with a lot of promise. He was obviously good; equally obviously, we didn't realise just how good. In his first outing on a Ducati, and his first on Bridgestone tyres, he rode what Valentino Rossi described as 'a perfect race'. It was an apposite adjective. Stoner was pressured all the way by the seven-times World Champion but never put a wheel wrong. It was a stunning display of maturity from a rider who many had written off as a crasher. Sure, the Aussie had been on pole at Losail twelve months previously, but he then failed to get on the front row for the rest of the season. Then there was the small matter of six crashes. You wouldn't have put money on Casey starting his career as a factory rider this way.

The doubters were proved wrong. Stoner used the speed of the Ducati on the long front straight to good advantage but also kept with Rossi when he forced past. Every time the Fiat Yamaha rider led onto the straight the youngster was able to pass him before the line. He did it for the first time at the end of the first lap, then again fifth time around after Valentino had pushed past at a slow left-hander. Casey also demonstrated that he was able to repass the Italian in the slowest corner on the track when the Italian ran wide.

After the early exchanges, the race boiled down to Rossi trying to harass Stoner into a mistake. Casey later said he had been riding well within himself, a point underlined by the fact he set the fastest lap of the race the final time round. Stoner was so composed that Rossi, in his own words, ran up the white flag two laps

Top & Below Pedrosa and Hopkins battle for third place was nine seconds behind the leaders at the flag. The surprise was the Honda's lack of pace

from home. The young Aussie led every lap despite Valentino attacking, harrying and trying to 'confuse' him for all but the last couple of laps. It was a stunning performance, aided and abetted by the jaw-dropping straight-line performance of the 800cc Ducati. All four Ducatis, the two satellite d'Antin bikes as well as the factory duo, were permanently grouped at the

top of the speed-gun charts. Stoner had top speed of the weekend, with 201.8mph in qualifying, while Alex Barros reached 195.1mph in the race, into a stiff headwind. Rossi's Yamaha managed 186.5mph in the race – and when Valentino did get onto the kilometre-long front straight first the Aussie didn't even have to use the slipstream to blast past.

'I DON'T GIVE A DAMN ABOUT QUALIFYING – AS LONG AS I'M ON THE FRONT TWO ROWS.'

CASEY STONER

Anyone expecting the new, lowered fuel limit to slow the red bikes down was soon disabused of that notion. Rossi told the Italian media that his crew suspected the Ducatis would hit fuel-consumption problems; they didn't. Ducati team-manager Livio Suppo couldn't – or didn't care to – tell the media exactly why his bikes were so fast. Ducati Corse has always operated on the principle that their machines can never have enough power and they pay particular attention to aerodynamics, which means that Ducatis tend to like a long straight. Suppo pointed out that Ducati are the only bikes using screamer rather than big-bang engines, then shrugged and said 'but I am not an engineer...'. HRC's Satoru Horiike is of the opinion that a rider's style will have much more influence on fuel consumption than firing order.

It was also clear that the Ducati team had thought very clearly about the race. To simplify the engine management set-up, the Dukes were only burning fuel on the straight and letting Casey do the work around the rest of the track. To make sure they didn't immediately lose what they had gained, the works bikes ran the big brake discs usually only seen at Donington and Motegi. That stopped Rossi and the agile Yamaha going past on the brakes at the end of the straight. It's usually Rossi's race engineer, Jerry Burgess, who is able to reduce all the variables of

Below Nicky Hayden had a tough start to his title defence. He lacked confidence in the front and didn't like the small fairing

Top Like most of the Honda riders, Marco Melandri suffered from lack of confidence in the RCV's front

Below Mario Ilien and his Ilmor team got one of their bikes on the grid, but Pitt didn't get to the flag

race set-up down to what really matters in that way.

While it was clear that the Ducati had a straight-line advantage, it didn't even look as if Casey had to use the slipstream to get past anyone; his was the only Desmosedici contending for the lead. The young Aussie did indeed ride the perfect race in that he used his machine's strengths to their best advantage and equally importantly didn't make a mistake in the areas where he didn't have an advantage. The only thing

he failed to do was take pole position. Asked if he was bothered about that, Stoner was typically straightforward: 'I don't give a damn about qualifying – as long as I'm on the front two rows.'

Behind Stoner and Rossi, John Hopkins tried hard to take third place off Dani Pedrosa. He didn't quite manage it, but for a man with a right hand the size of a cow's udder thanks to a crash in pre-season testing, this was a heroic ride. It also boded well for Suzuki. Hopper said the adrenaline took care of things during the race, but when he reached Turn 1 on the slow-down lap it felt as though someone had dropped a brick wall on his hand. Despite Pedrosa's rostrum finish, this was not a good weekend for Honda. World Champion Nicky Hayden looked like he was riding in reverse when a Ducati went past him on the straight, and he was outgunned by Vermeulen's Suzuki on the run to the flag; the American was also suffering from a lack of protection from his fairing. Gresini team-mates Melandri and Elias both showed at the front in the early laps but faded. Team Roberts and the embarrassingly out-gunned Ilmor were even worse off. It was difficult to gauge Kawasaki's progress as de Puniet crashed early on and the returning Olivier Jacque looked decidedly rusty. What did not happen was what everyone had thought would happen: Honda rolling out a bike that made the rest look silly, as they did at the start of the 990cc formula in 2002.

Like everyone else, Livio Suppo was stunned by his rider's maturity. After the race he asked Casey why he hadn't let Rossi past for a few laps. The reply was that Valentino was more likely to make a mistake or use up his tyres if he kept the pressure on – and Rossi thought he was the one trying to force his opponent into a mistake.

THE NEW RULES

This was the first MotoGP race under new technical regulations. Engine capacity was reduced from 990 to 800cc and fuel-tank capacity lowered from 22 to 21 litres. Despite this, the new bikes qualified faster than the 990s, demolished the lap record and took nearly 20 seconds off the race record. Top speeds were down by just over 6mph. Many people, including Valentino Rossi, thought Ducati would have to slow their bikes on race day to avoid running out of fuel; if they did take anything off the top end it was minimal and post-race scrutineering showed their tank size to be perfectly legal. However, that didn't stop some disbelievers making snide remarks about how Ducati could have such a power advantage. The counter-argument was that Yamaha erred on the safe side of that equation at a track where the M1 was known to be thirsty. Honda said categorically they had no worries about fuel consumption.

The new tyre rule also came into force. This limits riders to 31 tyres per race split 14/17 front to back. Tyres are pre-selected the day before practice starts and have a bar code fitted by technical director Mike Webb in addition to the code built in during construction. Only Michelin and Bridgestone have to do this – the regulation applies to manufacturers that have won a GP in the last two seasons – thus allowing Dunlop to use as many tyres as they wished as they strive to be competitive in the top class while developing their product with the Tech 3 Yamaha team. Most riders seemed have two qualifiers in their allocation. Perhaps because Losail is a track where both Michelin and Bridgestone users had tested only weeks before the race, the new system did not seem to affect anyone adversely. Jerry Burgess's view was that it made the engineering staff think harder about the bike rather than just throwing in a new tyre; Rossi hoped it would mark the end of tyres that only worked in a narrow temperature or humidity range and would thus make things safer.

Top Checking bar codes on one of Pedrosa's thirty-one tyres, part of the routine associated with the new regulations

Below Valentino Rossi congratulates Casey Stoner on his maiden MotoGP victory. The warmth wouldn't last the season

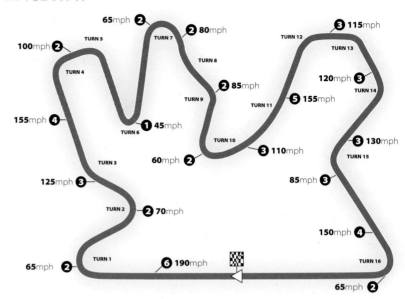

QATARI GP
LOSAIL INTERNATIONAL RACEWAY

ROUND 1
March 10

RACE RESULTS

CIRCUIT LENGTH 3.343 miles
NO. OF LAPS 22
RACE DISTANCE 73.546 miles
WEATHER Dry, 29°C
TRACK TEMPERATURE 45°C
WINNER Casey Stoner
FASTEST LAP 1m 56.528s,
103.280mph, Casey Stoner (record)
PREVIOUS LAP RECORD 1m 57.305s,
102.598mph, Valentino Rossi, 2006

QUALIFYING

	Rider	Nationality	Team	Qualifying	Pole +	Gap
1	Rossi	ITA	Fiat Yamaha Team	1m 55.002s		
2	Stoner	AUS	Ducati Marlboro Team	1m 55.007s	0.005s	0.005s
3	Edwards	USA	Fiat Yamaha Team	1m 55.233s	0.231s	0.226s
4	Elias	SPA	Honda Gresini	1m 55.358s	0.356s	0.125s
5	Pedrosa	SPA	Repsol Honda Team	1m 55.361s	0.359s	0.003s
6	Hopkins	USA	Rizla Suzuki MotoGP	1m 55.833s	0.831s	0.472s
7	Capirossi	ITA	Ducati Marlboro Team	1m 55.851s	0.849s	0.018s
8	De Puniet	FRA	Kawasaki Racing Team	1m 55.933s	0.931s	0.082s
9	Hayden	USA	Repsol Honda Team	1m 56.041s	1.039s	0.108s
10	Melandri	ITA	Honda Gresini	1m 56.222s	1.220s	0.181s
11	Nakano	JPN	Konica Minolta Honda	1m 56.306s	1.304s	0.084s
12	Checa	SPA	Honda LCR	1m 56.609s	1.607s	0.303s
13	Vermeulen	AUS	Rizla Suzuki MotoGP	1m 56.639s	1.637s	0.030s
14	Jacque	FRA	Kawasaki Racing Team	1m 56.754s	1.752s	0.115s
15	Barros	BRA	Pramac d'Antin	1m 56.814s	1.812s	0.060s
16	Guintoli	FRA	Dunlop Yamaha Tech 3	1m 57.257s	2.255s	0.443s
17	Hofmann	GER	Pramac d'Antin	1m 57.274s	2.272s	0.017s
18	Roberts Jr	USA	Team Roberts	1m 57.495s	2.493s	0.221s
19	Tamada	JPN	Dunlop Yamaha Tech 3	1m 58.024s	3.022s	0.529s
20	McWilliams	GBR	Ilmor GP	1m 59.606s	4.604s	1.582s
21	Pitt	AUS	Ilmor GP	1m 59.725s	4.723s	0.119s

FINISHERS

1 CASEY STONER First race on Bridgestones, first race with Ducati and first MotoGP victory to become the youngest Aussie ever to win in motorcycle racing's top class. And he made it look easy, setting a new lap record the final time round.

2 VALENTINO ROSSI Tried hard but couldn't get the gap he needed to stop the Ducati powering past on the front straight. Nevertheless, relieved to have a bike that worked as he wanted it to and delighted with the 46th pole position of his Grand Prix career.

3 DANI PEDROSA Never got within range of the top two after an early skirmish

with Rossi, but fought off a determined Hopkins to become the youngest rider ever to achieve 50 podium finishes in GPs.

4 JOHN HOPKINS Still riding hurt after a massive crash in testing a month before; hadn't even sat on a bike between then and set-up day for the GP. Took a couple of laps to get up to pace, then moved forward and was third for a short while.

5 MARCO MELANDRI An early charge took him to fourth place but he was losing time on the straight and trying to make it up on the brakes. That stressed the front tyre and slowed him until the fuel load lightened and the bike's balance returned.

6 COLIN EDWARDS A slow start off the front row was followed by a near-crash

– he held the bike up with his knee for 30 metres – putting him firmly in the chasing group and in a race-long fight with Melandri.

7 CHRIS VERMEULEN Starting from 13th and being slow off the grid put him back to 16th, which meant his front tyre was used up in the first half of the race. Up to eighth by half-distance but the gap to the men in front was too big.

8 NICKY HAYDEN An unhappy first race with the number-one plate. Front-end feel had been the problem all through testing and it remained Nicky's main problem at a track where he had crashed twice in pre-season tests and did not want to repeat the experience.

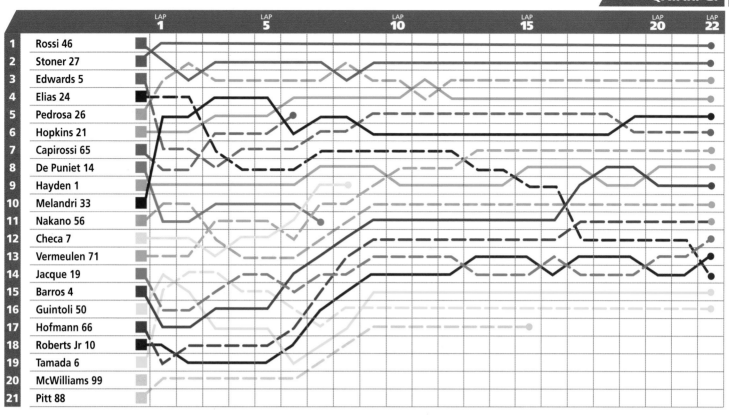

		LAP 1	LAP 5	LAP 10	LAP 15	LAP 20	LAP 22
1	Rossi 46						
2	Stoner 27						
3	Edwards 5						
4	Elias 24						
5	Pedrosa 26						
6	Hopkins 21						
7	Capirossi 65						
8	De Puniet 14						
9	Hayden 1						
10	Melandri 33						
11	Nakano 56						
12	Checa 7						
13	Vermeulen 71						
14	Jacque 19						
15	Barros 4						
16	Guintoli 50						
17	Hofmann 66						
18	Roberts Jr 10						
19	Tamada 6						
20	McWilliams 99						
21	Pitt 88						

RACE

	Rider	Motorcycle	Race Time	Time +	Fastest Lap	Average Speed
1	Stoner	Ducati	43m 02.788s		1m 56.528s	102.511mph
2	Rossi	Yamaha	43m 05.626s	2.838s	1m 56.717s	102.398mph
3	Pedrosa	Honda	43m 11.318s	8.530s	1m 56.951s	102.173mph
4	Hopkins	Suzuki	43m 11.859s	9.071s	1m 56.939s	102.151mph
5	Melandri	Honda	43m 20.221s	17.433s	1m 57.297s	101.823mph
6	Edwards	Yamaha	43m 21.435s	18.647s	1m 57.238s	101.776mph
7	Vermeulen	Suzuki	43m 25.704s	22.916s	1m 57.621s	101.609mph
8	Hayden	Honda	43m 25.845s	23.057s	1m 57.468s	101.604mph
9	Barros	Ducati	43m 28.749s	25.961s	1m 57.290s	101.490mph
10	Nakano	Honda	43m 31.244s	28.456s	1m 57.815s	101.393mph
11	Hofmann	Ducati	43m 37.817s	35.029s	1m 57.897s	101.139mph
12	Jacque	Kawasaki	43m 45.736s	42.948s	1m 58.388s	100.834mph
13	Roberts Jr	Kr212v	43m 45.765s	42.977s	1m 58.365s	100.832mph
14	Elias	Honda	43m 45.777s	42.989s	1m 57.581s	100.832mph
15	Guintoli	Yamaha	43m 54.427s	51.639s	1m 58.972s	100.501mph
16	Tamada	Yamaha	44m 00.641s	57.853s	1m 58.828s	100.264mph
	Pitt	Ilmor GP	30m 31.099s	7 Lap	2m 00.990s	98.585mph
	Checa	Honda	15m 53.958s	14 Lap	1m 57.406s	100.924mph
	De Puniet	Kawasaki	13m 56.908s	15 Lap	1m 57.710s	100.660mph
	Capirossi	Ducati	11m 53.279s	16 Lap	1m 57.234s	101.234mph
	McWilliams	Ilmor GP				

CHAMPIONSHIP

	Rider	Team	Points
1	Stoner	Ducati Marlboro team	25
2	Rossi	Fiat Yamaha Team	20
3	Pedrosa	Repsol Honda Team	16
4	Hopkins	Rizla Suzuki MotoGP	13
5	Melandri	Honda Gresini	11
6	Edwards	Fiat Yamaha Team	10
7	Vermeulen	Rizla Suzuki MotoGP	09
8	Hayden	Repsol Honda Team	08
9	Barros	Pramac d'Antin	07
10	Nakano	Konica Minolta Honda	06
11	Hofmann	Pramac d'Antin	05
12	Jacque	Kawasaki Racing Team	04
13	Roberts Jr	Team Roberts	03
14	Elias	Honda Gresini	02
15	Guintoli	Dunlop Yamaha Tech 3	01

9 ALEX BARROS Set the fastest race speed of the weekend, but a catastrophic start from the dirty side of the track put him at the back going into the first corner. Had a brilliant ride through the field from there and only lost out to Hayden after making a small mistake.

10 SHINYA NAKANO Suffered a big crash in qualifying and spent most of the race circulating with Hayden and Vermeulen, but couldn't find his trade-mark charge in the closing laps. Estimated he needed to find half a second a lap to be where he should be.

11 ALEX HOFMANN Got a good start, unlike team-mate Barros, only to have Vermeulen run into him at the first corner with enough force to take Alex's foot off

its footrest. He was 19th at the end of the first lap but then rode an excellent race for useful points.

12 OLIVIER JACQUE A depressing return to MotoGP: 18th in practice, 14th in qualifying, and with only Pitt and the Tech 3 Yamahas posting worse fastest laps. A hard rear tyre slid early on, but OJ had enough left to blast past Elias and Roberts out of the final corner.

13 KENNY ROBERTS A totally depressing weekend for the team. Neither the rider nor the team principal had anything good to say about the entire event.

14 TONI ELIAS Got away with the leaders but faded very quickly, then ran off track on lap 17 while ninth and lost three

places. Mugged by Jacque on the last lap to make it a thoroughly disappointing race.

15 SYLVAIN GUINTOLI The only rookie in the field impressed everyone by qualifying 16th and then picking up a point – which ensured he'd be Rookie of the Year! Outperformed his much more experienced team-mate all weekend.

16 MAKOTO TAMADA The Japanese rider has always said he simply cannot get on with the Losail circuit, and this race did nothing to change his opinion

NON-FINISHERS

ANDREW PITT Things looked good on Thursday, then went downhill, culminating

in a fuel-pump problem in the race. Corner entry was the main difficulty so he decided to maintain a steady pace and try to finish. It wasn't to be – and what no-one knew was that this might well have been the last time the Ilmor V4 turned a wheel at a racetrack.

CARLOS CHECA Had just passed Hayden for eighth place on lap nine when he lost the front due to a combination of too much brake and too much lean angle.

RANDY DE PUNIET Couldn't get close enough to Hayden to pass him on the brakes at the end of the straight, so tried to make up time in the corners and paid the penalty. Lost the front on lap eight after being passed by Vermeulen and Checa.

LORIS CAPIROSSI Another victim of bunching in the first corner. Carved through the pack and was up to sixth when he lost the front in the last corner of lap seven. Was the fastest man on the track when he crashed, but it was strange to see him overshadowed all weekend by his new team-mate.

NON-STARTER

JEREMY MCWILLIAMS A massive crash in qualifying resulted in trauma in the muscle around the still-healing femur broken in the Jerez test. If Jeremy says he can't race then you know it really, really hurts. Doubly frustrated, because he reckoned he would have had a chance of scoring points.

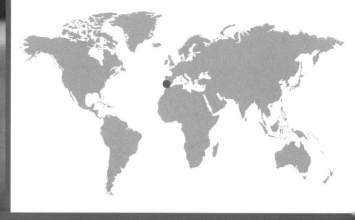

FOLLOW THE LEADER

Rossi reasserted his authority in a processional race, but the new tyre rule caused some problems along the way

Valentino Rossi reminded everyone who was the main man with a controlled and dominant win at a tense Spanish GP in front of the small matter of 138,000 fans. He pushed past pole-man Dani Pedrosa half-way round the first lap and was never headed again. His Fiat Yamaha team-mate, Colin Edwards, backed him up with a solid third place, the Texan's first rostrum for nearly a year. The top three never changed position after the first lap but tension came from the way the gaps fluctuated.

Casey Stoner's Ducati looked much less suited to the twists of Jerez than the kilometre-long straight of Losail but, despite being forced as far back as ninth early on, he was fifth at the flag. He blamed some 'dodgy' overtaking moves by 'overly aggressive' riders at the beginning, but it was noticeable that the Ducati was spinning its rear tyre coming out of corners all over the track through practice. Late in the race Stoner was the fastest man out there, and was only just over half a second from fourth at the flag.

According to the bookmakers this season was supposed to be a fight between Rossi and Pedrosa, but in two races the Spaniard had not laid a glove on the Doctor. The one time Dani appeared to take a big chunk out of Valentino's lead it was opened up again immediately. After the race Rossi maintained that he'd had to work hard and that he'd been worried about how his tyres would last, but it was difficult to pinpoint anywhere he could honestly be said to have had a significant problem. Colin had to stay honest to fend off a charging Toni Elias in the closing stages; he told the post-race press conference that when he saw Toni's name on his pit board he'd thought: 'Oh no, not Elias; not here in Spain!' This remark was notable for getting

Top Carlos Checa started from the front row and finished sixth – a good race in front of his home crowd

Below Nicky Hayden got a super start but faded in the race

'OH NO, NOT ELIAS; NOT HERE IN SPAIN!'
COLIN EDWARDS

a laugh out of Dani Pedrosa, who otherwise seemed unmoved by repeating his second place of last year.

One man who was in urgent need of a good start was Nicky Hayden – and he got it, going from eleventh on the grid to fifth after the first turn and fourth after the third. He held this position for over half the race, but then slid back as his tyre wore out. After the race he sounded totally exhausted. Randy Mamola commented that the experience of having a few hundredths taken out of you in every sector was like bleeding to death: 'Drip, drip, drip.' Getting the Honda to turn on the front is still the problem. Melandri had similar problems on different tyres.

Suzuki's good form continued, although Hopkins slid off just after moving into fourth place. One of the team's test riders, Kousuke Akiyoshi, got his first taste of a European GP, having ridden at the pre-season Jerez test. Team-manager Paul Denning was quick to praise the work he and Nobu Aoki do back in Japan: 'If they say something will work, it does.' This has not always been the case with Japanese testers, and both men were scheduled to make further wild-card appearances as a reward for their hard work and to make sure they understood the level of competition.

One of the unexpected factors at Jerez was the tension over tyre choice. Significant differences in temperature between morning and afternoon sessions led Rossi to describe the earlier outings as 'useless'. The Yamaha team also thought they were in trouble with their selection and were preparing to use their hardest tyre, the one put in the box in case of emergencies. The tactic is to have just two of these, out of the seventeen rears allowed, so when the team realised the majority of

Below Elias charged through from a slow start and nearly made the rostrum

Top Chris Vermeulen had a difficult race, not helped by a persistent cough

Below Rossi leads the charge onto Jerez's back staright, the fastest part of the track

their selection was too soft to last the distance all they could do was save one tyre for the race and use the other on Saturday afternoon. Which is why Rossi was only eighteenth fastest in the Saturday morning practice session. Fortunately for both Fiat Yamaha riders, track temperature dropped by nine degrees for race day and what had been a stop-gap solution, at best, became the

ideal. Before the race, all Valentino's comments related to tyre wear and how he expected the winner to be the man who managed that wear best during the last ten laps. His worries were unfounded: after the race he said the tyres 'went to the end'. Colin Edwards just grinned and said he had pulled the tyre from somewhere anatomically improbable.

For the second race running Michelin monopolised the front row but only 0.325 seconds covered the top ten, making it the closest in GP history. Add in the lack of overtaking at the front and some people worried that the new 800s were going down the F1 road to overwhelmingly efficient electronic control. However, the frantic fights behind the top three showed that there was life in the class yet, although it is definitely true that gaps (especially when the qualifying tyres go on) are now measured in hundredths and thousandths of a second rather than tenths, the inevitable conclusion being that more people can ride an 800 to the limit than could max out a 990. The reduction in both top speeds and race times also demonstrates that braking distances must be much lessened, thus reducing the chance of an outbraking manoeuvre. That effect is compounded by the 800s having a lack of excess power to blast out of corners if they get out of shape making a pass. It truly looked as if the new 800s were behaving like super-sized 250s, carrying lots of lean angle and corner speed. There again, the best race here at Jerez was an epic 250cc GP.

Rossi unveiled his first post-victory stunt for a while to celebrate ending the longest dry spell since his initial 500cc GP win at Donington in 2000. A bunch of his friends dressed as tenpins at which Vale bowled an invisible ball and scored a strike. Was this a celebration of ending his personal record run of six races without a win? The number of pins was the clue: eight of them. This was the celebration the fan club had prepared for Valencia 2006, to celebrate Rossi's eighth world title...

WHERE ARE ILMOR?

The biggest shock of the Spanish GP was the sight of the Ilmor team's trucks in the paddock but no activity in their pit garage. After Qatar, the team announced that they would be suspending racing operations but would continue to develop their bikes. Riders Jeremy McWilliams and Andrew Pitt were both at Jerez, and both professed surprise at the decision. There are two possible reasons for the pull-out. The first was shock at the impossibility of generating sponsorship income, resulting in Mario Ilien and his business partner deciding they couldn't go on spending money at the rate they had been doing. The second reason was professional embarrassment at being so far off the pace: well-informed paddock insiders reckoned some of the team had been expecting to be shooting for rostrums. Mario Ilien himself had no such illusions. He said his target, which he regarded as attainable, was to be getting into the 'top ten in the first year'. That sounds like a sensible ambition, including just the correct amount of optimism.

Winter testing provided a bit of a reality check. The Japanese 800s and the Ducati showed up the Ilmor's lack of development, although the gap did close before the first race. Unfortunately, Qatar was not a happy outing for the team. Although the bike was fast down the straight, riders McWilliams and Pitt were marooned on the back of the grid. Power delivery was still vicious, and the bike didn't look too clever going into corners either. However, Ilien's team was there 'till 4am as the boss went through the data byte by byte'. 'This is a 24-hour shirt,' one mechanic told me, pointing at his chest. McWilliams was impressed with the effort and hopeful of rapid improvement.

But there were frustrations. Ilmor naturally recruited from the labour pool they knew, signing a lot of staff with F1 experience. This made for communications problems – F1 technicians look at data readouts rather than listen to drivers – and some people took a while to accept that listening to the bloke in the leathers and crash helmet might be useful. As for listening to the tyre or suspension technician ... there only appeared to be rapid progress when Ilien himself was present.

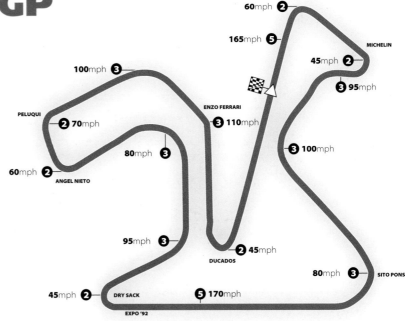

SPANISH GP
CIRCUITO DE JEREZ

ROUND 2
March 25

RACE RESULTS

CIRCUIT LENGTH 2.748 miles
NO. OF LAPS 27
RACE DISTANCE 119.421 miles
WEATHER Dry, 19°C
TRACK TEMPERATURE 31°C
WINNER Valentino Rossi
FASTEST LAP 1m 40.905s, 98.040mph, Valentino Rossi (record)
PREVIOUS LAP RECORD 1m 41.248s, 97.724mph, Loris Capirossi, 2006

QUALIFYING

	Rider	Nationality	Team	Qualifying	Pole +	Gap
1	Pedrosa	SPA	Repsol Honda Team	1m 39.402s		
2	Rossi	ITA	Fiat Yamaha Team	1m 39.453s	0.051s	0.051s
3	Checa	SPA	Honda LCR	1m 39.460s	0.058s	0.007s
4	Edwards	USA	Fiat Yamaha Team	1m 39.486s	0.084s	0.026s
5	Stoner	AUS	Ducati Marlboro Team	1m 39.524s	0.122s	0.038s
6	Hopkins	USA	Rizla Suzuki MotoGP	1m 39.625s	0.223s	0.101s
7	Nakano	JPN	Konica Minolta Honda	1m 39.632s	0.230s	0.007s
8	Elias	SPA	Honda Grisini	1m 39.660s	0.258s	0.028s
9	Melandri	ITA	Honda Grisini	1m 39.722s	0.320s	0.062s
10	Roberts Jr	USA	Team Roberts	1m 39.727s	0.325s	0.005s
11	Hayden	USA	Repsol Honda Team	1m 39.834s	0.432s	0.107s
12	De Puniet	FRA	Kawasaki Racing Team	1m 39.883s	0.481s	0.049s
13	Barros	BRA	Pramac d'Antin	1m 40.196s	0.794s	0.313s
14	Vermeulen	AUS	Rizla Suzuki MotoGP	1m 40.328s	0.926s	0.132s
15	Capirossi	ITA	Ducati Marlboro Team	1m 40.391s	0.989s	0.063s
16	Jacque	FRA	Kawasaki Racing Team	1m 40.405s	1.003s	0.014s
17	Tamada	JPN	Dunlop Yamaha Tech 3	1m 40.617s	1.215s	0.212s
18	Hofmann	GER	Pramac d'Antin	1m 40.710s	1.308s	0.093s
19	Akiyoshi	JPN	Rizla Suzuki MotoGP	1m 41.202s	1.800s	0.492s
20	Guintoli	FRA	Dunlop Yamaha Tech 3	1m 41.219s	1.817s	0.017s

FINISHERS

1 VALENTINO ROSSI His fifth win at Jerez made him the most successful rider ever at the Spanish track, and ended his longest barren spell since his first 500cc victory at Donington in 2000. More importantly, it was as emphatic a win as he could have hoped for: Vale led every lap and set fastest lap.

2 DANI PEDROSA Started from pole, led for half a lap, then kept in Vale's wheel tracks until around half-distance, after which he knew he couldn't win. Slower than Rossi for the second half of the race, so concentrated on keeping his focus and controlling Edwards in third.

3 COLIN EDWARDS Was pleased he pushed past Checa early on and tagged on to the leaders. In the closing stages harassed by a charging Elias and described the fast rights before the final corner with a worn tyre as 'a little hairy'.

4 TONI ELIAS The first Bridgestone rider home. Didn't get a brilliant start, couldn't get his tyres up to temperature and wasn't quick in the early laps, but when the opposition slowed Toni was able to maintain his pace and scare Edwards.

5 CASEY STONER The Ducati looked to be spinning everywhere and Casey was shuffled back to ninth in the first ten laps before a gutsy fight back. Said a few harsh words about some of the opposition's passing manoeuvres.

6 CARLOS CHECA Lower temperatures on race day compared to qualifying caught him out and couldn't match the pace that saw him start from the front row. Enjoyed the dice with Stoner and Elias but couldn't respond when they pushed with five laps to go.

7 NICKY HAYDEN Awful qualifying followed by a brilliant start that took him to sixth at Turn 1, and a blazing first lap when he passed Checa and Stoner. Unfortunately lacked the set-up to maintain this pace and used up his tyres early on – a different pattern from Qatar but just as frustrating.

8 MARCO MELANDRI Never ran with the top men and complained about the same problem as at Qatar: having to be

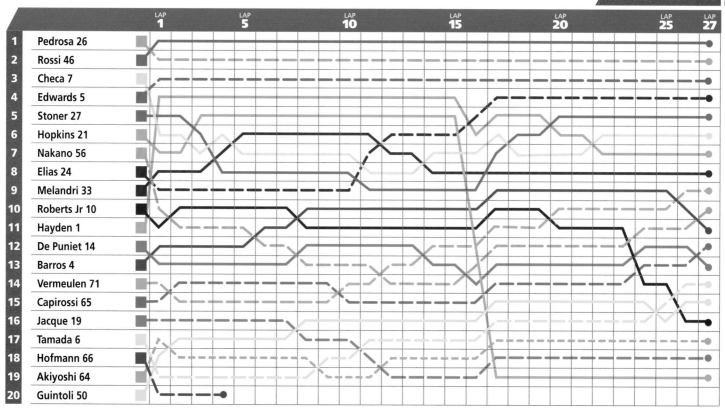

		LAP 1	LAP 5	LAP 10	LAP 15	LAP 20	LAP 25	LAP 27
1	Pedrosa 26							
2	Rossi 46							
3	Checa 7							
4	Edwards 5							
5	Stoner 27							
6	Hopkins 21							
7	Nakano 56							
8	Elias 24							
9	Melandri 33							
10	Roberts Jr 10							
11	Hayden 1							
12	De Puniet 14							
13	Barros 4							
14	Vermeulen 71							
15	Capirossi 65							
16	Jacque 19							
17	Tamada 6							
18	Hofmann 66							
19	Akiyoshi 64							
20	Guintoli 50							

RACE

	Rider	Motorcycle	Race Time	Time +	Fastest Lap	Average Speed
1	Rossi	Yamaha	45m 53.340s		1m 40.905s	97.023mph
2	Pedrosa	Honda	45m 54.586s	1.246s	1m 41.014s	96.979mph
3	Edwards	Yamaha	45m 56.041s	2.701s	1m 41.174s	96.278mph
4	Elias	Honda	45m 57.691s	4.351s	1m 41.395s	96.869mph
5	Stoner	Ducati	45m 58.333s	4.993s	1m 41.443s	96.847mph
6	Checa	Honda	46m 03.340s	10.000s	1m 41.421s	96.612mph
7	Hayden	Honda	46m 07.486s	14.146s	1m 41.441s	96.527mph
8	Melandri	Honda	46m 13.309s	19.969s	1m 41.303s	96.324mph
9	Vermeulen	Suzuki	46m 18.126s	24.786s	1m 42.037s	96.157mph
10	Nakano	Honda	46m 18.295s	24.955s	1m 42.024s	96.151mph
11	Barros	Ducati	46m 18.348s	25.008s	1m 41.812s	96.149mph
12	Capirossi	Ducati	46m 19.192s	25.852s	1m 41.876s	96.120mph
13	De Puniet	Kawasaki	46m 19.785s	26.445s	1m 41.967s	96.099mph
14	Tamada	Yamaha	46m 29.993s	36.653s	1m 42.456s	95.748mph
15	Guintoli	Yamaha	46m 30.084s	36.744s	1m 42.291s	95.745mph
16	Roberts Jr	Kr212v	46m 42.251s	48.911s	1m 42.024s	95.329mph
17	Akiyoshi	Suzuki	46m 44.124s	50.784s	1m 42.555s	95.266mph
18	Jacque	Kawasaki	46m 54.241s	1m 00.901s	1m 42.327s	94.923mph
19	Hopkins	Suzuki	46m 56.711s	1m 03.371s	1m 40.938s	94.840mph
	Hofmann*	Ducati			1m 41.904s	

*Excluded

CHAMPIONSHIP

	Rider	Team	Points
1	Rossi	Fiat Yamaha Team	45
2	Stoner	Ducati Marlboro Team	36
3	Pedrosa	Repsol Honda Team	36
4	Edwards	Fiat Yamaha Team	26
5	Melandri	Honda Gresini	19
6	Hayden	Repsol Honda Team	17
7	Vermeulen	Rizla Suzuki MotoGP	16
8	Elias	Honda Gresini	15
9	Hopkins	Rizla Suzuki MotoGP	13
10	Nakano	Konica Minolta Honda	12
11	Barros	Pramac d'Antin	12
12	Checa	Honda LCR	10
13	Hofmann	Pramac d'Antin	05
14	Jacque	Kawasaki Racing Team	04
15	Capirossi	Ducati Marlboro Team	04
16	Roberts Jr	Team Roberts	03
17	De Puniet	Kawasaki Racing Team	03
18	Tamada	Dunlop Yamaha Tech 3	02
19	Guintoli	Dunlop Yamaha Tech 3	02

ultra-aggressive on the brakes to make a pass and using up the tyre. Complained long and loud about Honda's treatment of him after the race.

9 CHRIS VERMEULEN A repeat of his Qatar race: disappointing qualifying followed by a bit of contact in Turn 1 and a tough race for a few points. Chris wasn't helped by suffering from a cough so bad his boots kept coming off their footrests.

10 SHINYA NAKANO Didn't have the confidence to push hard early on thanks to a fast crash in warm-up. When the bike felt better balanced he suffered from chatter at the front. Managed to ambush Barros on the last lap to get a top-ten finish.

11 ALEX BARROS Up to ninth in the first half of the race, then handicapped by a front tyre that didn't want to keep working hard. A tough last-lap pass by Vermeulen opened the door for Nakano, so lost two places on the final lap.

12 LORIS CAPIROSSI Too old? Fazed by his new, younger team-mate? Not a bit of it – merely preoccupied by the imminent birth of his and wife Ingrid's first child. Ricardo Capirossi duly arrived eight days later.

13 RANDY DE PUNIET Salvaged some points from what was a disastrous weekend for the Kawasaki team. Lost touch with the fight for ninth after a couple of small mistakes, battled back to the group only to be severely hampered when Roberts's bike suffered a transmission problem.

14 MAKOTO TAMADA Held up by Akiyoshi early on, then enjoyed a good dice with his team-mate before half-distance. Finished the race four seconds quicker than in 2006, on a Michelin-shod 990cc Honda, which pleased both team and rider – not to mention Dunlop.

15 SYLVAIN GUINTOLI Another impressive race from the class rookie at a track where he's never done well. A good, aggressive start followed by a dice with his team-mate saw the Frenchman finish the race ten seconds quicker than Checa did on the Yamaha in 2006, in a race time that was four seconds quicker than last year's.

16 KENNY ROBERTS Looked set for a solid top-ten finish until he suffered a major transmission problem on lap 24 out

of 27. Kenny's bike decided to put itself into second gear in the middle of a corner; thought he'd have to pull in but was able to finish.

17 KOUSUKE AKIYOSHI Suzuki's test rider had participated in the Jerez test when Hopkins was injured and came back for the GP to help him understand the level of competition in MotoGP.

18 OLIVIER JACQUE Reported a total lack of grip after just three laps and would have been last and ten seconds adrift of the field but for Hopkins's crash. The team was deeply unhappy that he was over a second a lap slower than his team-mate.

19 JOHN HOPKINS Crashed out of fourth place when he ran wide and lost the front

a lap after he'd passed Hayden. Thankfully did no further damage to his injured wrist and was able to pick up the bike and ride to the flag.

EXCLUDED

ALEX HOFMANN Problems with a new clutch led to a comedy of errors and a black flag. Came in after a couple of laps with terminal power-delivery problems and changed to his spare bike. Unfortunately this is totally illegal...

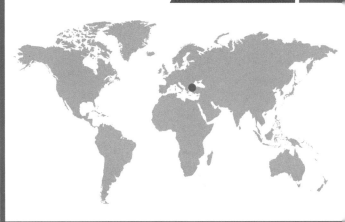

DUCATI DELIGHT

**Stoner wins and Ducati fill
three of the top four places
as Rossi suffers from the first
signs of the tyre troubles that
would dog his season**

Amid the post-race arguments, tyre post-mortems and political intrigue over the future of the Turkish GP it was easy to overlook the achievement of Casey Stoner. The young Aussie took his second win in three races and retook the championship lead while the rest fought among themselves in his wake.

It had all looked so good for Fiat Yamaha until half-way round the first lap. Rossi and Edwards qualified first and second and Valentino made an uncharacteristically aggressive start, then ran off track on the first lap at the fastest corner in the MotoGP calendar. He lost the front going in, pushing too hard on a tyre that was probably not yet up to temperature. Stoner found himself in the lead. Moments later the pack got to the hardest braking effort on the lap, going right down the gearbox from over 180mph to around 45mph. Olivier Jacque, running in about tenth, missed his braking marker and arrived at the corner 8mph faster than the man in front of him. The French rider tried to avoid a crash by running up the inside kerb but clipped Dani Pedrosa and then brought down Colin Edwards. Chris Vermeulen's Suzuki then ended up surfing on top of Pedrosa's Honda, which at least enabled the Aussie to get back into the race.

The multiple pile-up left a hole in the pack – Stoner, Capirossi, Hopkins, Rossi, Elias and Hayden were nearly two seconds ahead of the pursuers, who were led by Melandri, Barros and de Puniet. Stoner was never headed. He had a lead of a second by lap four and had doubled it by lap ten. Capirossi had been second early on, but by this time Elias had come through after a war with Hopkins and putting a pass on Rossi that reminded everyone of that incident with Gibernau at Jerez in 2005.

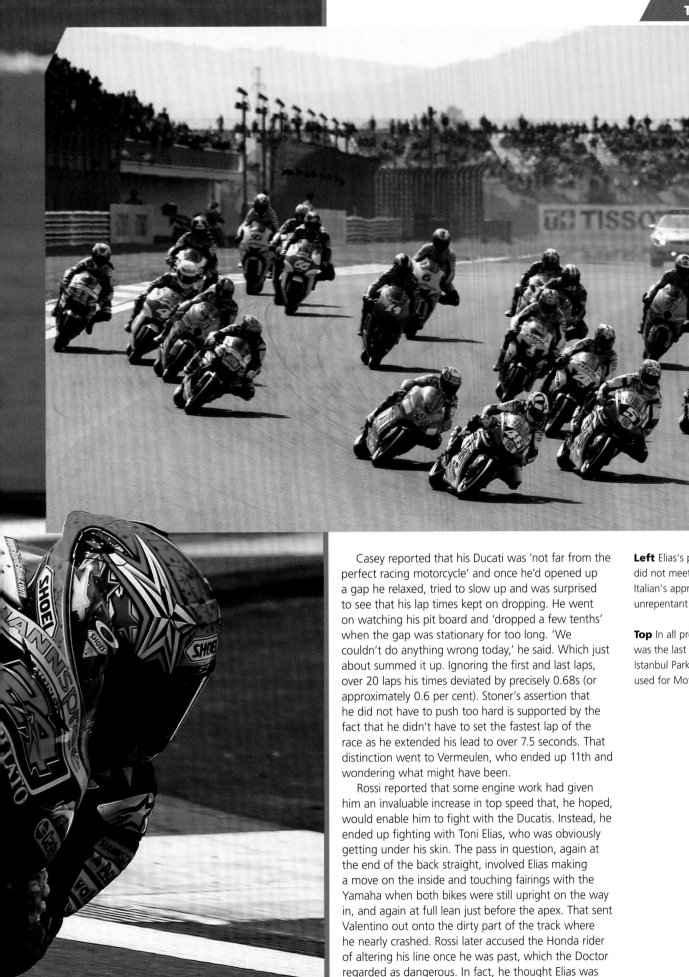

Casey reported that his Ducati was 'not far from the perfect racing motorcycle' and once he'd opened up a gap he relaxed, tried to slow up and was surprised to see that his lap times kept on dropping. He went on watching his pit board and 'dropped a few tenths' when the gap was stationary for too long. 'We couldn't do anything wrong today,' he said. Which just about summed it up. Ignoring the first and last laps, over 20 laps his times deviated by precisely 0.68s (or approximately 0.6 per cent). Stoner's assertion that he did not have to push too hard is supported by the fact that he didn't have to set the fastest lap of the race as he extended his lead to over 7.5 seconds. That distinction went to Vermeulen, who ended up 11th and wondering what might have been.

Rossi reported that some engine work had given him an invaluable increase in top speed that, he hoped, would enable him to fight with the Ducatis. Instead, he ended up fighting with Toni Elias, who was obviously getting under his skin. The pass in question, again at the end of the back straight, involved Elias making a move on the inside and touching fairings with the Yamaha when both bikes were still upright on the way in, and again at full lean just before the apex. That sent Valentino out onto the dirty part of the track where he nearly crashed. Rossi later accused the Honda rider of altering his line once he was past, which the Doctor regarded as dangerous. In fact, he thought Elias was dangerous in the general sense but was saving the special stuff for him. Jerry Burgess was more measured, mentioning the impetuosity of youth but also suggesting that if Toni wanted to win the race it would have been a

Left Elias's pass on Rossi did not meet with the Italian's approval. Toni was unrepentant

Top In all probability, this was the last time the splendid Istanbul Park circuit will be used for MotoGP

> ## 'DEPENDS HOW YOU LOOK AT IT… I DON'T THINK I DID ANYTHING WRONG; IF HE IS ANGRY WHAT CAN I DO?'
> **TONI ELIAS**

better idea to follow Valentino for a few laps and see if he got towed close enough to Stoner.

Elias later reported that he did try to close on Stoner for three or four laps but then 'I decide to be intelligent'. That remark was delivered with a grin and raised a laugh from the post-race press conference. His view of the overtaking move was markedly different from Rossi's, and was also delivered wittily and received with sympathy. 'Depends how you look at it,' he said with a grin. 'I don't think I did anything wrong; if he is angry what can I do?' Shrug, end of subject. He was pleased that he could 'finally show my style is good for MotoGP' and mentioned that he had 'found a good solution' at the first corner. That would have been a solution to starting from the fourth row. It was, by the way, obvious that the Italian media pack was not siding with Rossi in this argument.

Valentino's real problem came from his rear tyre. At mid-distance his lap times suddenly increased by a second; it was painfully obvious that he couldn't carry any speed into a corner and he dropped to tenth. A long meeting ensued behind closed garage doors after which Rossi said of his tyre supplier: 'Michelin have to work like us and have to give heart like us.' The tyre had felt like it was falling apart, but there was no repeat of the chunking that had happened at Laguna the previous season. Nevertheless, the offending hoop was whisked away to Clermont-Ferrand for a post-mortem. Michelin's top finisher was Hayden, in seventh; he just survived a big moment on the last lap but was happier than in the first two races, despite having worked his front tyre hard early on.

Top Rossi's front tyre trouble saw him drop down the order

Below The World Champion was severely handicapped by a lack of power on the fast Turkish track

Nicky was part of the frantic battle for third which raged behind Stoner and Elias that, on the last lap, came down to a fight between the Ducatis of Capirossi and Barros. When the Italian lost the front going into the fast right and got in the mother of all tank-slappers Barros powered past. It looked all over – the Brazilian is still one of the latest brakers in MotoGP – but somehow Loris not only edged past but resisted Alex's counter-attacks in the tight triple bend that ends the lap. 'Twenty days ago was the best day of my life,' said Loris, referring to the birth of his son. 'My championship starts here.'

The only depressing thing about this, the third Turkish GP, was that it was the last for the foreseeable future. Despite being built primarily for Formula One the Istanbul Park circuit had proved perfect for bike racing, but the organisers made a thumping loss each year and Turkey's slot in the 2008 calendar was taken by the USA's second GP, at Indianapolis.

Top Loris Capirossi just beat out Alex Barros in a frantic fight for third place

Below The paddock main street doesn't look like it suffers from a lack of finance, but the private teams are strapped for cash

MONEY, MONEY, MONEY

Everything in the MotoGP garden looked rosy – TV viewing figures and track attendances both increasing healthily and the racing as close as it's ever been. And yet there is one major problem: money – or rather the lack of it. In the past couple of seasons the MotoGP paddock has lost the WCM and Sito Pons teams, and all the satellite teams left on the grid have varying degrees of financial worry.

So how to address the perplexing lack of sponsorship? Dorna convened a meeting in Barcelona just before the Turkish GP, attended by representatives of all the teams, the MSMA and IRTA to try and find some answers. The forum's discussions covered such diverse subjects as negative press and professional presentation without coming up with any earth-shattering suggestions. However, one idea that hasn't met with universal approval does appear to be heading towards reality. That is the inner paddock that shuts the 125 and 250 classes out of the MotoGP teams' territory, the objective being to make the sponsors go to MotoGP teams if they want their guests and staff to get anywhere near the big class. Or to put it another way, it would stop the guy who supplies a 125 team with a few nuts and bolts rubbing shoulders with Valentino Rossi. Bar-coded paddock passes that are scanned on entering and leaving the paddock were introduced this season in preparation for this, as well as to counter problems with forgery.

Bernie Ecclestone was in Istanbul to buy the lease on the circuit. His view? 'Be a man and get your own sponsorship.'

TURKISH GP
ISTANBUL PARK

ROUND 3
April 22

RACE RESULTS

CIRCUIT LENGTH 3.311 miles
NO. OF LAPS 22
RACE DISTANCE 72.838 miles
WEATHER Dry, 23°C
TRACK TEMPERATURE 38°C
WINNER Casey Stoner
FASTEST LAP 1m 54.026s,
104.760mph, Chris Vermeulen
PREVIOUS LAP RECORD 1m 52.877s,
105.830mph, Toni Elias, 2006

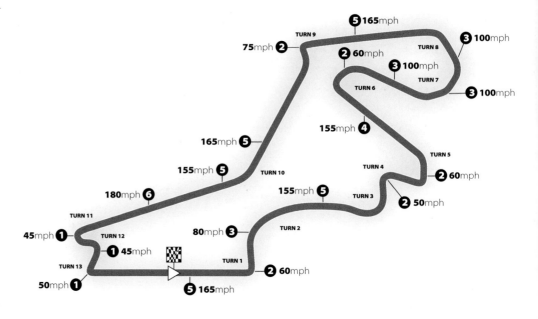

QUALIFYING

	Rider	Nationality	Team	Qualifying	Pole +	Gap
1	Rossi	ITA	Fiat Yamaha Team	1m 52.795s		
2	Edwards	USA	Fiat Yamaha Team	1m 52.944s	0.149s	0.149s
3	Pedrosa	SPA	Repsol Honda Team	1m 52.971s	0.176s	0.027s
4	Stoner	AUS	Ducati Marlboro Team	1m 53.375s	0.580s	0.404s
5	Capirossi	ITA	Ducati Marlboro Team	1m 53.559s	0.764s	0.184s
6	Hayden	USA	Repsol Honda Team	1m 53.613s	0.818s	0.054s
7	Hopkins	USA	Rizla Suzuki MotoGP	1m 53.637s	0.842s	0.024s
8	De Puniet	FRA	Kawasaki Racing Team	1m 53.706s	0.911s	0.069s
9	Vermeulen	AUS	Rizla Suzuki MotoGP	1m 53.771s	0.976s	0.065s
10	Elias	SPA	Honda Gresini	1m 53.835s	1.404s	0.064s
11	Jacque	FRA	Kawasaki Racing Team	1m 53.847s	1.052s	0.012s
12	Nakano	JPN	Konica Minolta Honda	1m 53.988s	1.193s	0.141s
13	Barros	BRA	Pramac d'Antin	1m 54.082s	1.287s	0.094s
14	Melandri	ITA	Honda Gresini	1m 54.143s	1.348s	0.061s
15	Tamada	JPN	Dunlop Yamaha Tech 3	1m 54.206s	1.411s	0.063s
16	Checa	SPA	Honda LCR	1m 54.221s	1.426s	0.015s
17	Hofmann	GER	Pramac d'Antin	1m 54.421s	1.626s	0.200s
18	Roberts Jr	USA	Team Roberts	1m 54.527s	1.732s	0.106s
19	Guintoli	FRA	Dunlop Yamaha Tech 3	1m 54.845s	2.050s	0.318s

FINISHERS

1 CASEY STONER Was describing his bike when he used the phrase 'not far from perfect' but could have been describing his whole race. Once Rossi gifted him the lead on the first lap it was a matter of watching his pit board, with every lap except the first and last within 0.7s. You believed him when he said he could've gone a lot quicker at the end.

2 TONI ELIAS Rode like a stocky version of Kevin Schwantz and really yanked Rossi's chain when he put a tough pass on the Italian at the end of the back straight. Unfortunately lost him time on the leader so Toni decided to 'be intelligent' and settle for second.

3 LORIS CAPIROSSI Back with his mind on racing and enjoying himself again. Seemed happy to let his team-mate set a faster pace, but quite willing to put everything on the line on the last lap to fight off Barros.

4 ALEX BARROS Got a good start despite a bout of flu and qualifying on the fifth row, and in the second half worked his way past Hayden, Rossi, Hopkins and Melandri – and Capirossi on the last lap – but was denied a rostrum finish by a vintage, last-gasp Loris move.

5 MARCO MELANDRI Came to the circuit where he'd won both previous events convinced that everything and everyone were conspiring against him. Qualifying did nothing to dispel the depression, but

the race did. Took him a while to find his confidence in the 2006 model RCV; looks like history could repeat itself.

6 JOHN HOPKINS Another fantastically gutsy effort: after a great start his late, late braking made him very difficult to pass and in the second half of the race he was part of the mass brawl for the final rostrum position.

7 NICKY HAYDEN Looked to be in terrible trouble until he used Michelin's qualifier to lop nearly two seconds off his time. Made a good start but used up his front tyre under hard braking to make up for lack of top end. Had a major moment in the fast right on the last lap, which let Hopkins past. It could have been a lot worse.

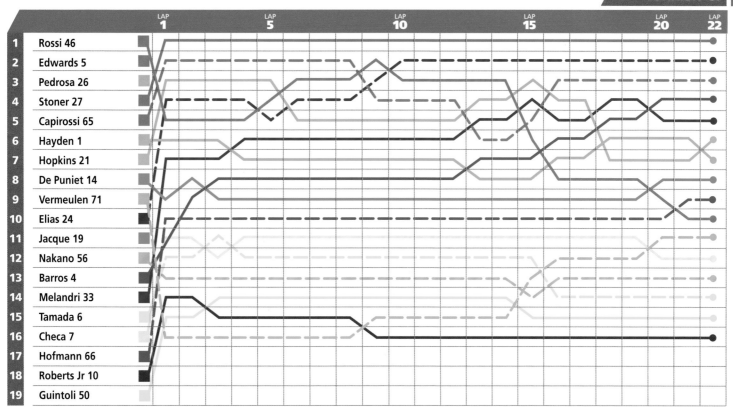

		LAP 1	LAP 5	LAP 10	LAP 15	LAP 20	LAP 22
1	Rossi 46						
2	Edwards 5						
3	Pedrosa 26						
4	Stoner 27						
5	Capirossi 65						
6	Hayden 1						
7	Hopkins 21						
8	De Puniet 14						
9	Vermeulen 71						
10	Elias 24						
11	Jacque 19						
12	Nakano 56						
13	Barros 4						
14	Melandri 33						
15	Tamada 6						
16	Checa 7						
17	Hofmann 66						
18	Roberts Jr 10						
19	Guintoli 50						

RACE

	Rider	Motorcycle	Race Time	Time +	Fastest Lap	Average Speed
1	Stoner	Ducati	42m 02.850s		1m 54.210s	104.165mph
2	Elias	Honda	42m 09.057s	6.207s	1m 54.224s	103.910mph
3	Capirossi	Ducati	42m 10.952s	8.102s	1m 54.461s	103.832mph
4	Barros	Ducati	42m 10.985s	8.135s	1m 54.224s	103.831mph
5	Melandri	Honda	42m 11.139s	8.289s	1m 54.391s	103.824mph
6	Hopkins	Suzuki	42m 13.036s	10.186s	1m 54.268s	103.747mph
7	Hayden	Honda	42m 13.089s	10.239s	1m 54.396s	103.745mph
8	De Puniet	Kawasaki	42m 17.584s	14.734s	1m 54.530s	103.561mph
9	Hofmann	Ducati	42m 18.892s	16.042s	1m 54.820s	103.507mph
10	Rossi	Yamaha	42m 21.849s	18.999s	1m 54.066s	103.387mph
11	Vermeulen	Suzuki	42m 29.099s	26.249s	1m 54.026s	103.093mph
12	Checa	Honda	42m 32.396s	29.546s	1m 55.043s	102.960mph
13	Nakano	Honda	42m 39.772s	36.922s	1m 55.266s	102.663mph
14	Tamada	Yamaha	42m 41.390s	38.540s	1m 55.428s	102.598mph
15	Guintoli	Yamaha	42m 42.187s	39.337s	1m 55.663s	102.567mph
16	Roberts Jr	Kr212v	43m 12.186s	1m 09.336s	1m 56.953s	101.379mph
	Jacque	Kawasaki				
	Pedrosa	Honda				
	Edwards	Yamaha				

CHAMPIONSHIP

	Rider	Team	Points
1	Stoner	Ducati Marlboro Team	61
2	Rossi	Fiat Yamaha Team	51
3	Pedrosa	Repsol Honda Team	36
4	Elias	Honda Gresini	35
5	Melandri	Honda Gresini	30
6	Edwards	Fiat Yamaha Team	26
7	Hayden	Repsol Honda Team	26
8	Barros	Pramac d'Antin	25
9	Hopkins	Rizla Suzuki MotoGP	23
10	Vermeulen	Rizla Suzuki MotoGP	21
11	Capirossi	Ducati Marlboro team	20
12	Nakano	Konica Minolta Honda	15
13	Checa	Honda LCR	14
14	Hofmann	Pramac d'Antin	12
15	De Puniet	Kawasaki Racing Team	11
16	Tamada	Dunlop Yamaha Tech 3	04
17	Jacque	Kawasaki Racing Team	04
18	Guintoli	Dunlop Yamaha Tech 3	03
19	Roberts Jr	Team Roberts	03

8 RANDY DE PUNIET His first MotoGP top-ten finish. Made a bad start but avoided the first-lap crash. Took a long time to pass the struggling Rossi, which meant he couldn't catch the big fight for third.

9 ALEX HOFFMAN Severely beaten up by a crash in morning warm-up, which damaged his ribs and made breathing uncomfortable. Still able to smile about the fact he overtook Rossi in a race for the first time in his career.

10 VALENTINO ROSSI Looked like he was on for a repeat of his Qatar fight with Stoner, but Elias's overtake cost Valentino more than a second and then his rear tyre started to give problems – thought it was losing rubber and was forced to slow his pace considerably.

11 CHRIS VERMEULEN Unsung hero of the Turkish GP: caught up in the first-lap crash but managed to remount and chase the pack; 22 seconds behind Stoner at the end of lap one but lost less than four seconds in the rest of the race; set the fastest lap on the penultimate circuit. Surely he should have been on the rostrum.

12 CARLOS CHECA Suffered all the Honda woes and was anonymous for most of the weekend. Reported problems with both the engine and the front end; adopted a no-risk strategy for the race.

13 SHINYA NAKANO An identical weekend to fellow Honda rider Checa, with Shinya's main problem lack of feedback from the front and extreme sensitivity to minor setting changes.

14 MAKOTO TAMADA There were signs of the confidence he needs so badly returning. Happy with the Dunlops' performance, which remained constant despite dropping from their early, impressive level.

15 SYLVAIN GUINTOLI Would surely have scored more than one point if he hadn't 'had to do a bit of gardening' to avoid the big first-lap crash, losing about ten seconds in the process. Another impressive weekend's work.

16 KENNY ROBERTS Couldn't find a set-up for new, stiffer swinging arms in practice but thought the team had found a solution in warm-up, only for the rear tyre to feel like it was flat right from the sighting lap.

NON-FINISHERS

OLIVIER JACQUE By his own admission the instigator of the big crash at the end of the back straight on the first lap. Missed his braking marker and arrived faster than the men around him, clipping Edwards first, then Pedrosa, whose bike took Vermeulen out. Hurt his coccyx when he landed from a great height and banged his head.

DANI PEDROSA The best Honda qualifier and looking set for a good race, then involved in Jacque's crash. Banged on chest and neck when his bike was hit by the Kawasaki and ended up underneath Vermeulen's Suzuki. The damage was enough to prevent him testing on the Monday after the race.

COLIN EDWARDS Lost a few places in the first corners as he struggled to get heat in his tyre, which put him in the wrong place when Jacque had his rush of blood. Took a bang on his knee, which swelled up after he got back to his pit garage.

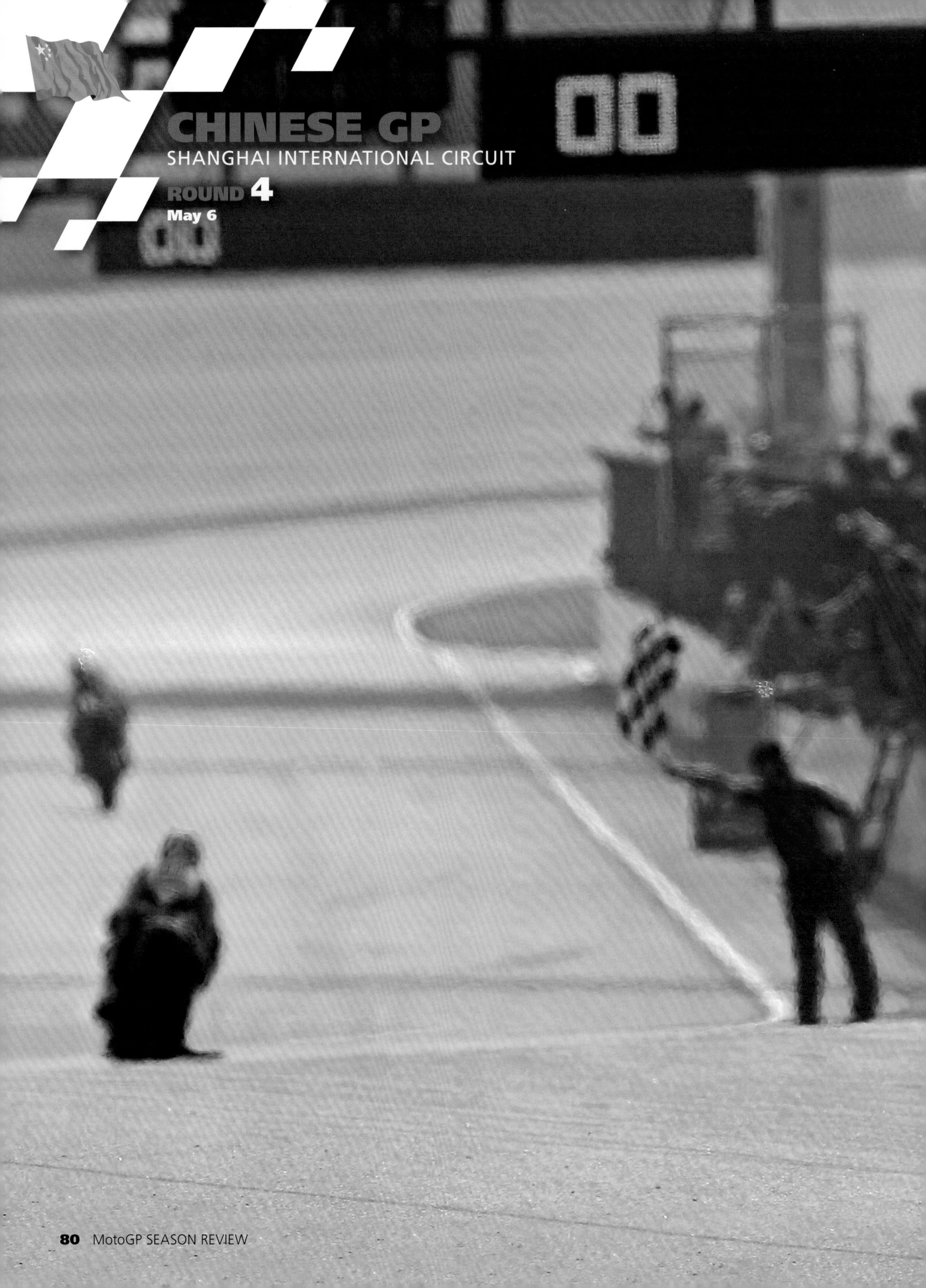

CHINESE GP
SHANGHAI INTERNATIONAL CIRCUIT
ROUND 4
May 6

CHINA SYNDROME

Stoner unleashes the full potential of the Ducati on the longest straight of the year, Rossi fights heroically, Hopkins gets his first rostrum in Grand Prix racing

After the first race of the year Rossi estimated that he'd need to lead Stoner onto the main straight at Losail by around 0.6s to avoid being overtaken before the first corner of the next lap. What, he was asked, would be necessary when he got to the Shanghai circuit's 0.8-mile straight? Valentino thought about it for a moment, muttered something about losing 0.6–0.7s a lap, came to an abrupt halt, looked up from his timing sheets and said: 'I need a gun.'

He wasn't far wrong, but for the third time in four races Rossi put the Yamaha on pole with a quite astounding lap that was 0.89s faster than second-placed John Hopkins, the biggest gap between first and second places on the grid in the MotoGP era. As third-placed Colin Edwards said of the Yamaha: 'It goes round in circles better than anything out there.'

The big problem for the Yamahas and the other Japanese bikes at Shanghai is that there are not one but two straights. The back straight may be the longest of the year but the front one is fairly substantial too. Casey Stoner used both of them to advantage on the first lap, driving past Edwards and Hopkins on the main straight to take second and then picking off Rossi just after they crossed the line for the first time. The Doctor had pushed past Hopkins and opened up a gap as they went onto the back straight, but his hopes of opening up a significant lead were not realised.

The leaders were lucky to escape a multiple pile-up in the never-ending first corner, instigated by Toni Elias. His optimistic charge up the inside put Barros and Hayden on the grass and the man himself on the floor and out of the race. Elias had also got on Stoner's wick during free practice, leading to an outbreak of fist-shaking.

Rossi's criticism of Elias after the Turkish race had not gone down well at home in Italy and he had revised his opinion significantly by the time he got to China. 'It's racing, it happens' was the new refrain. But Vale could have reverted to his original opinion again after Turn 1 and found very few dissenters.

It would have been very easy for Valentino Rossi to accept the inevitable and settle for second place, but he did not. As he had under similar circumstances in Qatar, he harried Stoner as hard as he could, passing him three times only to be repassed almost immediately. The first time was at one-third distance. Rossi forced through in the tight left before the right that unwinds onto the back straight only to have the Ducati blast past half-way to the hairpin. Rossi tried to repass on the brakes but went wide. A couple of laps later Valentino repeated the pass and Casey powered past again.

While all this was transpiring, John Hopkins managed to stay with them. 'I knew those two were my ticket to a breakaway,' he said later. At two-thirds distance John had visions of splitting the pair after Rossi hit a bump in the braking area at the end of the main straight and ran off the track, but it only took Vale two laps to regain second place. The rostrum was a just reward for Hopper who had been up front in every race so far this year, and usually involved in a fight with Rossi. Suzuki team staff struggled onto their flights to Europe next day in varying states of disarray following their rider-led celebrations.

Behind the close battle for the rostrum places the Hondas faded, despite Melandri showing well in the early laps. Lack of top speed and insufficient confidence in the front end were again the problems. The works

Left The tight opening part of the lap was instrumental in causing the first-lap pile-up

Below Was this the start of negotiations? Loris Capirossi will be a Suzuki rider in 2008

genuinely impressive, as was his fellow-countryman de Puniet, who was sixth for much of the race. Randy was carrying the Kawasaki flag alone after Olivier Jacque suffered a deep gash to his forearm during Friday practice.

On paper this may look like a predictable, even boring, race but it was a lot closer than the numbers would have you believe. The issue was only settled by Rossi's excursion on lap 16. Until then, the Doctor was using his handling advantage in the long corners and infield and Stoner was riding equally brilliantly to keep the Italian behind him. The Yamaha had certainly improved its top end since Qatar, but the speed with which the Ducati was able to pull alongside the Yamaha and then open a gap was breathtaking. If Valentino got onto the straight in its slipstream he could just about stay there and regain the lost ground on the brakes and in the hairpin at the end of the straight. The Ducati was notably less nimble, with Stoner reporting that the long right-hander onto the back straight was his biggest problem, but he didn't make a mistake despite the unrelenting pressure.

The young Aussie did, though, show signs of irritation with the media's highlighting of the Desmosedici's top speed, reminding everyone that it can also go round corners.

Casey wasn't the only one in a red shirt who was irritated. Ever since the Qatar race there had been whispers about the legality of the Ducati, gleefully amplified by the Italian press, despite the bike having had its tank and fuel temperature measured. This time MotoGP technical director Mike Webb checked the

Top Nicky Hayden gets back on track after being punted by a wayward Toni Elias on the first lap

Below Stoner and Rossi's duel lasted until the Italian made a mistake on the brakes just two laps from the chequered flag

Repsol machines had a little more top-end power and at least looked competitive. The satellite teams languished downfield and the Honda-engined Team Roberts bike was embarrassingly outgunned both on the straights and in the turns. After Nicky Hayden got back on track, following the first-corner incident, he was shadowed for ten laps by Sylvain Guintoli on the Dunlop-shod Tech 3 Yamaha. The only rookie in the MotoGP field was

'I KNEW THOSE TWO WERE MY TICKET TO A BREAKAWAY'
JOHN HOPKINS

capacity and, of course, found it perfectly legal. Marlboro Ducati team-manager Livio Suppo took exception to a quote attributed to Fiat Yamaha boss Davide Brivio: his reply began, 'As an Italian, I am proud...' Great stuff! Talk up your own engineering and impugn the patriotism of the other guy while you're at it.

Another Italian, Mr Rossi, was surprisingly happy.

He'd enjoyed himself riding at the limit and put in a fastest lap only 0.027s slower than Stoner's, which shows how hard he was pushing in the corners. Vale was quick to praise both Yamaha and Michelin for giving him the tools to take the fight to Ducati and Bridgestone. When he looked at the points table and Stoner's 15-point lead, though, he couldn't stop himself harking back to his tyre problems in the previous round.

Top Alex Hofmann at speed on the Pramac d'Antin satellite team Ducati

THE VIEW FROM HRC

It was the signal the Honda riders had been waiting for. Once HRC MD Satoru Horiike had given the press his opinion on the Honda V4's slow start to the year and admitted to some mistakes, the riders started to voice theirs. Horiike-san was gracious enough to congratulate Ducati on the great job they were doing, but he also defended the concept of the V4. There was, he said, nothing wrong with the basic idea, but the company had failed to give their riders the tools they needed. HRC had concentrated on manoeuvrability and the ability to change direction quickly – hence the vestigial fairing: 'We thought that the reduction in engine capacity would highlight agility and corner speed.' So HRC concentrated their efforts on the chassis.

Ducati's approach was to use a screamer motor and produce as much power as possible, then control it with electronics. Ironically, there are echoes here of HRC and Mick Doohan ditching their big-bang engines and reverting to a screamer motor when unleaded petrol became compulsory for the 500s.

After the race Dani Pedrosa was heard to utter his first public criticism of the Honda, while Nicky Hayden was able to articulate at least some of the discontent he'd been bottling up.

The other subject that attracted Horiike's attention was the future of the 250cc class, something that is preoccupying the MSMA. Emphasising that this was a decision for them, Horiike-san nevertheless offered his personal opinion. He was strongly against prototype four-strokes on cost grounds and anything based on 600cc production motors, as that would impinge on the territory of the World Superbike and Supersport Championships. The suggestion that the only series production motors left that would fit the bill were the sort of 400–450cc motors currently used in enduro and motocross was met with something close to enthusiasm, not least because companies like Aprilia and KTM would still be able to compete.

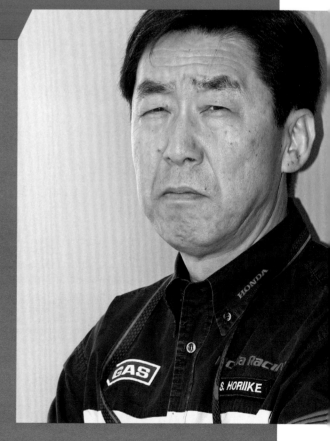

Above HRC's MD Satoru Horiike made the company's first public admission that the form of their 800 had been disappointing

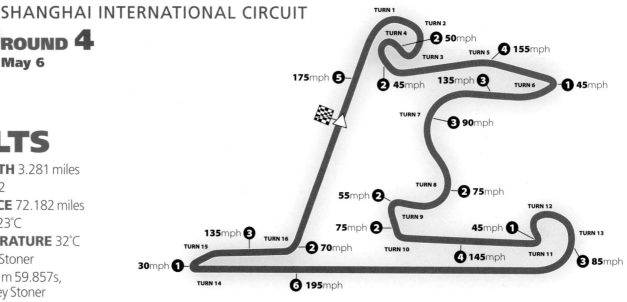

CHINESE GP
SHANGHAI INTERNATIONAL CIRCUIT
ROUND 4
May 6

RACE RESULTS

CIRCUIT LENGTH 3.281 miles
NO. OF LAPS 22
RACE DISTANCE 72.182 miles
WEATHER Dry, 23°C
TRACK TEMPERATURE 32°C
WINNER Casey Stoner
FASTEST LAP 1m 59.857s, 98.570mph, Casey Stoner
PREVIOUS LAP RECORD 11m 58.424s, 99.750mph, Valentino Rossi, 2006

QUALIFYING

	Rider	Nationality	Team	Qualifying	Pole +	Gap
1	Rossi	ITA	Fiat Yamaha Team	1m 58.424s		
2	Hopkins	USA	Rizla Suzuki MotoGP	1m 59.315s	0.891s	0.891s
3	Edwards	USA	Fiat Yamaha Team	1m 59.406s	0.982s	0.091s
4	Stoner	AUS	Ducati Marlboro Team	1m 59.516s	0.092s	0.110s
5	Pedrosa	SPA	Repsol Honda Team	1m 59.602s	1.178s	0.086s
6	Melandri	ITA	Honda Gresini	1m 59.863s	1.439s	0.261s
7	De Puniet	FRA	Kawasaki Racing Team	1m 59.985s	1.561s	0.122s
8	Barros	BRA	Pramac d'Antin	2m 00.052s	1.628s	0.067s
9	Hayden	USA	Repsol Honda Team	2m 00.087s	1.663s	0.035s
10	Nakano	JPN	Konica Minolta Honda	2m 00.157s	1.733s	0.070s
11	Hofmann	GER	Pramac d'Antin	2m 00.175s	1.751s	0.018s
12	Elias	SPA	Honda Gresini	2m 00.205s	1.781s	0.030s
13	Checa	SPA	Honda LCR	2m 00.319s	1.895s	0.114s
14	Capirossi	ITA	Ducati Marlboro Team	2m 00.369s	1.945s	0.050s
15	Vermeulen	AUS	Rizla Suzuki MotoGP	2m 00.680s	2.256s	0.311s
16	Roberts Jr	USA	Team Roberts	2m 00.763s	2.339s	0.083s
17	Guintoli	FRA	Dunlop Yamaha Tech 3	2m 00.157s	2.733s	0.394s
18	Tamada	JPN	Dunlop Yamaha Tech 3	2m 01.178s	2.754s	0.021s
19	Jacque	FRA	Kawasaki Racing Team			

FINISHERS

1 CASEY STONER Another frighteningly fast, faultless performance from the young Aussie under race-long pressure from Rossi. Ducati's power was a major weapon but Casey used it to maximum effect, limiting any losses in the corners. The only problem was getting distracted in qualifying and missing pole.

2 VALENTINO ROSSI Said he wasn't letting Stoner win without a fight, and was as good as his word. Passed and repassed the Ducati before a major moment when he hit a bump at the end of the main straight on the brakes, putting him wide and breaking the tow. Much happier with his bike, and especially his tyres, than in Turkey.

3 JOHN HOPKINS His first MotoGP rostrum finish after 82 starts. Hopper started from the front row for the first time since Assen '06 and used his elbows in the first few corners to make sure he got away with Stoner and Rossi. Only settled for third in the last couple of laps, and dedicated the podium to his late father.

4 DANI PEDROSA The Chinese GP summed up Honda's season so far: 14 seconds adrift of the winner at a track where Dani won last year. Started well and had a good dice with Melandri but could never run the pace of the leaders.

5 MARCO MELANDRI Beginning to look more like his old self after a troubled start to the year but, like the other Honda riders, complained of lack of top speed and front-end stability on corner entry. Ran as high as second early on before hitting chatter.

6 LORIS CAPIROSSI Started from 14th thanks to a crash with Vermeulen in qualifying, then only just avoided the first-lap pile-up. Had problems on the brakes but defended his position at the head of a four-man group. Starting to express some dissatisfaction with the new 800.

7 CHRIS VERMEULEN Started from 15th, next to Capirossi, after their qualifying crash, then spent most of the race dicing with the Italian. An even better ride than it looks on paper – Chris was riding hurt, having lost most of the flesh off two toes in that crash.

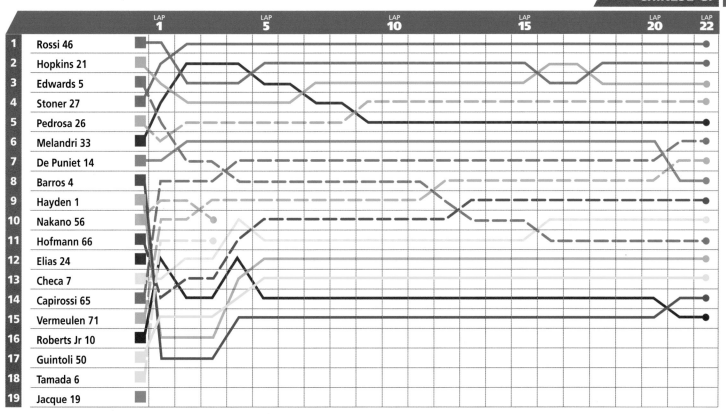

		LAP 1	LAP 5	LAP 10	LAP 15	LAP 20	LAP 22
1	Rossi 46						
2	Hopkins 21						
3	Edwards 5						
4	Stoner 27						
5	Pedrosa 26						
6	Melandri 33						
7	De Puniet 14						
8	Barros 4						
9	Hayden 1						
10	Nakano 56						
11	Hofmann 66						
12	Elias 24						
13	Checa 7						
14	Capirossi 65						
15	Vermeulen 71						
16	Roberts Jr 10						
17	Guintoli 50						
18	Tamada 6						
19	Jacque 19						

RACE

	Rider	Motorcycle	Race Time	Time +	Fastest Lap	Average Speed
1	Stoner	Ducati	44m 12.891s		1m 59.857s	97.965mph
2	Rossi	Yamaha	44m 15.927s	3.036s	1m 59.884s	97.853mph
3	Hopkins	Suzuki	44m 19.554s	6.663s	2m 00.065s	97.720mph
4	Pedrosa	Honda	44m 26.981s	14.090s	2m 00.523s	97.448mph
5	Melandri	Honda	44m 30.167s	17.276s	2m 00.715s	97.332mph
6	Capirossi	Ducati	44m 39.147s	26.256s	2m 00.946s	97.005mph
7	Vermeulen	Suzuki	44m 39.482s	26.591s	2m 01.177s	96.993mph
8	De Puniet	Kawasaki	44m 39.916s	27.025s	2m 00.781s	96.977mph
9	Hofmann	Ducati	44m 40.999s	28.108s	2m 01.040s	96.938mph
10	Checa	Honda	44m 45.848s	32.957s	2m 01.360s	96.763mph
11	Edwards	Yamaha	44m 47.944s	35.053s	2m 01.405s	96.688mph
12	Hayden	Honda	44m 50.218s	37.327s	2m 01.525s	96.606mph
13	Guintoli	Yamaha	45m 03.596s	50.705s	2m 01.865s	96.128mph
14	Barros	Ducati	45m 08.155s	55.264s	2m 00.383s	95.967mph
15	Roberts Jr	Kr212v	45m 10.627s	57.736s	2m 02.452s	95.879mph
	Nakano	Honda	06m 11.246s	19 Laps	2m 02.032s	95.461mph
	Tamada	Yamaha	06m 11.956s	19 Laps	2m 01.588s	95.279mph
	Elias	Honda				

CHAMPIONSHIP

	Rider	Team	Points
1	Stoner	Ducati Marlboro Team	86
2	Rossi	Fiat Yamaha Team	71
3	Pedrosa	Repsol Honda Team	49
4	Melandri	Honda Gresini	41
5	Hopkins	Rizla Suzuki MotoGP	39
6	Elias	Honda Gresini	35
7	Edwards	Fiat Yamaha Team	31
8	Capirossi	Ducati Marlboro Team	30
9	Hayden	Repsol Honda	30
10	Vermeulen	Rizla Suzuki MotoGP	30
11	Barros	Pramac d'Antin	27
12	Checa	Honda LCR	20
13	De Puniet	Kawasaki Racing Team	19
14	Hofmann	Pramac d'Antin	19
15	Nakano	Konica Minolta Honda	15
16	Guintoli	Dunlop Yamaha Tech 3	06
17	Roberts Jr	Team Roberts	04
18	Tamada	Dunlop Yamaha Tech 3	04
19	Jacque	Kawasaki Racing Team	04

8 RANDY DE PUNIET Flew the Kawasaki flag alone, finishing where the team thought he would. A hint of disappointment, however, as he lost two places in the closing stages. The good news was the bike now looked as good as most out there.

9 ALEX HOFMANN Lost a bit of time in the first-lap mêlée, then spent the first half of the race getting past traffic before latching onto the back of the Capirossi–Vermeulen dice.

10 CARLOS CHECA Another victim of the domino effect that followed the Elias incident on the first lap. Had to run wide to avoid Hofmann and slipped to 13th, but was able to run the same times as the group in front of him later in the race.

11 COLIN EDWARDS Three front-row starts in four races, but a slightly different choice of rear tyre from his team-mate condemned Colin to a depressing slide through the field.

12 NICKY HAYDEN The principal victim of that first-lap incident, and lucky not to fall or come back on track in the middle of the pack. Continued, with damage to his swinging arm and vibration from the rear, to rescue a few points. Doubly disappointing as he was fifth fastest in warm-up.

13 SYLVAIN GUINTOLI Off the pace in qualifying but able to follow Hayden closely for over ten laps in the middle of the race before making a mistake that allowed the gap to open up. The best race so far of his short MotoGP career.

14 ALEX BARROS Unluckiest man of the weekend. Came to a dead stop in Turn 1 with his stalled bike jammed against Elias's fallen Honda, got it started and set the fourth-fastest lap of the race. Would probably have been able to challenge Hopkins for third place if he'd been luckier.

15 KENNY ROBERTS A depressing weekend: managed a point but was in a solid last place. Team Roberts is finding it impossible to develop their bike with the twin constraints of the new tyre regulations and having just one machine. Lack of top-end power didn't help either.

NON-FINISHERS

SHINYA NAKANO Stone last through most of practice as he struggled with lack of feel from his front tyre, but disguised the problem with a good run on the qualifier. Taken out in the race by Tamada at the end of the straight on lap three.

MAKOTO TAMADA More confident than so far this season but made a mistake on lap three when following Nakano. Caught out because Shinya was going slower than he realised, tried to dive to the inside of the corner but hit the Honda. Apologised to Nakano and his team.

TONI ELIAS Added to his growing notoriety with a kamikaze first-bend move that resulted in Toni himself crashing, Barros and Hayden having their races ruined and several other riders having to take avoiding action.

NON-STARTER

OLIVIER JACQUE Suffered a deep gash to his forearm during Friday practice.

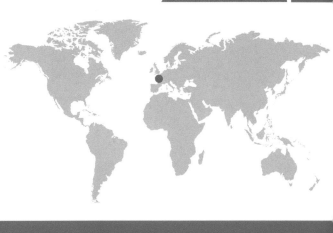

RAIN MAN

Chris Vermeulen gave Suzuki their first victory of the MotoGP era and cemented his own reputation as the best wet-weather rider in the world

This was supposed to be where Casey Stoner and the big red Ducati lost ground. Rossi had said at the first race of the season that the championship would really start in France, when the circus got back to tracks where the teams and tyre companies had stacks of data. Yamahas have always gone well here, Valentino himself has won twice on one at Le Mans, and the French track, of course, has no long straight on which the Ducati can stretch its legs. Stoner was therefore likely to get tangled up with the pack, as he had in Jerez. And it looked for a while as if the race was going to pan out according to the Doctor's script.

Team-mate Colin Edwards took pole, with Rossi right behind him in fourth, and once Valentino had forced past Hopkins and Stoner in the first two corners he looked to be opening out a winning lead. Then came the rain, which had been threatening all day. Surely this would make life even more difficult for Stoner? It certainly made life difficult for Rossi.

At first it was little more than a shower, but it did persuade the leader to back off the throttle just a fraction. Not so local heroes Sylvain Guintoli and Randy de Puniet who, between them, led for three laps before crashing. That was enough to send the massed ranks of motards into a noisy delirium. Guintoli had told his team-manager on the grid that he intended to lead the race, if only for one lap. De Puniet hurt a shoulder and was peeved that his fall got a negative reaction from his team while Guintoli was universally praised. The difference between what is expected from a privateer, grabbing a moment in the limelight, and the leading rider of a factory team had to be carefully explained to him. The Frenchmen's

crashes were the signal for the first of two distinct waves to head into pit lane to switch bikes – the second time the 'flag-to-flag' wet-weather rules had been used. Once the picture cleared, it seemed that neither bunch had gained a significant advantage.

However, it cannot be a coincidence that the men who finished first and second in that first bike-swapping extravaganza at Phillip Island in 2006 also emerged at the front of the pack this time. Chris

Vermeulen went into the pits in eighth place with the first wave at the end of lap nine, emerged in sixth and a lap later was in the lead. That was on lap 11, by which time everyone had come in and changed bikes. One lap later Melandri emerged from the confusion as the only challenger to the smooth-riding Suzuki man. Visibly willing to take more risks than the Aussie, in just four laps Marco reduced the gap from just over 1.5 seconds to a mere two-tenths. However, he hadn't had time to put double-thickness sliders on his leathers and 'because I have little legs' could not get his knee down and 'control the front'. When he had a heart-stopping front-end slide going into the first corner he decided to say, 'Okay, Chris, this race is yours.'

By this time the weather had turned really nasty, and heavy rain over the final ten laps played into the hands of the Bridgestone users. At Phillip Island the track had dried towards the end of the race and it was the Michelin men who had grip in the closing stages with the Bridgestone runners suffering. This time the track got wetter and the Japanese rubber stayed intact while the home team got it badly wrong.

All the Michelin runners bar Pedrosa used medium-hard or hard wet tyres as advised by the French company, which obviously expected conditions to ameliorate not deteriorate. But the weather got worse and Rossi suffered accordingly: he had no grip at the rear, suffered engine-braking problems with his clutch and ran wide or had the back end come round at the least provocation. In the last half-dozen laps he was passed by Hayden, Stoner, Pedrosa and Hofmann and later described those laps as the most difficult of his career. Only Repsol Honda, of all the Michelin teams,

Below Guintoli was able to remount after his crash and finish a heroic tenth

'OK, CHRIS, THIS RACE IS YOURS'
MARCO MELANDRI

looked comfortable: Hayden was having his best race of the year, until he crashed heavily, while Pedrosa all but put to rest his reputation as a total aquaphobic. Dani habitually takes a softer tyre than the other Michelin men and had done so again for his wet bike. He found himself with the right set-up for the conditions and used it extremely effectively.

Amid the confusion the man who, according to all the predictions, would suffer in these conditions on this track rode another mistake-free race to the rostrum. Stoner said he merely tried to 'play it smart', but most observers saw it as much better than that. The brutally powerful Ducati should not have been manageable around the tight and twisty Le Mans circuit, let alone in a deluge, yet Casey stayed on, finished third and extended his points lead. He looked mildly surprised by the way things had panned out over the weekend. The opposition was now wondering what would happen at the next two races, on tracks that the script said would suit the Ducati.

Chris Vermeulen greeted his maiden MotoGP victory with his customary restraint. No late-night celebrations, no histrionics, just polite answers to every question and the rather surprising admission that he hates racing in the wet. Suzuki's first win in MotoGP was a long time coming for a factory with their history, and justified their decision to spend 2006 developing many of the systems used on their 800, including the pneumatic valve operation. The last man to win a GP on a Suzuki was Sete Gibernau at Valencia in the immediate aftermath of 9/11. Following on from Hopkins's rostrum in China the status of the Rizla Suzukis had undergone a subtle shift from gutsy also-rans to genuine contenders in the first five races of the year. There were also signs that the Kawasakis were far from uncompetitive and the green team's real problem was the lack of a top-drawer rider. The changes in the technical and tyre regulations were starting to take effect.

The weekend's biggest losers were Michelin. They'd already had to suffer one Bridgestone clean sweep of the rostrum and now had to host Bridgestone's first wet-weather win and endure another clean sweep on their home turf. Rossi was nearly as unhappy with them as he'd been after Turkey. The balance of power appeared to be moving inexorably away from the combination of Honda and Michelin that had taken the title in ten of the thirteen preceding seasons.

Opposite Chris Vermeulen becomes the first Suzuki rider of the MotoGP era to stand on top of the rostrum

Below Chaos in pitlane as riders change from their slick-shod bikes to their second machines with wet-weather set-up

BLUES FOR FINDLAY

On the day that Suzuki took their first MotoGP victory news came through of the death of the first man to win a 500cc GP on a Suzuki, Jack Findlay. He had a lengthy career as a rider after he came to Europe from Australia in 1958. Findlay didn't retire until 1978, having won three 500cc GPs, and was still quick enough to win the FIM Formula 750 prize, forerunner of the F750 World Championship, on a Yamaha in 1975, beating Barry Sheene by one point. His best finish in the World Championship was second behind Agostini in 1968 when he rode British Norton and Matchless singles against the mighty four-cylinder MV Agusta. Jack's first win, at the 1971 Ulster GP, was also Suzuki's first in the 500s and the first in the class using a two-stroke engine. He was also Michelin's first GP winner, and from 1992 until 2001 he was the FIM's Grand Prix Technical Director.

But Findlay will always be remembered as the archetypal privateer, the man who could ride and win on anything from a Manx Norton to a Suzuki RG500 and do it on any type of track – he won an Isle of Man TT and he won at the Salzburgring, filling the gaps between the then infrequent GPs with the many international meetings that at least offered decent prize money.

Fortunately the French film producer Jerome Laperrousaz made his cult film Continental Circus *during the 1968 season. It was first screened at the 1971 Cannes Film Festival and vividly illustrates the hand-to-mouth existence of the privateer in an era when most GPs were held on road circuits and safety was almost non-existent. Jack was the focus of the film and his trademark blue crash helmet with the white kangaroo appeared on the film poster and the album artwork of the soundtrack by prog rock pioneers Gong. The nigh-on eight-minute opening track is entitled* Blues for Findlay, *and there's an instrumental version on the B-side.*

Both the film and soundtrack can still be found, and are well worth the effort for their insights into the way racing was back in the 1960s.

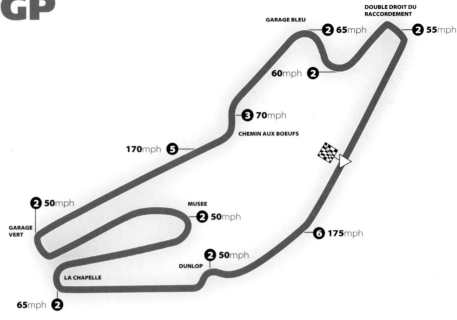

FRENCH GP
LE MANS

ROUND 5
May 20

RACE RESULTS

CIRCUIT LENGTH 2.597 miles
NO. OF LAPS 28
RACE DISTANCE 72.716 miles
WEATHER Wet, 13°C
TRACK TEMPERATURE 16°C
WINNER Chris Vermeulen
FASTEST LAP 1m 38.678s, 94.760mph, Loris Capirossi
PREVIOUS LAP RECORD 1m 33.516s, 99.880mph, Colin Edwards, 2006

QUALIFYING

	Rider	Nationality	Team	Qualifying	Pole +	Gap
1	Edwards	USA	Fiat Yamaha Team	1m 33.616s		
2	Stoner	AUS	Ducati Marlboro Team	1m 33.710s	0.094s	0.094s
3	Checa	SPA	Honda LCR	1m 33.859s	0.243s	0.149s
4	Rossi	ITA	Fiat Yamaha Team	1m 33.875s	0.259s	0.016s
5	Hopkins	USA	Rizla Suzuki MotoGP	1m 34.102s	0.486s	0.227s
6	Elias	SPA	Honda Gresini	1m 34.125s	0.509s	0.023s
7	Hayden	USA	Repsol Honda Team	1m 34.247s	0.631s	0.122s
8	De Puniet	FRA	Kawasaki Racing Team	1m 34.318s	0.702s	0.071s
9	Melandri	ITA	Honda Gresini	1m 34.360s	0.744s	0.042s
10	Pedrosa	SPA	Repsol Honda Team	1m 34.412s	0.796s	0.052s
11	Guintoli	FRA	Dunlop Yamaha Tech 3	1m 34.507s	0.891s	0.095s
12	Vermeulen	AUS	Rizla Suzuki MotoGP	1m 34.574s	0.958s	0.067s
13	Barros	BRA	Pramac d'Antin	1m 34.817s	1.201s	0.243s
14	Nakano	JPN	Konica Minolta Honda	1m 34.834s	1.218s	0.017s
15	Capirossi	ITA	Ducati Marlboro Team	1m 34.903s	1.287s	0.069s
16	Tamada	JPN	Dunlop Yamaha Tech 3	1m 35.346s	1.730s	0.443s
17	Hofmann	GER	Pramac d'Antin	1m 35.578s	1.962s	0.232s
18	Roberts Jr	USA	Team Roberts	1m 35.681s	2.065s	0.103s
19	Nieto	SPA	Kawasaki Racing Team	1m 36.312s	2.696s	0.631s

FINISHERS

1 CHRIS VERMEULEN Claims not to like riding in the wet but is now the undisputed rain master. Was in eighth, but only took a lap to get to the front after everyone swapped machines, then didn't put a foot wrong. It was his first win, Suzuki's first under MotoGP rules and Bridgestone's first wet-weather MotoGP victory.

2 MARCO MELANDRI Looked to be catching the leader before the rain became torrential, then had a couple of moments which persuaded him that second place and his first rostrum of the year weren't a bad idea. The rain disguised his continuing problems with set-up and feel.

3 CASEY STONER Another great weekend. Le Mans was supposed to be a track where the Ducati wouldn't work, with problems which should've been exacerbated in the wet. Instead, another faultless performance saw Casey come away with an increased championship lead.

4 DANI PEDROSA For a guy who isn't supposed to be able to ride in the wet this was a stunning performance in a landmark race – his 100th GP – making him the youngest rider ever to reach a century of starts. Top Michelin finisher as well as finally burying the wet-weather rabbit tag.

5 ALEX HOFMANN A career-best result from the very back row of the grid. Had been ready to go home after disastrous practice and qualifying sessions but

gambled on an early change to his wet bike and it paid off. It was, he said, the only good decision he made all weekend.

6 VALENTINO ROSSI Dominant in the dry but hamstrung in the wet by the decision to set the second bike up for damp rather than fully wet conditions. No grip at the rear saw him running wide into corners, making him easy prey – a lost chance to close in on Stoner.

7 JOHN HOPKINS Yet again very rapid at the start of the race but lost out when the rains came. Set the fastest lap of the race on his way from 12th to leading on lap nine. His wet bike lacked feeling and he ran off track as a result. A disappointing end to a weekend that promised much.

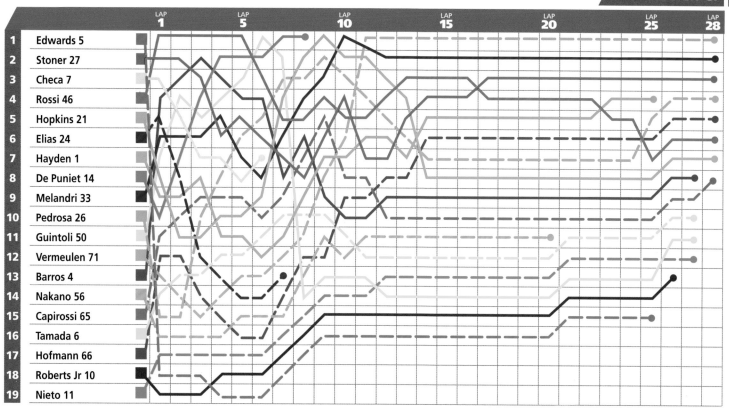

		LAP 1	LAP 5	LAP 10	LAP 15	LAP 20	LAP 25	LAP 28
1	Edwards 5							
2	Stoner 27							
3	Checa 7							
4	Rossi 46							
5	Hopkins 21							
6	Elias 24							
7	Hayden 1							
8	De Puniet 14							
9	Melandri 33							
10	Pedrosa 26							
11	Guintoli 50							
12	Vermeulen 71							
13	Barros 4							
14	Nakano 56							
15	Capirossi 65							
16	Tamada 6							
17	Hofmann 66							
18	Roberts Jr 10							
19	Nieto 11							

RACE

	Rider	Motorcycle	Race Time	Time +	Fastest Lap	Average Speed
1	Vermeulen	Suzuki	50m 58.713s		1m 39.477s	85.595mph
2	Melandri	Honda	51m 11.312s	12.599s	1m 40.050s	85.243mph
3	Stoner	Ducati	51m 26.060s	27.347s	1m 39.537s	84.836mph
4	Pedrosa	Honda	51m 36.041s	37.328s	1m 38.744s	84.563mph
5	Hofmann	Ducati	51m 47.879s	49.166s	1m 40.161s	84.241mph
6	Rossi	Yamaha	51m 52.276s	53.563s	1m 40.273s	84.122mph
7	Hopkins	Suzuki	51m 59.786s	1m 01.073s	1m 38.678s	83.919mph
8	Capirossi	Ducati	51m 19.954s	1m 21.241s	1m 38.678s	83.380mph
9	Tamada	Yamaha	51m 34.842s	1 Lap	1m 38.915s	81.574mph
10	Guintoli	Yamaha	51m 40.165s	1 Lap	1m 38.825s	81.434mph
11	Nieto	Kawasaki	51m 50.572s	1 Lap	1m 43.681s	81.162mph
12	Edwards	Yamaha	51m 06.769s	3 Laps	1m 48.875s	76.223mph
	Barros	Ducati	50m 05.770s	1 Lap	1m 39.970s	83.992mph
	Roberts Jr	Kr212v	50m 16.009s	2 Laps	1m 51.967s	80.606mph
	Hayden	Honda	45m 50.382s	3 Laps	1m 39.485s	84.991mph
	Nakano	Honda	36m 48.570s	8 Laps	1m 40.004s	84.674mph
	De Puniet	Kawasaki	13m 35.554s	20 Laps	1m 39.522s	91.721mph
	Elias	Honda	12m 00.579s	21 Laps	1m 39.288s	90.833mph
	Checa	Honda	10m 15.683s	22 Laps	1m 39.866s	91.122mph

CHAMPIONSHIP

	Rider	Team	Points
1	Stoner	Ducati Marlboro Team	102
2	Rossi	Fiat Yamaha Team	81
3	Pedrosa	Repsol Honda Team	62
4	Melandri	Honda Gresini	61
5	Vermeulen	Rizla Suzuki MotoGP	55
6	Hopkins	Rizla Suzuki MotoGP	48
7	Capirossi	Ducati Marlboro Team	38
8	Elias	Honda Gresini	35
9	Edwards	Fiat Yamaha Team	35
10	Hayden	Repsol Honda Team	30
11	Hofmann	Pramac d'Antin	30
12	Barros	Pramac d'Antin	27
13	Checa	Honda LCR	20
14	De Puniet	Kawasaki Racing Team	19
15	Nakano	Konica Minolta Honda	15
16	Guintoli	Dunlop Yamaha Tech 3	12
17	Tamada	Dunlop Yamaha Tech 3	11
18	Nieto	Kawasaki Racing Team	5
19	Roberts Jr	Team Roberts	4
20	Jacque	Kawasaki Racing Team	4

8 LORIS CAPIROSSI His team issued a public apology after the race. The wet bike had not had its engine mapping changed and Loris had to deal with much too aggressive power delivery. In the circumstances performed a minor miracle to get home and score useful points.

9 MAKOTO TAMADA Best result of the season so far under the most difficult conditions, and a breakthrough for the Tech 3 team who got both their riders in the top ten. Makoto was happiest with his Dunlop tyres in the very wet conditions.

10 SYLVAIN GUINTOLI Blazingly quick in practice and qualifying, passed Rossi in the race and led for a lap before crashing and remounting. The new hero of the fans – and not just the locals at Le Mans.

11 FONSI NIETO Hard to imagine more difficult circumstances when starting a 100th GP, but Fonsi coped with a rack of firsts – first MotoGP ride, first ride on Bridgestones, first ride on the Kawasaki ZX-RR without any testing – in a professional manner that left his team mightily impressed.

12 COLIN EDWARDS A crushing anti-climax after his first pole position in MotoGP. No grip in the damp sent Colin in for his wet bike too early and he came in again to change wheels, all of which put him three laps behind the winner.

NON-FINISHERS

ALEX BARROS Much happier in the dry than the wet. Crashed on the last lap while trying to take seventh place off Hopkins.

KENNY ROBERTS Gambled on fitting wet tyres at the start but the rain didn't come soon enough for it to pay off. Regained some ground when the weather got nasty but then stopped on the last lap when the engine failed 'in a big way', according to its dispirited rider.

NICKY HAYDEN Just when things looked to be going well at last he crashed at speed at the Chemin aux Boeufs chicane, locking the front brake three laps from home.

Doubly frustrating as he had just overtaken both Rossi and his team-mate Pedrosa.

SHINYA NAKANO Crashed while closing on the group in front of him as the weather turned really bad, probably because he felt happier in the wet than the dry.

RANDY DE PUNIET Cheered the French fans, along with Guintoli, by leading the race before crashing. Was in front for two laps before crashing heavily but, unlike his fellow-countryman, was unable to restart.

TONI ELIAS Crashed just as he was trying to work out when to come in and change bikes. Took a big hit to his back but thankfully didn't suffer any serious injury.

CARLOS CHECA One of his best tracks, as he proved by qualifying on the front row. Lost the front when trying to take a tight line inside Barros, after Rossi slowed dramatically, and the pack took evasive action.

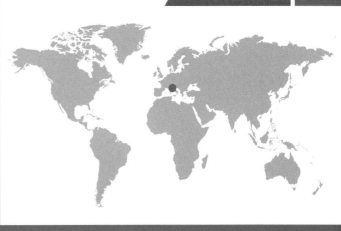

HEART AND SOUL

Italian passion and careful planning – plus a little assistance from the weather – helped Rossi overcome the speed and power of the Italian motorcycles

Given the speed of the Stoner–Ducati combination so far this season, you would have bet the mortgage on them winning the Italian Grand Prix. After all, Mugello's lap record stands at over 106mph and the front straight is both long and the fastest in the calendar, with even the new 800s attaining speeds approaching 200mph. Add in the proximity of Bologna, Ducati's home town, and this was a race they would have expected to win by a distance.

It didn't work out that way. Valentino Rossi remains undefeated on a MotoGP bike at Mugello and in the process became the first man ever to win his home race six times in a row.

This was the first of four races in June, a month Rossi knew was vital to his championship chances. Mugello and the next venue, Barcelona, are his two favourite circuits and they were followed by his next choices, Donington Park and Assen. The erosion of Stoner's points lead had to start here. Yamaha helped by bringing a bit more horsepower for the long straights and fitted new ultra-wide Ohlins fork legs held in a redesigned top yoke that was obviously intended to put back the flex that the forks eliminated. The M1 was still slower through the speed trap than the Ducati, but by around half the deficit that had caused jaws to drop in Qatar, that is 3.75mph.

Rossi and Jerry Burgess knew what to do about that. As Burgess pointed out, there was only one straight but five fast ess-bends plus five more bends of varying speeds, cambers and entries. Get them right and a few mph extra at the end of the long straight didn't matter. All through practice Valentino could be seen working on his corner exits, cracking the throttle

open a metre or two earlier each lap until he discovered the limit. Factor in the improved stability on the brakes, always an M1 strong point, and Rossi was getting the Yamaha onto and along the short straights between corners better than any of the opposition. Typical Burgess; he never dwells on what his bike can't do but optimises what it can. Yamaha were not alone in making improvements. Suzuki had a new big-bang motor and Kawasaki had found yet another four or five horsepower and added different bodywork.

JB's cunning plan was eventually helped by the weather, although it didn't look like it after qualifying. Rain on both Friday and Saturday afternoons, including the decidedly non-Tuscan sight of hail delaying qualifying, should have handed the advantage to Stoner and Ducati – this is their test track, after all – and Valentino shouldn't have had enough time to get things right, especially as he slipped off on Friday. And when Stoner set pole, that's the way it looked. It looked like that after the start as well: the young Aussie led the charge to Turn 1 with Rossi back in eighth after he wheelied off the line. Yet this time Casey could neither do the disappearing act he performed in Turkey nor fight like he had in Qatar.

It all looked very good for Ducati early on, with Stoner leading and, at the end of the first lap, Capirossi blasting past Vermeulen's Suzuki to go second, then taking the lead off his team-mate two laps later. That move allowed Melandri and Pedrosa, who had been fastest whenever practice was dry, to join in the dice for the lead. Rossi has being saying that one of the problems with his Michelin tyres was that they were

Opposite Dani Pedrosa was by far the most competitive of the Hondas despite only qualifying eighth

Top The pack chase the fast disappearing Ducatis of Stoner and Capirossi in the early laps

Below Capirossi got a special motor from Ducati, led early on but was relegated to seventh by Elias on the last lap

'WE ARE PROUD TO SHOW OUR SATELLITE TEAM IS SO COMPETITIVE'

LIVIO SUPPO

Top Alex Barros on the satellite team's Ducati has just taken third place off Casey Stoner on the factory bike

Opposite Joyous scenes under the rostrum as most of the population of Italy join in with the national anthem

taking considerably longer to get up to working temperature than the Bridgestones, which seem to perform at full potential from the moment the lights go out. The Doctor suited the action to the words. On lap six he passed Capirossi going into Materassi, repassed the troublesome Hopkins at Scarperia and got Melandri at Bucine. That put him right behind Stoner and Pedrosa, who had just taken the lead. Rossi then repeated his Materassi move on Stoner and latched onto Pedrosa. Dani had set the fastest lap of the race the third time round – what was that about the Honda–Michelin combination being slow? – and the Spaniard's pace strung the leaders out just enough to ensure Casey couldn't get back in range. Rossi took the lead at Scarperia on lap nine and was only headed when Pedrosa got his nose ahead on the straight three corners later.

It was as brilliant a few minutes of racing as you could hope to see, and the crowd loved it. The action stirred them into a scarily premature track invasion, which Rossi wasn't referring to when he said the race had been 'great, great fun', although he didn't have enough power to pass on the straight despite the fact that 'the engine for me is perfect'.

Casey's difficulties stemmed from the disrupted free

practice that prevented the team from getting the perfect set-up. It was becoming clear that if the new 800cc MotoGP bikes lost a mere a tenth of a second through technical problems then even riders like Rossi and Stoner could not make up the difference. The Honda rider's problem was that he couldn't get out of the final corner with enough speed to get past before the braking zone for Turn 1 and so wasn't able to challenge the leaders.

Three laps from home Stoner's problem was the rapidly approaching Alex Barros on the satellite d'Antin team's Pramac Ducati. Anyone who expected the Brazilian to defer to the factory team was soon disabused of that notion. Barros went past on the brakes with three laps to go and held Casey off to the flag.

'I hope Ducati will still help us,' said Alex. The finish made Barros only the third rider after Mick Doohan and Rossi to pass the milestone of 2000 premier-class points.

'We are proud to show our satellite team is so competitive,' said Livio Suppo.

Those were the public pronouncements, anyway.

'He's good on braking,' Casey noted, echoing what GP racers have been saying about Alex since 1986, the year after the Aussie was born.

Valentino Rossi always sports a special crash-helmet design for his home race, often with a cryptic message in the artwork. This time it was easy to decode: a big heart on a white background. Some sections of the Italian press had been suggesting that Vale had lost the heart to fight for the title. The man himself said that he had 'to make a point' in the month of June. He had more than made one at Mugello.

TEAM ROBERTS SUFFERS

It was difficult to believe it, here at Mugello, but at the end of the 2006 season Team KR had been a contender. The team had scored front-row starts and rostrum finishes, but now their bike was the perennial backmarker. What had gone wrong?

The answer was the new technical regulations. First, as the only independent constructor on the grid they had to design and build a brand-new motorcycle over the winter break. Without the time or the budget to test, and with only enough resources to field a single bike, the machine was far from optimised when it came to the grid for the first time. The fact that no Honda privateer was suffering from an excess of power didn't help either.

Then there was the tyre rule. How can a limited number of tyres be selected for a motorcycle that's never been tested? It's not possible, of course – well, not with any accuracy. It was quickly obvious that the chassis needed a major redesign, which the team achieved before the half-way point of the season. However, rider Kenny Roberts Junior was having trouble with his motivation. As he'd shown last year, when the bike was working the World Champion of 2000 was still capable of racing with anyone on the grid. Now, though, he had no intention of taking risks on a bike incapable of getting into the top ten.

Kenny's younger brother Kurtis was drafted in for Mugello to help the team speed up their development work. There were only two bikes in the pit so both riders lost considerable amounts of time when adjustments were needed, but the process of data collection was given a useful boost. Short term, the plan was for Kurtis to stay for the next race and then for British Superbike star Jonathan Rea to ride the second bike at Donington. Long-term? Well...no-one could imagine the MotoGP paddock without Kenny Junior, but...

Above The brothers Roberts, Kurtis on the left, Kenny on the right, compare notes after a wet practice session

ITALIAN GP
MUGELLO
ROUND 6
June 3

RACE RESULTS

CIRCUIT LENGTH 3.259 miles
NO. OF LAPS 23
RACE DISTANCE 74.794 miles
WEATHER Dry, 24°C
TRACK TEMPERATURE 29°C
WINNER Valentino rossi
FASTEST LAP 1m 50.357s, 106.320mph, Dani Pedrosa
PREVIOUS LAP RECORD 1m 48.969s, 107.670mph, Sete Gibernau, 2006

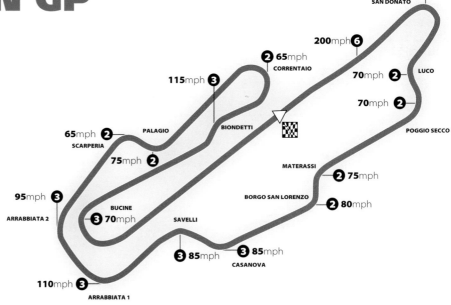

Circuit map with corner speeds:
- 55mph SAN DONATO (2)
- 200mph (6)
- 65mph CORRENTAIO (2)
- 70mph LUCO (2)
- 115mph (3)
- 70mph (2)
- 70mph (2)
- PALAGIO
- BIONDETTI
- POGGIO SECCO
- 65mph SCARPERIA (2)
- 75mph (2)
- MATERASSI
- 75mph (2)
- 95mph (3)
- BUCINE
- BORGO SAN LORENZO
- 80mph (2)
- ARRABBIATA 2
- 70mph (3)
- SAVELLI
- 85mph (3)
- 85mph (3)
- CASANOVA
- 110mph (3)
- ARRABBIATA 1

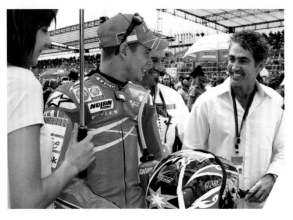

QUALIFYING

	Rider	Nationality	Team	Qualifying	Pole +	Gap
1	Stoner	AUS	Ducati Marlboro Team	2m 00.359s		
2	Vermeulen	AUS	Rizla Suzuki MotoGP	2m 01.381s	1.022s	0.022s
3	Rossi	ITA	Fiat Yamaha Team	2m 01.695s	1.336s	0.314s
4	Jacque	FRA	Kawasaki Racing Team	2m 01.709s	1.350s	0.014s
5	Capirossi	ITA	Ducati Marlboro Team	2m 01.797s	1.438s	0.088s
6	Melandri	ITA	Honda Gresini	2m 02.001s	1.642s	0.204s
7	De Puniet	FRA	Kawasaki Racing Team	2m 02.443s	2.084s	0.442s
8	Pedrosa	SPA	Repsol Honda Team	2m 02.776s	2.417s	0.333s
9	Hopkins	USA	Rizla Suzuki MotoGP	2m 02.932s	2.573s	0.156s
10	Barros	BRA	Pramac d'Antin	2m 03.025s	2.666s	0.093s
11	Hofmann	GER	Pramac d'Antin	2m 03.920s	3.561s	0.895s
12	Nakano	JPN	Konica Minolta Honda	2m 04.185s	3.826s	0.265s
13	Hayden	USA	Repsol Honda Team	2m 04.353s	3.994s	0.168s
14	Checa	SPA	Honda LCR	2m 04.971s	4.612s	0.618s
15	Elias	SPA	Honda Gresini	2m 05.592s	5.233s	0.621s
16	Edwards	USA	Fiat Yamaha Team	2m 06.254s	5.895s	0.662s
17	Guintoli	FRA	Dunlop Yamaha Tech 3	2m 06.426s	6.067s	0.172s
18	Roberts Jr	USA	Team Roberts	2m 06.660s	6.301s	0.234s
19	Roberts K.	USA	Team Roberts	2m 07.571s	7.212s	0.911s
20	Tamada	JPN	Dunlop Yamaha Tech 3	2m 09.080s	8.721s	1.509s

FINISHERS

1 VALENTINO ROSSI No-one else has won an Italian GP under MotoGP rules and this time nobody else looked likely to. The winning margin was the biggest he's managed at Mugello and put him equal with Doohan's record of 95 podium finishes in the top class. No-one has had more...

2 DANI PEDROSA Led early on, set the fastest lap of the race (but didn't break Biaggi's record) and kept Rossi in sight until the last five laps when both tyres started sliding in corners. Pleased with his weekend, given the conditions in practice and qualifying.

3 ALEX BARROS The first rostrum for the d'Antin team since Qatar 2004, made doubly satisfying by being at the home track of both Ducati and sponsor Pramac. Alex didn't hesitate to pass Stoner's factory Ducati and just held him off to the flag.

4 CASEY STONER Blamed lack of dry track time due to the mixed conditions on Friday and Saturday for a set-up that wouldn't let him take that vital tenth of a second a lap out of the opposition. Reported his main problems came in the long corners and that he lacked a little bit of traction.

5 JOHN HOPKINS In the thick of the action in the early laps, swapping places with Rossi. Gave his tyres a hard time

trying to stay with the Ducatis and lost touch with the dice for third in the later stages of the race.

6 TONI ELIAS A typical all-action Elias race: blasted up to the leaders from 15th on the grid, then suffered from a too-soft front tyre. Raced with his team-mate in the middle of the race, then passed Capirossi on the final lap.

7 LORIS CAPIROSSI Ducati delivered some of the engine characteristics he'd been demanding but that seemed to involve a trade-off in top speed. Didn't stop him leading a couple of laps early on, but big scares when he lost the front at Arrabbiata 1 and 2 in quick succession forced him to slow.

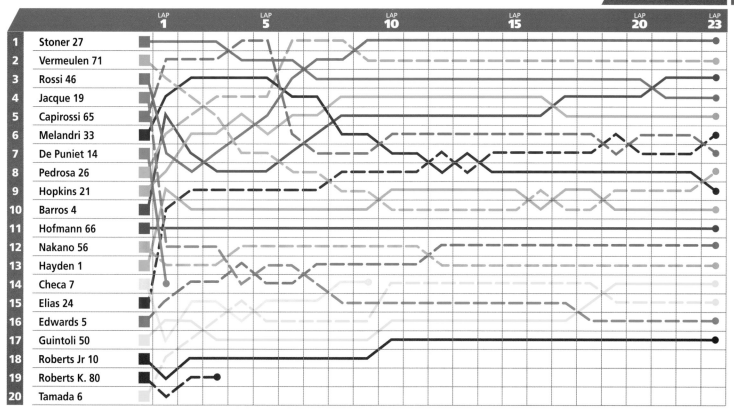

		LAP 1	LAP 5	LAP 10	LAP 15	LAP 20	LAP 23
1	Stoner 27						
2	Vermeulen 71						
3	Rossi 46						
4	Jacque 19						
5	Capirossi 65						
6	Melandri 33						
7	De Puniet 14						
8	Pedrosa 26						
9	Hopkins 21						
10	Barros 4						
11	Hofmann 66						
12	Nakano 56						
13	Hayden 1						
14	Checa 7						
15	Elias 24						
16	Edwards 5						
17	Guintoli 50						
18	Roberts Jr 10						
19	Roberts K. 80						
20	Tamada 6						

RACE

	Rider	Motorcycle	Race Time	Time +	Fastest Lap	Average Speed
1	Rossi	Yamaha	42m 42.385s		1m 50.504s	105.313mph
2	Pedrosa	Honda	42m 45.459s	3.074s	1m 50.357s	105.186mph
3	Barros	Ducati	42m 48.341s	5.956s	1m 50.853s	105.069mph
4	Stoner	Ducati	42m 48.397s	6.012s	1m 50.807s	105.066mph
5	Hopkins	Suzuki	42m 55.629s	13.244s	1m 50.524s	104.773mph
6	Elias	Honda	43m 01.640s	19.255s	1m 50.764s	104.527mph
7	Capirossi	Ducati	43m 02.031s	19.646s	1m 50.482s	104.512mph
8	Vermeulen	Suzuki	43m 05.195s	22.810s	1m 51.125s	104.384mph
9	Melandri	Honda	43m 05.222s	22.837s	1m 50.637s	104.382mph
10	Hayden	Honda	43m 06.798s	24.413s	1m 51.153s	104.319mph
11	Hofmann	Ducati	43m 07.166s	24.781s	1m 51.553s	104.304mph
12	Edwards	Yamaha	43m 10.386s	28.001s	1m 51.615s	104.175mph
13	Nakano	Honda	43m 19.118s	36.733s	1m 51.676s	103.824mph
14	Guintoli	Yamaha	43m 27.483s	45.098s	1m 52.236s	103.491mph
15	Tamada	Yamaha	43m 27.530s	45.145s	1m 51.495s	103.489mph
16	Jacque	Kawasaki	43m 27.602s	45.217s	1m 51.721s	103.487mph
17	Roberts Jr	Kr212v	44m 09.607s	1m 27.222s	1m 53.735s	101.846mph
	Checa	Honda	16m 59.065s	14 Laps	1m 51.500s	103.769mph
	Roberts K.	Kr212v	06m 00.621s	20 Laps	1m 57.409s	97.604mph
	De Puniet	Kawasaki	02m 00.523s	22 Laps	2m 00.523s	97.348mph

CHAMPIONSHIP

	Rider	Team	Points
1	Stoner	Ducati Marlboro Team	115
2	Rossi	Fiat Yamaha Team	106
3	Pedrosa	Repsol Honda Team	82
4	Melandri	Honda Gresini	68
5	Vermeulen	Rizla Suzuki MotoGP	63
6	Hopkins	Rizla Suzuki MotoGP	59
7	Capirossi	Ducati Marlboro Team	47
8	Elias	Honda Gresini	45
9	Barros	Pramac d'Antin	43
10	Edwards	Fiat Yamaha Team	39
11	Hayden	Repsol Honda Team	36
12	Hofmann	Pramac d'Antin	35
13	Checa	Honda LCR	20
14	De Puniet	Kawasaki Racing Team	19
15	Nakano	Konica Minolta Honda	18
16	Guintoli	Dunlop Yamaha Tech 3	14
17	Tamada	Dunlop Yamaha Tech 3	12
18	Nieto	Kawasaki Racing Team	5
19	Roberts Jr	Team Roberts	4
20	Jacque	Kawasaki Racing Team	4

8 CHRIS VERMEULEN Another stunning performance in wet qualifying put him on the front row. Says he is still a bit naive about the Mugello track, but managed to pass Hayden and Melandri in the last five laps.

9 MARCO MELANDRI Still hasn't been on the rostrum at Mugello. Started well but faded rapidly. Said the bike started skipping around and this was the same problem he'd been having since the season started.

10 NICKY HAYDEN Another thoroughly dispiriting weekend. Never found a set-up he was at all comfortable with and had problems in the fast turns that abound at Mugello. The bike's balance was never right so it never felt 'planted' in the corners and he had a few 'moments'.

11 ALEX HOFMANN Not the way he hoped his 100th GP would finish. Knew right from the start he had problems, coming from the rear of the bike, and couldn't run the pace he had in dry practice.

12 COLIN EDWARDS Suffered again at his bogey track. Put some 16-inch tyres in his allocation, which turned out not to work as well as testing had suggested, so his whole weekend was compromised from the start.

13 SHINYA NAKANO Happy with the first half of the race but then ran into chatter and slowed, allowing Edwards past.

14 SYLVAIN GUINTOLI Impressed everyone again and, despite using Dunlop's

16-inch front tyre for the first time, was able to beat a former GP winner and a former 250 World Champion.

15 MAKOTO TAMADA Also happy with Dunlop's new 16-inch front tyre. Reported much-improved feel and excellent grip at the start and only slight drop-off, after which performance remained stable.

16 OLIVIER JACQUE A superb fourth in qualifying, but his injury from China meant he had no strength in his right arm. Getting to the flag after a two-race lay-off was his ambition and with gritted teeth he managed it.

17 KENNY ROBERTS Had a very lonely race after the first couple of

corners. Spent the race experimenting with electronics – traction control and engine braking – to try and match his time from Friday.

NON-FINISHERS

CARLOS CHECA Crashed out before half-distance trying to make up places despite 'not having a comfortable feeling'. Could see Nakano and Edwards, thought they were catchable, pushed too hard and fell out of 14th place.

KURTIS ROBERTS King Kenny Roberts's younger son was drafted in to try and speed up the team's development work. Went to the line with some experimental chassis settings which turned out not to

be raceworthy. As agreed with the team, pulled in to save unnecessary wear on engine parts.

RANDY DE PUNIET Crashed hard at Arrabbiata on the second lap trying to make up for a start that dropped him from seventh to 14th place. Got in too fast and ran wide onto the bumps; lucky not to do further damage to the shoulder he injured at Le Mans, but hurt his left knee.

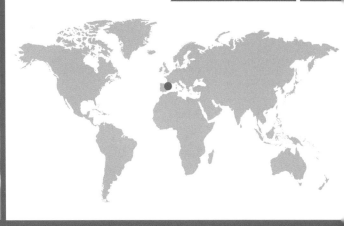

PERFECT STORM

The closest race so far, with Stoner taking his fourth win of the year despite the race-long attentions of Valentino Rossi and Dani Pedrosa

This was what the season had been waiting for – no advantage for one tyre company or the other, no first-lap multiple pile-ups, no interventions from the weather, just a magnificent race-long dice between the top three riders in the championship on three different machines. Casey Stoner, Valentino Rossi and, to the joy of the home crowd, Dani Pedrosa were rarely covered by more than a second, but the real battle was between the Ducati and the Yamaha. Third-place man Pedrosa was later moved to remark that he enjoyed watching the fight in front of him because they weren't overtaking in 'typical places'. He wasn't wrong.

The only other racer to get among the top three was John Hopkins who, yet again, gave Rossi a fight early on and then set the fastest lap of the race eighth time round while trying to stay in touch with the disappearing Doctor. Hopper only dropped back from the leaders in the last third of the race, but he entertained the crowd mightily throughout the weekend. Did he get his elbow down at La Caixa in qualifying?

It took six laps for Rossi to recover from a relatively slow start off pole position and get up to Stoner and Pedrosa, who had led the first lap. Dani's Honda did not appear to be suffering too much when it came to a drag race down the straight with Casey's Ducati. Rossi took second on the brakes at the start of lap 11 and within one lap was on Stoner's back wheel; he immediately tried a dive up the inside at the slow left-hander, ran wide and then settled back to stalk the Australian. For the next half-dozen laps Valentino was content to watch and wait as Pedrosa first lost and

Top Both Yamaha Tech 3's men got in the points; here they sandwich Alex Hofmann

Opposite Valentino Rossi regards Catalunya as one of his favourite circuits

Below John Hopkins was the only man to trouble the top three all weekend: here he is at La Caixa in qualifying

then regained ground. The next attack came in the big right-hander of Turn 3 on lap 18. Once again Rossi forced down the inside of the Ducati and again ran wide, but this time he had the inside line for the downhill left-hander. For once Stoner couldn't get past on the main straight, although that might have had something to do with the Italian cutting very firmly across his nose into the first corner. There followed half a lap of merciless action as the pair repeatedly swapped positions, only for Casey to get a break when Valentino ran wide on the exit of La Caixa. It wasn't the first time he'd had a problem in a left-hander, and the other Michelin user, Pedrosa's Honda, had been spinning up in the two slow lefts in the infield section since the early laps.

Dani later said that he had felt the problem on the warm-up lap and gone to the line knowing he would have difficulty in left-handers, although anytime he got alongside Rossi it was on the brakes that he was beaten. Rossi was now obviously having problems driving out of the slowest left, which is exited on full lean, and also out of the final left-hander. However, the Yamaha was working well in the stadium section and the succession of right-handers that end the lap. For a bike that was supposed to be a straight-line weapon and little else, though, the Ducati was quite capable of fighting back in the twisty bits.

The move of the race – and this was a race full of breathtaking manoeuvres – was Rossi's third-gear inside pass on Stoner at the last corner, a place where no-one

'WHEN HE STOPS PASSING
ME ON THE STRAIGHT, I'LL
STOP DOING THAT!'
VALENTINO ROSSI

Top Casey Stoner is congratulated by his Bridgestone technician in parc fermé

Opposite The top four race through the fast right-handers that end the Catalunya lap

Below Randy de Puniet scored his best ever result in MotoGP despite carrying a collection of painful injuries from crashes at the previous two races

could remember anyone passing before. Valentino then defended his lead with another very tough move on the brakes at the end of the straight, and to show he meant it did it again a lap later. But as hard as Rossi worked there was no denying the combination of the Ducati's speed and Casey's faultless riding, both in a straight line and in the corners, no matter where Rossi attacked. Two laps from the flag Stoner squeezed past on the straight, Rossi made him use the pit-lane exit, and then Casey wasn't headed again. Vale did consider another pass at the final corner but talked himself out of it on the grounds that Stoner would overtake him by the line.

Behind the epic fight for the lead, and the increasingly impressive Hopkins, came the heroic Randy de Puniet for his best-ever MotoGP finish. The Frenchman was suffering from an injured right

collarbone, the legacy from crashing out of the lead at his home GP, as well as a right knee the size of a football thanks to his 100mph crash at Mugello the previous weekend. His leathers company had to put a bit of extra room in the leg, after which he got on the front row of the grid. Early in the race he took a big whack to that knee from Elias's Honda, after Toni had made a big lunge up the inside of Hopkins at Turn 1, and then found himself almost stopped in Turn 2, right where a fast-approaching Kawasaki couldn't avoid him. No wonder Randy said he was having trouble breathing after the race. It was a performance that more than made up for some of his lapses of judgement earlier in the year.

As has become their habit, Rossi and Stoner said nice things about each other and about the race after the event. Casey couldn't resist a dig at those who said 'we couldn't win at European tracks', a reference to the fact that this is a circuit where Bridgestone have suffered in the past. His team-manager said the rest: 'It's not the top speed, it's the man!' The Aussie also declared himself 'disappointed' by one of Rossi's overtaking moves, one of at least three very close shaves at the end of the straight where Valentino cut across the Ducati's nose. When this was relayed to Rossi he laughed out loud and offered Casey a deal: 'When he stops passing me on the straight, I'll stop doing that!' It was a good line, but Valentino now knew as well as anyone that there was much more to Casey's championship challenge than a motorcycle that happened to be quick in a straight line.

MERCI, OJ

An innocuous-looking crash at the track's slowest corner during Saturday morning's free practice put an end to the career of the 2000 250cc World Champion, Olivier Jacque. The Kawasaki rider tweaked his neck, but on top of the nasty cut to his arm sustained in China and the back injury from the pile-up he instigated in Turkey it was enough for him to decide to call it a day.

Jacque won seven 250cc GPs from 80 starts, three of them with Honda, the rest on a Yamaha. He won his world title for Yamaha, then moved up to the 500cc class with the Tech 3 team. Olivier only got on the rostrum in the top class once, while deputising for the injured Kawasaki rider Alex Hofmann in the 2005 Chinese GP. At the time it was Kawasaki's best finish in the top class. However, the Frenchman was well on his way to winning the 2002 German GP when he was brought down by Alex Barros. It was the last hurrah of the two-stroke in the top class, and the Sachsenring circuit was at the time the only place they were likely to beat the new 990cc four-strokes.

Thirty-three-year-old Jacque had intended to spend the 2007 season as Kawasaki's test rider, as he had done in '06; he had recently married and was soon to become a father. However, he was talked into coming back to racing because Kawasaki were anxious for continuity in development of their new 800.

OJ never quite fulfilled his potential on the big bikes, but he will always be remembered for winning his 250 title by a wheel when he out-dragged team-mate Shinya Nakano from the last corner at Phillip Island. It was the coolest piece of racecraft you could wish to see. There again, Olivier is always cool, on and off the track.

Above Olivier Jacque decided it was time to bring down the curtain on his career as a racer; he will stay with the Kawasaki team as an an advisor

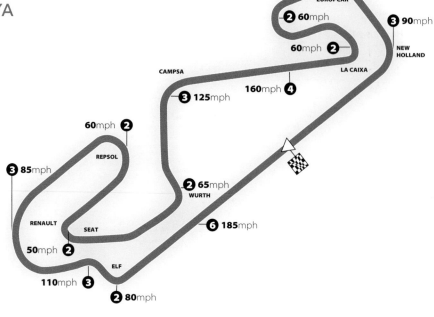

CATALAN GP
CIRCUIT DE CATALUNYA

ROUND 7
June 10

RACE RESULTS

CIRCUIT LENGTH 2.937 miles
NO. OF LAPS 25
RACE DISTANCE 73.425 miles
WEATHER Dry, 31°C
TRACK TEMPERATURE 43°C
WINNER Casey Stoner
FASTEST LAP 1m 43.252s, 102.410mph, John Hopkins
PREVIOUS LAP RECORD 1m 43.048s, 102.617mph, Nicky Hayden, 2006

QUALIFYING

	Rider	Nationality	Team	Qualifying	Pole +	Gap
1	Rossi	ITA	Fiat Yamaha Team	1m 41.840s		
2	De Puniet	FRA	Kawasaki Racing Team	1m 41.901s	0.061s	0.061s
3	Pedrosa	SPA	Repsol Honda Team	1m 42.002s	0.162s	0.101s
4	Stoner	AUS	Ducati Marlboro team	1m 42.117s	0.277s	0.115s
5	Hopkins	USA	Rizla Suzuki MotoGP	1m 42.233s	0.393s	0.115s
6	Edwards	USA	Fiat Yamaha Team	1m 42.283s	0.443s	0.050s
7	Hayden	USA	Repsol Honda Team	1m 42.522s	0.682s	0.239s
8	Elias	SPA	Honda Gresini	1m 42.607s	0.767s	0.085s
9	Melandri	ITA	Honda Gresini	1m 42.623s	0.783s	0.016s
10	Hofmann	GER	Pramac d'Antin	1m 42.860s	1.020s	0.237s
11	Vermeulen	AUS	Rizla Suzuki MotoGP	1m 42.967s	1.127s	0.107s
12	Nakano	JPN	Konica Minolta Honda	1m 43.334s	1.494s	0.367s
13	Guintoli	FRA	Dunlop Yamaha Tech 3	1m 43.557s	1.717s	0.223s
14	Barros	BRA	Pramac d'Antin	1m 43.722s	1.882s	0.165s
15	Checa	SPA	Honda LCR	1m 43.729s	1.889s	0.007s
16	Tamada	JPN	Dunlop Yamaha Tech 3	1m 43.947s	2.107s	0.218s
17	Capirossi	ITA	Ducati Marlboro Team	1m 43.948s	2.108s	0.001s
18	Roberts Jr	USA	Team Roberts	1m 44.263s	2.423s	0.315s
19	Roberts K.	USA	Team Roberts	1m 45.223s	3.383s	0.960s
	Jacque	FRA	Kawasaki Racing Team			

FINISHERS

1 CASEY STONER Yet another fault-free race under intense pressure from Rossi showed he must already be considered a genuine title contender, even if he refused to discuss it. Now matter how or where Valentino passed him, the Aussie was able to go straight back to the front. A masterful display.

2 VALENTINO ROSSI Didn't have the best of starts and took a while to get past Hopkins. Then tried everything he knew to put Stoner off his stride but admitted there was nothing he could do: 'Casey rode like a god.' Some consolation in setting a new record for the number of podiums in the top class: 96.

3 DANI PEDROSA Led the first lap, never lost touch with the leaders, but never threatened them either, despite finishing only 0.3s behind Rossi. Used a harder tyre than he normally does and reported some troubles.

4 JOHN HOPKINS Went head to head with Rossi in the early stages for the second week running, then set the fastest lap of the race as he tried to prevent the front three breaking away. Couldn't hold on to them and had a lonely if impressive race to fourth.

5 RANDY DE PUNIET An heroic ride from his first front-row start to his best finishing position in MotoGP, despite a knee so swollen after his Mugello crash that Spidi had to build an extra 10cm into the left leg of his leathers. Elias then stuck his handlebar into that knee a few laps in – and his shoulder remained strapped up after Le Mans. Still pulled a giant wheelie to celebrate.

6 LORIS CAPIROSSI Reverted to the same engine spec as his team-mate but was depressed after dire qualifying. Changed everything for warm-up and found something that worked. Not surprisingly, after the events of the previous year, cautious into the first corner but then got into an impressive rhythm and cut through the field.

7 CHRIS VERMEULEN Again suffered from a slightly disappointing qualifying which was compounded by losing a couple of places in the first corner. After

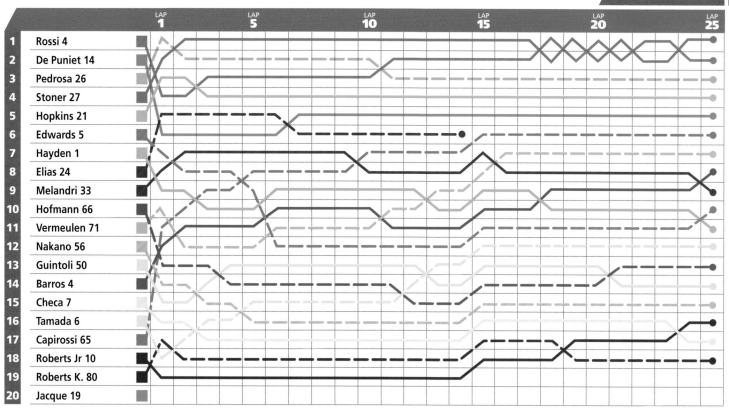

		LAP 1	LAP 5	LAP 10	LAP 15	LAP 20	LAP 25
1	Rossi 4						
2	De Puniet 14						
3	Pedrosa 26						
4	Stoner 27						
5	Hopkins 21						
6	Edwards 5						
7	Hayden 1						
8	Elias 24						
9	Melandri 33						
10	Hofmann 66						
11	Vermeulen 71						
12	Nakano 56						
13	Guintoli 50						
14	Barros 4						
15	Checa 7						
16	Tamada 6						
17	Capirossi 65						
18	Roberts Jr 10						
19	Roberts K. 80						
20	Jacque 19						

RACE

	Rider	Motorcycle	Race Time	Time +	Fastest Lap	Average Speed
1	Stoner	Ducati	43m 16.907s		1m 43.317s	101.793mph
2	Rossi	Yamaha	43m 16.976s	0.069s	1m 43.324s	101.791mph
3	Pedrosa	Honda	43m 17.297s	0.390s	1m 43.376s	101.778mph
4	Hopkins	Suzuki	43m 24.721s	7.814s	1m 43.252s	101.489mph
5	De Puniet	Kawasaki	43m 34.760s	17.853s	1m 43.642s	101.099mph
6	Capirossi	Ducati	43m 36.316s	19.409s	1m 43.834s	101.039mph
7	Vermeulen	Suzuki	43m 36.402s	19.495s	1m 43.996s	101.036mph
8	Barros	Ducati	43m 41.769s	24.862s	1m 44.111s	100.829mph
9	Melandri	Honda	43m 41.870s	24.963s	1m 43.836s	100.825mph
10	Edwards	Yamaha	43m 52.255s	35.348s	1m 44.466s	100.427mph
11	Hayden	Honda	43m 53.208s	36.301s	1m 43.987s	100.391mph
12	Tamada	Yamaha	43m 55.627s	38.720s	1m 44.267s	100.299mph
13	Hofmann	Ducati	43m 57.841s	40.934s	1m 44.600s	100.214mph
14	Guintoli	Yamaha	44m 01.306s	44.399s	1m 44.478s	100.083mph
15	Nakano	Honda	44m 11.010s	54.103s	1m 44.972s	99.716mph
16	Roberts Jr	Kr212v	44m 16.562s	59.655s	1m 45.354s	99.508mph
17	Checa	Honda	44m 19.222s	1m 02.315s	1m 45.314s	99.408mph
18	Roberts K.	Kr212v	44m 20.229s	1m 03.322s	1m 45.702s	99.371mph
	Elias	Honda	24m 23.184s	11 Laps		

CHAMPIONSHIP

	Rider	Team	Points
1	Stoner	Ducati Marlboro Team	140
2	Rossi	Fiat Yamaha Team	126
3	Pedrosa	Repsol Honda Team	98
4	Melandri	Honda Gresini	75
5	Vermeulen	Rizla Suzuki MotoGP	72
6	Hopkins	Rizla Suzuki MotoGP	72
7	Capirossi	Ducati Marlboro Team	57
8	Barros	Pramac d'Antin	51
9	Elias	Honda Gresini	45
10	Edwards	Fiat Yamaha Team	45
11	Hayden	Repsol Honda Team	41
12	Hofmann	Pramac d'Antin	38
13	De Puniet	Kawasaki Racing Team	30
14	Checa	Honda LCR	20
15	Nakano	Konica Minolta Honda	19
16	Guintoli	Dunlop Yamaha Tech 3	16
17	Tamada	Dunlop Yamaha Tech 3	16
18	Nieto	Kawasaki Racing Team	5
19	Roberts Jr	Team Roberts	4
20	Jacque	Kawasaki Racing Team	4

that he fought the Ducatis of Capirossi and Barros, leading the Italian on the last lap only to be out-dragged on the straight.

8 ALEX BARROS Never happy with his set-up yet improved on his qualifying position by six places in the race. Had to fight hard early on and had problems with the front in the closing stages. A good result from a difficult weekend.

9 MARCO MELANDRI Suffering from a total loss of confidence in his chassis and lost all feel from the front end after a few laps, dropping back through the field. The situation was now bad enough for his team-manager to make a public appeal to HRC for help.

10 COLIN EDWARDS A replay of his nightmare at Mugello, although the situation was masked by good qualifying. No rear grip from the start, which may have been related to Michelin's experiments with 16-inch rear tyres.

11 NICKY HAYDEN Finally got the exhausts his team-mate had been using for a while and reported a distinct improvement in driveability. His race was compromised by a wheel or tyre going out of balance, after which he dropped back. Proof that when your luck is out it's really out.

12 MAKOTO TAMADA Second-best result of the season so far, aided by new 16-inch front and rear Dunlops. Reckoned he could've challenged the two men in

front of him if he hadn't had problems with chatter in the middle of the race.

13 ALEX HOFMANN Everything looked good up until the beginning of the race, but a bad start and a lack of acceleration made life difficult. Disappointing, after a good Friday and Saturday.

14 SYLVAIN GUINTOLI Continued his record of scoring points in every race so far in his rookie MotoGP season. Like team-mate Tamada suffered from chatter on the new-design Dunlops. This dropped him off the back of Edwards, who wasn't pulling away.

15 SHINYA NAKANO Another suffering Honda privateer. Things looked good in warm-up but when Shinya pushed

in the race he ran wide in corners. Still experiencing lack of feeling at the front, and chatter.

16 KENNY ROBERTS Followed his brother for the first two-thirds of the race before draughting past on the front straight and closing down on Checa.

17 CARLOS CHECA Couldn't remember having a worse feeling in a race, a situation exacerbated by this being his home GP. Suffered the same problems as all the other Honda riders, with the possible exception of the Repsol team.

18 KURTIS ROBERTS Reckoned it was the first time he'd led his brother in a race, which messed with his concentration. Reported the bike was sliding everywhere.

NON-FINISHERS

TONI ELIAS In stark contrast to his team-mate, Toni was having a good race until his engine stopped on the 14th lap while he was lying sixth and convinced he could have got past de Puniet.

NON-STARTER

OLIVIER JACQUE A seemingly innocuous crash in practice on Saturday morning at the slowest corner on the track sent OJ to hospital with a neck injury. The team made the decision to withdraw him from the race.

BRITISH GP

DONINGTON PARK

ROUND 8

June 24

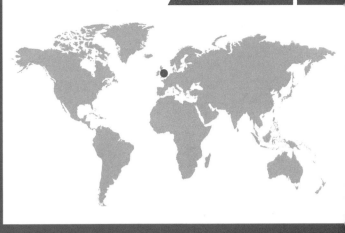

WEATHER MAN

Wet or dry, it doesn't matter to Casey Stoner. This time it was wet and he drove through the field after a bad start to extend his championship lead over a disgruntled Rossi

Donington Park is not a circuit that rewards power above all else; it is also notoriously treacherous in the wet. Neither of these factors could possibly be thought of as advantageous to Casey Stoner and the brutally quick Ducati, yet despite fluffing the start, the Aussie was able to keep his head in the hectic opening skirmishes, hunt down Colin Edwards and win with ease. Apart from that start it was another faultless display, although Casey maintained he did have a perfect start but the bike spun up after he'd got moving, probably on a white line. Nobody could describe the races of the reigning World Champion or his predecessor as perfect, although Nicky Hayden was a lot happier than he'd been all season, despite crashing out of contention. Valentino Rossi's fourth place meant Stoner's championship lead was now 26 points, or more than a race win's worth.

Hayden was with the leading group when he crashed out, but his change of mood could be traced back to the test after the Catalan GP. His team had dialled out a lot of traction control: 'I haven't forgotten how to ride, but when I pushed I crashed,' said Nicky. 'With less traction control I can push harder, you don't need it like with a 990.' He then went on to prove his point by being fastest in the final free practice session, although he just missed out on the front row in qualifying. He didn't seem too disappointed: 'Lately, good days have been hard to come by.'

Rossi wasn't having a good time. He crashed twice in practice, once in the first free session and again when he ran off the edge of the track at the first corner after he emerged from the pits and looked over his shoulder. The first one was painful, the second muddy and embarrassing. His race wasn't much better. The Doctor

was shuffled to the back of the eight-man leading group in the first four laps and took the next six to get up to third, which he did with a breathtaking move on Hopkins at the Old Hairpin only to run off track at Coppice and give the place back. Valentino spent the next two laps getting back to third but when he got there he was eight seconds behind the leading duo of Edwards and Stoner. It was the closest he got to the leaders. Four laps later Colin had a couple of scares on the front end, one of which sent him wide at the Melbourne Loop, and Stoner was through. Casey made the rest look easy.

The race had started in the rain, but by half-distance a dry line was appearing and Rossi was heading for trouble with his full-wet treaded tyres. Yet again it appeared that the Bridgestone runners were having an easier time than the Michelin men. Once Stoner had gone past him, Edwards realised he 'had nothing for him'. He had to manage the wheelspin by short-shifting out of corners with some very small throttle openings. Nevertheless, Colin rode his best race of the year from his second pole position, a very different outcome from the disaster of Le Mans.

Meanwhile Rossi's on-board TV camera, facing backwards from under the seat, was showing shreds of rubber peeling off the right side of his tyre. He managed the problem well until a few laps from home. Chris Vermeulen, who had come through from a crash-happy practice and 12th on the grid, closed down a gap of over six seconds and took third on the brakes at Foggy's. 'It was like Vermeulen had changed tyre,' said Rossi afterwards, while bemoaning the fact that his tyre was

'I'M NOT WORRIED FOR 26 POINTS, MORE FOR OWN PROBLEMS. THIS YEAR IS MORE DIFFICULT THAN '06. LAST YEAR WE FOUGHT LUCK, THIS YEAR A REAL RIVAL. WE HAVE PROBLEMS, PEDROSA HAS BIGGER PROBLEMS!'
VALENTINO ROSSI

Top Pole sitter Edwards leads the sodden charge to the first corner

Right Rossi never showed at the front and was not happy with his tyre supplier

Opposite Casey Stoner gets both wheels off the ground under the Dunlop bridge, the fastest part of the course, in free practice

Top The Suzukis heading for third and fifth places: Vermeulen would overtake his team-mate and then overhaul Rossi

Right The form book said Ducati couldn't win in the wet: Casey Stoner thought otherwise, but had to get past a very fast Colin Edwards to do it

slick on the right side: 'I never see a tyre like this in my career.' This despite the French factory being able to use their old advantage of flying tyres in overnight – the 31-tyre allowance only applies to slicks, with teams allowed as many full wets as they like – and more fuel for his festering resentment of Michelin, which had started at the Portuguese Grand Prix the previous season. As for the fourth place, 'This was our potential today' although he also said, 'I could have done better today.' Was he worried that Stoner now had a 26-point lead? 'I'm not worried for 26 points, more for own problems. This year is more difficult than '06. Last year we fought luck, this year a real rival. We have problems, Pedrosa has bigger problems!'

Dani certainly did. He had led the opening laps but plummeted down the order and only just held off Hofmann in the closing stages. It may be that his light weight didn't work his soft rear tyre enough to get heat in it and he had to swap to his second bike after the sighting lap, but that didn't stop Pedrosa making it very clear to his Japanese bosses that if things didn't get better he'd be seeking an alternative employer.

But, once again, if you took Casey Stoner out of the equation it was difficult to say that Ducati, certainly, or to a lesser extent Bridgestone, had a major advantage. Where, for example, was Alex Barros, a noted rain man and rostrum finisher at Donington only two years previously? Rossi and others made the point that the Michelins had a different problem from the one suffered at Le Mans. This time they couldn't cope with a drying track; in France it was a track that changed from wet to flooded as the race went on that did for the French tyres. More significantly, Donington Park showed that the Stoner–Ducati–

THE THIRD AUSSIE

There were two Aussies on the rostrum, but a third attracted nearly as much applause as Stoner and Vermeulen. Anthony West, drafted into the Kawasaki team to replace Olivier Jacque, lived up to his reputation as a master of wet conditions by being fastest in Sunday morning warm-up and getting as high as fourth in the race before running off track at Coppice. He avoided the wall with some high-speed drifts only to topple over at walking pace, then rejoined the race and worked his way back up to 11th.

Not bad for a rider who started the year on a private 250 Aprilia, split with the team after conspicuous lack of success and then went to the factory Yamaha World Supersport team, for whom he immediately won two races, one in the wet, one in the dry. After riding the Kawasaki at the Barcelona test he was offered the MotoGP ride and bought himself out of the Yamaha contract. It was money well spent.

The Australian trio's success at Donington begs the question why they should be so good in the wet. After all, Australia is hardly noted for its rainfall levels. The answer may be that all of them started racing young in dirt-track competition on oil-slicked ovals. Not long ago schoolboy motocross was a necessary prerequisite for a successful road-racing career, but more recently champions like Rossi, Melandri and Kato came from a background of minibike competition and arrived in GPs without having used a knobbly tyre in anger.

Whatever the reason, Ant's ride at Donington turned not just his season but his career around. One of the paddock's nearly-men was now well and truly in the frame for a full-time MotoGP ride with a factory team.

Above Nobody is quicker on a soaking wet track than Ant West

Bridgestone combination could cope with yet another set of conditions that nobody would possibly have thought was to their advantage. The Ducati team-manager Livio Suppo is normally keen to mention his technical partners Shell and Bridgestone in any press or TV interview, but when he was asked to comment on the efficacy of Bridgestone's wet-weather tyres he gave a one-word answer: 'Rider!' Then, to make sure his audience understood, he said 'Rider!' And then he said 'Rider!'

When that rider criticises the Donington Park surface on Friday, wins the race by nearly 12 seconds in ultra-tricky drying conditions, then repeats his opinion that the surface was probably the worst of the year, it is difficult to argue with his manager's opinion.

BRITISH GP
DONINGTON PARK

ROUND 8
June 24

RACE RESULTS

CIRCUIT LENGTH 2.500 miles
NO. OF LAPS 30
RACE DISTANCE 74.993 miles
WEATHER Wet, 14°C
TRACK TEMPERATURE 18°C
WINNER Casey Stoner
FASTEST LAP 1m 41.428s, 88.720mph, Toni Elias
PREVIOUS LAP RECORD 1m 27.676s, 102.641mph, Dani Pedrosa, 2006

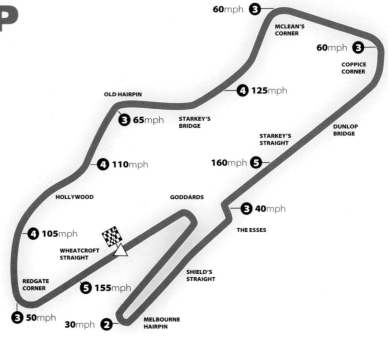

QUALIFYING

	Rider	Nationality	Team	Qualifying	Pole +	Gap
1	Edwards	USA	Fiat Yamaha Team	1m 28.531s		
2	Rossi	ITA	Fiat Yamaha Team	1m 28.677s	0.146s	0.146s
3	Pedrosa	SPA	Repsol Honda Team	1m 28.863s	0.332s	0.186s
4	Hayden	USA	Repsol Honda Team	1m 29.025s	0.494s	0.162s
5	Stoner	AUS	Ducati Marlboro Team	1m 29.061s	0.530s	0.036s
6	Hopkins	USA	Rizla Suzuki MotoGP	1m 29.073s	0.542s	0.012s
7	Checa	SPA	Honda LCR	1m 29.281s	0.750s	0.208s
8	De Puniet	FRA	Kawasaki Racing Team	1m 29.415s	0.884s	0.134s
9	Melandri	ITA	Honda Gresini	1m 29.498s	0.967s	0.083s
10	Elias	SPA	Honda Gresini	1m 29.711s	1.180s	0.213s
11	Nakano	JPN	Konica Minolta Honda	1m 29.718s	1.187s	0.007s
12	Vermeulen	AUS	Rizla Suzuki MotoGP	1m 29.793s	1.262s	0.075s
13	Capirossi	ITA	Ducati Marlboro Team	1m 29.900s	1.369s	0.107s
14	Hofmann	GER	Pramac d'Antin	1m 29.911s	1.380s	0.011s
15	Barros	BRA	Pramac d'Antin	1m 30.071s	1.540s	0.160s
16	Guintoli	FRA	Dunlop Yamaha Tech 3	1m 30.271s	1.740s	0.200s
17	West	AUS	Kawasaki Racing Team	1m 30.718s	2.187s	0.447s
18	Tamada	JPN	Dunlop Racing Tech 3	1m 30.800s	2.269s	0.082s
19	Roberts K.	USA	Team Roberts	1m 31.543s	3.012s	0.743s

FINISHERS

1 CASY STONER Another one Casey and Ducati weren't supposed to win, let alone in the wet, yet win he did, and easily, despite a bad start, to increase his lead in the championship. Team-manager Livio Suppo described Casey's race management as the work of a genius.

2 COLIN EDWARDS Second podium of the year from his second pole position, equalling his best career finish – he'd been runner-up three times previously, twice in 2004, once in 2005. Managed a worn rear Michelin very well and led for ten laps once Pedrosa had run into problems.

3 CHRIS VERMEULEN Three crashes, including a major get-off down Craner Curves on Saturday morning, weren't the best preparation, but again he showed his mastery of wet conditions. Only real problem was a misting visor that caused him to run off track on lap eight.

4 VALENTINO ROSSI A strange weekend, with two crashes in practice and an off-track race excursion that put him down to eighth. Fast in dry qualifying but his rear Michelin couldn't cope with the drying track. Only consolation was becoming top scorer in the history of the top class, with 2303 points.

5 JOHN HOPKINS His top wet-race finishing position. Was in third early on but the dry line that emerged didn't

coincide with the line he uses! It was his fifth top-five finish of the year.

6 RANDY DE PUNIET Put in another impressive race, despite a bad start and still suffering from Le Mans and Mugello injuries. Considered it his toughest, and best, race and, after eight rounds, had scored more points than he did in the entire 2006 season.

7 ALEX BARROS Gave himself problems by choosing a front tyre that was too soft for the drying track but was helped by a rear tyre that came good as the race went on. Not a bad result from 15th on the grid.

8 DANI PEDROSA Had to change his bike after the sighting lap due to a clutch

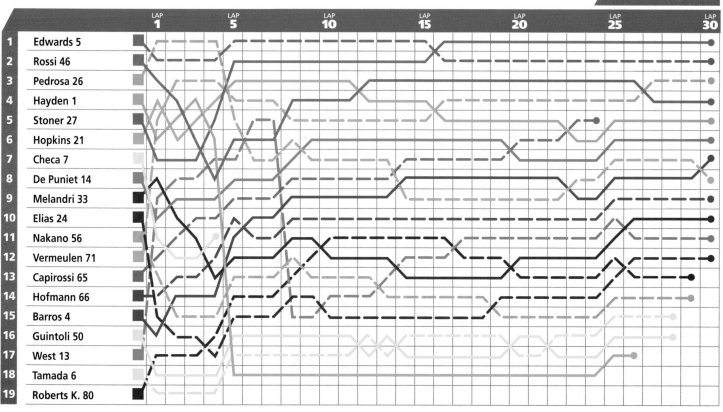

		LAP 1	LAP 5	LAP 10	LAP 15	LAP 20	LAP 25	LAP 30
1	Edwards 5							
2	Rossi 46							
3	Pedrosa 26							
4	Hayden 1							
5	Stoner 27							
6	Hopkins 21							
7	Checa 7							
8	De Puniet 14							
9	Melandri 33							
10	Elias 24							
11	Nakano 56							
12	Vermeulen 71							
13	Capirossi 65							
14	Hofmann 66							
15	Barros 4							
16	Guintoli 50							
17	West 13							
18	Tamada 6							
19	Roberts K. 80							

RACE

	Rider	Motorcycle	Race Time	Time +	Fastest Lap	Average Speed
1	Stoner	Ducati	51m 40.739s		1m 41.797s	87.067mph
2	Edwards	Yamaha	51m 52.507s	11.768s	1m 41.843s	86.738mph
3	Vermeulen	Suzuki	51m 56.417s	15.678s	1m 42.102s	86.630mph
4	Rossi	Yamaha	52m 02.566s	21.827s	1m 42.081s	86.459mph
5	Hopkins	Suzuki	52m 16.257s	35.518s	1m 42.836s	86.082mph
6	De Puniet	Kawasaki	52m 17.213s	36.474s	1m 42.813s	86.055mph
7	Barros	Ducati	52m 18.833s	38.094s	1m 42.213s	86.011mph
8	Pedrosa	Honda	52m 19.731s	38.992s	1m 42.257s	85.987mph
9	Hofmann	Ducati	52m 19.978s	39.239s	1m 41.822s	85.980mph
10	Melandri	Honda	52m 42.265s	1m 01.526s	1m 41.473s	85.374mph
11	West	Kawasaki	52m 47.225s	1m 06.486s	1m 43.039s	85.240mph
12	Elias	Honda	53m 14.813s	1m 34.074s	1m 41.428s	84.504mph
13	Roberts K.	Kr212v	51m 47.281s	1 Lap	1m 44.531s	83.988mph
14	Nakano	Honda	52m 50.579s	1 Lap	1m 46.069s	82.312mph
15	Tamada	Yamaha	52m 41.346s	2 Laps	1m 50.101s	79.705mph
16	Guintoli	Yamaha	52m 54.413s	2 Laps	1m 50.304s	79.377mph
17	Hayden	Honda	52m 58.768s	4 Laps	1m 45.475s	73.606mph
	Capirossi	Ducati	41m 47.579s	6 Laps	1m 41.794s	86.130mph
	Checa	Honda	07m 18.101s	26 Laps	1m 46.051s	82.165mph

CHAMPIONSHIP

	Rider	Team	Points
1	Stoner	Ducati Marlboro Team	165
2	Rossi	Fiat Yamaha Team	139
3	Pedrosa	Repsol Honda Team	106
4	Vermeulen	Rizla Suzuki MotoGP	88
5	Hopkins	Rizla Suzuki MotoGP	83
6	Melandri	Honda Gresini	81
7	Edwards	Fiat Yamaha Team	65
8	Barros	Pramac d'Antin	60
9	Capirossi	Ducati Marlboro Team	57
10	Elias	Honda Gresini	49
11	Hofmann	Pramac d'Antin	45
12	Hayden	Repsol Honda Team	41
13	De Puniet	Kawasaki Racing Team	40
14	Nakano	Konica Minolta Honda	21
15	Checa	Honda LCR	20
16	Tamada	Dunlop Yamaha Tech 3	17
17	Guintoli	Dunlop Yamaha Tech 3	16
18	West	Kawasaki Racing Team	5
19	Nieto	Kawasaki Racing Team	5
20	Roberts Jr	Team Roberts	4
21	Jacque	Kawasaki Racing Team	4
22	Roberts K.	Team Roberts	3

problem. Unfortunately the second bike had too-soft tyres – Dani's choice – and still had the dry-weather gearbox in it – the team's mistake. Uncharacteristically vocal after the race in his criticism of Honda.

9 ALEX HOFMANN After his wet-weather heroics in France this was a let-down. Closing on the men in front of him when he had a major moment at Goddard's and lost touch.

10 MARCO MELANDRI Finished well but struggled to find grip when the track was fully wet; only when it started to dry did he pick up the pace. Had set fastest lap of the race until his team-mate went even faster two laps from the flag.

11 ANTHONY WEST An eventful and very promising debut as a full-time MotoGP rider, after replacing Jacque in the Kawasaki team. Up to fourth when the weather was at its worst, ran across the gravel trap at Coppice and fell at walking pace, getting back on track in 15th.

12 TONI ELIAS A race of several very different parts, starting with a high-speed run across the grass at Craner Curves, then complicated by tyres that wouldn't get up to temperature and lack of stability on the brakes. Things got better as the dry line appeared; set the fastest lap of the race on lap 28 of 30.

13 KURTIS ROBERTS Team Roberts's best result since the first race of the season and a personal best in MotoGP for Kurtis.

Up to 11th early on, despite a fall in warm-up, then found his soft wet-weather tyre didn't work for long on the drying track. Kenny Senior reckoned the wet weekend taught the team nothing.

14 SHINYA NAKANO Another race that followed the emerging pattern of frustrating practice disguised by bravery with the qualifying tyres promoting him five places up the grid. The race started well, but Shinya was another Michelin man who suffered as the race went on, and had the indignity of being lapped.

15 MAKOTO TAMADA Dunlop's wet tyres never let the Tech 3 Yamaha men run with the opposition. They had to circulate on their own, losing a couple of seconds a lap, and being lapped twice.

16 SYLVAIN GUINTOLI Had scored points in every race so far but the inadequacies of his Dunlops in the wet brought that run to an end. Doubly disappointing as Donington is his second 'home race': he lives less than half-an-hour's drive from the track.

17 NICKY HAYDEN Happier than he'd been all season thanks to post-Barcelona tests. Qualified the best he'd done all year and was running with the leading group when he crashed at McLean's. Got back to the pits for running repairs and then circulated with stones in his clutch, hoping to pick up a point or two.

NON-FINISHERS

LORIS CAPIROSSI Never an outstanding wet-weather rider, but still up to fifth place and looking confident as he challenged Vermeulen, then crashed five laps from the flag.

CARLOS CHECA Very quick in dry qualifying but crashed out of the race on lap five, making his personal record four crashes in eight races.

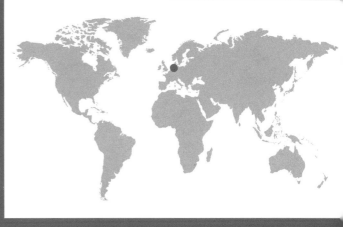

FANCY DRESS PARTY

**It was just like old times –
Rossi at his imperious best
on what, despite the recent
modifications, is still a
great track**

It is a measure of what we have come to expect from Valentino Rossi that the fact he won this race from 11th on the grid hardly merited a mention in most race reports. After all, he'd won from the same grid position in Germany the previous season and at Donington in 2001, so who cared about something as commonplace as a win from the fourth row? Assen in 2007 was a flashback to the past in more than one way: Rossi took time to work his way up from midfield, setting new fastest laps six times in eight laps as he worked his way up to Stoner, who had led from the start. He then stalked the Aussie for ten laps before applying the coup de grâce four laps from home. When he made the move, at that favourite Assen passing place, the chicane that ends the lap, he immediately opened up a decisive gap. There was even some serious posing for the cameras on the slow-down lap. Just like old times, indeed.

The only thing that didn't go according to plan was qualifying, which was wet and turned into a benefit for the Bridgestone users. In dry free practice and the race there didn't appear to be an advantage to any tyre brand, but after the race, mindful no doubt of his early-season sniping, Rossi was very quick to praise his Michelin tyres.

Casey Stoner wasn't unduly worried by losing – 'not after the season we've had'. He was happy to have run the best pace he could but readily acknowledged that Rossi 'had the better package'. For the first time, Stoner reported an issue with his machinery. The big Ducati fairing that had served him so well on the straights of Losail and Catalunya did not like the strong wind that gusted across the flatlands of Holland. After

Right Alex Barros's normally neat riding style deserts him as he wrestles his Pramac Ducati into submission

two serious scares when he nearly lost the front going into corners, the Aussie said later, his confidence on the brakes was 'destroyed'. This description may have been a little overstated – Casey is never anything less than intense when talking about a race – but his reaction to the problem was calm and considered. He ran the pace he could but wasn't tempted to over-ride to catch Rossi. It's not a reaction you'd usually associate with a 21-year-old racer. He'd watched Valentino's progress on the big screens around the circuit (in itself a pretty cool thing to do) and accepted the inevitable. Right after he got past Hopkins for second place, Rossi set the fastest lap of the race as he instantaneously demolished the one-second gap to Stoner. For once the Doctor admitted that it had felt like hard work. The effort meant that 'I arrived quite tired, me and my tyres. And my mouth was dry, so I decide to wait.'

Maybe he did need a rest, maybe it was the old sense of theatre, but TV viewers and the sections of the massive Assen crowd who could see the big screens were treated to some fabulous footage from Rossi's on-board camera as he followed Stoner through the high-speed sweeps that lead back to the chicane. Two laps after he made the pass, Rossi's lead was 1.5 seconds.

If Rossi's win from 11th was impressive, then Nicky Hayden's third from two places lower on the grid was even more so. The reigning World Champion had endured a deeply depressing first half to the season but had finally found some feeling from his bike in the post-Catalunya test. Like Rossi, he was nowhere in

qualifying but felt better than he had all season in warm-up. Time, he decided, to 'fight like a dog'. Matching the deed to the thought, Nicky raged round the outside of most of the field in the first turn. He was briefly third but was pushed back to fifth from where he rode with all the aggression of the top-flight dirt-tracker he used to be. The pass on Vermeulen at the end of the back straight was made with the bike sideways on the brakes.

Hayden never said so, but beating his team-mate must

Top Once Rossi hit the front it was clear that he had the pace to pull away from Stoner

Below As usual, John Hopkins was fast early on, but he's about to lose third to Hayden

resulted in a spiral fracture of the femur and the prospect of another lengthy convalescence.

The Assen track came in for a fair amount of stick, with Edwards and Stoner laying into the latest modifications in no uncertain terms at the pre-race press conference. There was evidence of another twist in the tale on the slow-down lap. Both Stoner and Hayden ran out of petrol. Had the additional hard acceleration out of slow corners made the Circuit van Drenthe even more marginal on fuel than it was when more time was spent with throttles wide open? Both men said it was simply a matter of more spinning in the race than in practice, throwing the teams' calculations slightly out.

At the start of the month Rossi had said that he needed to 'make a point' in the four races in June. They were on his four favourite tracks and Valentino knew he had to take points from Stoner if he wanted to regain his crown. Vale was well aware of the significance of his Dutch victory for himself, and for Yamaha and Michelin. Given the schisms that seemed to be developing between the tyre company and the rider, his statement that the win was 'very important for me and all the team' carried more significance than the usual post-race blandishments. However, when the scores for June were added up, Rossi and Stoner had identical records: two wins, a second and a fourth place for 83 points apiece. Not what the Doctor ordered.

It was also a significant result for the Yamaha factory, their 150th victory in the premier class of motorcycle racing. The first win was back in 1972 on Barcelona's Montjuich Park circuit thanks to the British privateer Chas Mortimer, riding an over-bored 350 twin. Valentino always did have a sense of history.

Top All three men on the rostrum had reasons to be cheerful

have been nearly as pleasing as getting back on the rostrum. Nicky wasn't too upbeat, pointing out that he'd never seen an HRC contract with bonuses for rostrum finishes. Typically, he was quick to praise his crew for the hours they put in when things weren't going well. It was heartening to see how pleased the rest of the paddock was for him. Both Rossi and Stoner made a point of talking about him, Casey saying he was 'stoked' (Australian for very pleased) for Nicky. It was a much less happy weekend for Toni Elias. What looked like a high-speed but essentially harmless slide into the gravel

Left Nicky Hayden's bike is still banked to the right but the rider is already shifting his weight to the left ready for another of Assen's interlinked corners

Top Randy de Puniet was a little too anxious to make up for his bad start; this ill-advised move on Vermeulen put them both in the gravel

Right Shy, retiring Colin Edwards entering into the retro spirit of the Fiat Yamaha team's colour scheme

DRESSING UP

The factory Yamaha team raced in distinctly unconventional colours to celebrate sponsor Fiat's new-model Cinquecento due to be unveiled the following week, exactly 50 years after the original iconic design was launched. The theme was very 1950s, with lots of pastel pinstripes and the sort of graphic illustrations seen on record sleeves of the era – couples doing the Twist and musical notes. Just to make sure everyone noticed, the fairing front was a wonderfully clashing Italian tricolore flag.

Naturally, Valentino Rossi took things further with a special helmet featuring a vinyl 45rpm record on top and a spoof poster on the back advertising 'Valentino and the Chihuahuas live at Assen'. Colin Edwards was slightly more restrained, with illustrations of classic guitars on his one-off lid, although he cast subtlety aside on the grid with a magnificently bequiffed Elvis wig and shades from the King's Las Vegas period.

Paddock inhabitants with a nostalgic bent were heard to sigh on seeing the number '500' on the side of a fairing again.

DUTCH TT
TT CIRCUIT ASSEN

ROUND 9
June 30

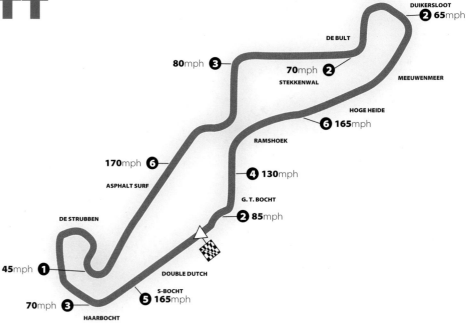

MANDEVEEN
DUIKERSLOOT
2 65mph
DE BULT
80mph **3**
70mph **2**
STEKKENWAL
MEEUWENMEER
HOGE HEIDE
6 165mph
RAMSHOEK
170mph **6**
4 130mph
ASPHALT SURF
G. T. BOCHT
2 85mph
DE STRUBBEN
DOUBLE DUTCH
45mph **1**
S-BOCHT
5 165mph
70mph **3**
HAARBOCHT

RACE RESULTS

CIRCUIT LENGTH 2.830 miles
NO. OF LAPS 26
RACE DISTANCE 73.592 miles
WEATHER Dry, 21°C
TRACK TEMPERATURE 32°C
WINNER Valentino Rossi
FASTEST LAP 1m 37.433s,
104.577mph, Valentino Rossi
PREVIOUS LAP RECORD 1m 37.106s,
104.934mph, Nicky Hayden, 2006 (record)

QUALIFYING

	Rider	Nationality	Team	Qualifying	Pole +	Gap
1	Vermeulen	AUS	Rizla Suzuki MotoGP	1m 48.555s		
2	Stoner	AUS	Ducati Marlboro Team	1m 48.572s	0.017s	0.017s
3	De Puniet	FRA	Kawasaki Racing Team	1m 49.579s	1.024s	0.007s
4	Melandri	ITA	Honda Gresini	1m 49.679s	1.124s	0.100s
5	Hopkins	USA	Rizla Suzuki MotoGP	1m 49.684s	1.129s	0.005s
6	Edwards	USA	Fiat Yamaha Team	1m 49.691s	1.136s	0.007s
7	West	AUS	Kawasaki Racing Team	1m 49.807s	1.252s	0.116s
8	Hofmann	GER	Pramac d'Antin	1m 49.927s	1.372s	0.120s
9	Pedrosa	SPA	Repsol Honda Team	1m 50.132s	1.577s	0.205s
10	Capirossi	ITA	Ducati Marlboro Team	1m 50.169s	1.614s	0.037s
11	Rossi	ITA	Fiat Yamaha Team	1m 50.392s	1.837s	0.223s
12	Barros	BRA	Pramac d'Antin	1m 50.402s	1.847s	0.010s
13	Hayden	USA	Repsol Honda Team	1m 50.581s	2.026s	0.179s
14	Roberts K.	USA	Team Roberts	1m 51.259s	2.704s	0.678s
15	Nakano	JPN	Konica Minolta Honda	1m 51.827s	3.272s	0.568s
16	Checa	SPA	Honda LCR	1m 53.271s	4.716s	1.444s
17	Guintoli	FRA	Dunlop Yamaha Tech 3	1m 54.253s	5.698s	0.982s
18	Tamada	JPN	Dunlop Yamaha Tech 3	1m 57.525s	8.970s	3.272s
	Elias	SPA	Honda Gresini			

FINISHERS

1 VALENTINO ROSSI A masterful display to give Yamaha their 150th win in the premier class – and all from 11th on the grid! Didn't get a great start and took half the race to work his way onto Stoner's back wheel. Made his move four laps from the flag and instantly pulled out a decisive gap.

2 CASEY STONER Happy enough with second place, limiting the damage to his championship lead. Unable to fight with Rossi because he lost his confidence on the brakes after the strong wind caused the front to push a couple of times going into corners – thought the big Ducati fairing might be to blame.

3 NICKY HAYDEN At last, the defending World Champion got a rostrum finish. Started even further back on the grid than Rossi, rode a stunning first bend and then outpaced his team-mate. Looked like the old Nicky: proof that whatever the team found at the Barcelona test had worked.

4 DANI PEDROSA Shadowed his team-mate for most of the race but couldn't match his pace in the last quarter. Again aimed some thinly veiled criticism at Honda by saying, after the race, that the problem was lack of traction, and it wasn't the first time he'd suffered from it this season.

5 JOHN HOPKINS Pushed hard in the opening stages to try and stay with Stoner but ran into some vibration after half-distance. Nevertheless, this was his sixth top-five finish of the year and he retook fourth place in the table from his team-mate.

6 COLIN EDWARDS Yamaha and Michelin's best qualifier. Got tangled up with Melandri and Vermeulen early on and then, once past them, hit a problem. Was able to up his pace again in the closing laps but Hopkins had then gapped him by over two seconds.

7 ALEX BARROS Like Stoner thought the strong wind might have affected his bike, the main problem being a tendency to run wide on corner exits. Add in a first-lap mistake that put him back to 15th and it's clear he had a very busy race.

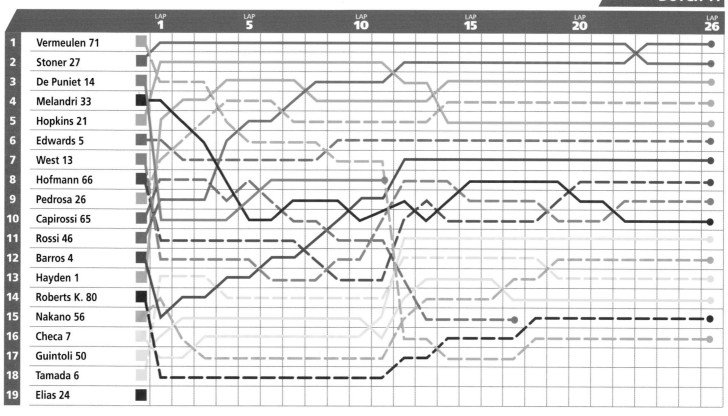

		LAP 1	LAP 5	LAP 10	LAP 15	LAP 20	LAP 26
1	Vermeulen 71						
2	Stoner 27						
3	De Puniet 14						
4	Melandri 33						
5	Hopkins 21						
6	Edwards 5						
7	West 13						
8	Hofmann 66						
9	Pedrosa 26						
10	Capirossi 65						
11	Rossi 46						
12	Barros 4						
13	Hayden 1						
14	Roberts K. 80						
15	Nakano 56						
16	Checa 7						
17	Guintoli 50						
18	Tamada 6						
19	Elias 24						

RACE

	Rider	Motorcycle	Race Time	Time +	Fastest Lap	Average Speed
1	Rossi	Yamaha	42m 37.149s		1m 37.433s	103.599mph
2	Stoner	Ducati	42m 39.058s	1.909s	1m 37.906s	103.522mph
3	Hayden	Honda	42m 43.226s	6.077s	1m 37.797s	103.354mph
4	Pedrosa	Honda	42m 47.614s	10.465s	1m 37.837s	103.177mph
5	Hopkins	Suzuki	42m 50.287s	13.138s	1m 37.848s	103.070mph
6	Edwards	Yamaha	42m 52.288s	15.139s	1m 37.931s	102.989mph
7	Barros	Ducati	43m 13.224s	36.075s	1m 38.845s	102.158mph
8	Hofmann	Ducati	43m 18.917s	41.768s	1m 38.878s	101.935mph
9	West	Kawasaki	43m 20.754s	43.605s	1m 38.835s	101.863mph
10	Melandri	Honda	43m 20.945s	43.796s	1m 39.114s	101.855mph
11	Checa	Honda	43m 20.975s	43.826s	1m 38.986s	101.854mph
12	Nakano	Honda	43m 25.045s	47.896s	1m 39.233s	101.694mph
13	Tamada	Yamaha	43m 31.217s	54.068s	1m 38.985s	101.454mph
14	Guintoli	Yamaha	43m 34.867s	57.718s	1m 39.102s	101.312mph
15	Roberts K.	Kr212v	44m 05.786s	1m 28.637s	1m 40.213s	100.129mph
16	Vermeulen	Suzuki	44m 11.957s	1m 34.808s	1m 38.582s	99.895mph
	Capirossi	Ducati	28m 48.517s	9 Laps		
	De Puniet	Kawasaki	18m 14.507s	15 Laps		

CHAMPIONSHIP

	Rider	Team	Points
1	Stoner	Ducati Marlboro Team	185
2	Rossi	Fiat Yamaha Team	164
3	Pedrosa	Repsol Honda Team	119
4	Hopkins	Rizla Suzuki MotoGP	94
5	Vermeulen	Rizla Suzuki MotoGP	88
6	Melandri	Honda Gresini	87
7	Edwards	Fiat Yamaha Team	75
8	Barros	Pramac d'Antin	69
9	Capirossi	Ducati Marlboro Team	57
10	Hayden	Repsol Honda Team	57
11	Hofmann	Pramac d'Antin	53
12	Elias	Honda Gresini	49
13	De Puniet	Kawasaki Racing Team	40
14	Nakano	Konica Minolta Honda	25
15	Checa	Honda LCR	25
16	Tamada	Dunlop Yamaha Tech 3	20
17	Guintoli	Dunlop Yamaha Tech 3	18
18	West	Kawasaki Racing Team	12
19	Nieto	Kawasaki Racing Team	5
20	Roberts Jr	Team Roberts	4
21	Roberts K.	Team Roberts	4
22	Jacque	Kawasaki Racing Team	4

Rode through the big dice and pulled five seconds on them, though.

8 ALEX HOFMANN Followed his team-mate home after pulling away from the big dice in the last couple of laps to put both Pramac d'Antin bikes in the top ten. Scared by the way his clutch behaved off the start – feared he might have to retire, then suffered cramp in his right arm that hampered his braking.

9 ANTHONY WEST Followed up his Donington debut with another truly impressive ride. Despite lack of track time on the Kawasaki, Ant was able to fight with much more experienced MotoGP riders and get a top-ten finish in his first dry race.

10 MARCO MELANDRI The usual depressing story: chatter in practice followed by chatter in the race that stopped him capitalising on a flying start which saw him fourth at the end of lap one. Rumoured to have told Honda head man Fukui-san exactly what he thought of his V4.

11 CARLOS CHECA Part of the midfield dice that entertained the crowd for much of the race but once again had no confidence in the front, especially under brakes. Happy to have been fighting for a top-ten position and to have scored points for only the second time in five races.

12 SHINYA NAKANO Tried a harder tyre than usual but to little effect. Doubly depressing as he'd finished on the Assen rostrum in 2006.

13 MAKOTO TAMADA Relieved to get in the points again after the disaster of Donington. Fading grip from the right side of the front tyre dropped him out of the group dice, the first time he'd experienced problems with his front Dunlop.

14 SYLVAIN GUINTOLI Thought he was faster than his team-mate at the end but decided not to try a pass. His problem was the rear tyre.

15 KURTIS ROBERTS The team tried some big changes for race day but the bike still suffered from the same problems. It was fine in banked corners but he reckoned he was losing lots of time in the four flat corners.

16 CHRIS VERMEULEN Started from pole for the third time in his career but couldn't run the pace of the leaders. Rammed off track by de Puniet, then nursed his damaged bike home.

NON-FINISHERS

LORIS CAPIROSSI Pulled in complaining of clutch and front-tyre problems. The noises coming out of the team garage didn't seem entirely sympathetic.

RANDY DE PUNIET Qualified third but made a mess of the start – 12th at the end of the first lap – then worked up to eighth until, just before half-distance, got frustrated trying to pass Vermeulen and hit the Suzuki from behind. Lucky to escape unhurt but unable to restart.

NON-STARTERS

TONI ELIAS What looked like a harmless slide into a gravel trap in first practice turned into a nightmare: hit the gravel with his left leg tucked under him and suffered a complicated fracture of the femur. Fortunately, the surgeon discovered things weren't quite as bad as first suspected, but no-one could envisage him being back in action before Misano, at the earliest.

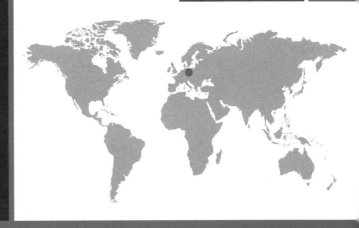

HONDA AT LAST!

Pedrosa dominated the weekend and delivered the Honda RC212V's first win of the 800 era; Rossi failed to take advantage of Stoner's tyre problems

Dani Pedrosa's third MotoGP race win came in the manner of the first two – a runaway victory during which he was only headed for one corner. The winning margin was the greatest in MotoGP history for a dry race. It was also Dani's first win for over a year and the Repsol Honda's first since Nicky Hayden triumphed at Laguna in 2006, and it all took place in the presence of new HRC President Masumi Humane, who was on a mission to assure the troops that things would get better. The task didn't look too easy after Hayden grenaded a motor in the most public and spectacular manner during Friday's practice, but Humane-san must have felt a lot better about his new job two days later as he watched both Repsol bikes finish on the rostrum.

The unhappiest man on Sunday was Valentino Rossi. This should have been the day he took points back off Casey Stoner: the Aussie, in common with most Bridgestone riders, ran into tyre problems. It didn't work out like that. A minor problem with his qualifying tyre put Rossi on the end of the second row of the grid, although he was actually less than a quarter of a second slower than pole; this was the closest qualifying ever in MotoGP, with the top 16 separated by just 0.8s. The Doctor's real problem came when he got stuck behind Randy de Puniet and the old Yamaha bugbear of overheating started to make itself felt. Rossi found he didn't have the speed to pass in the usual places – on the brakes at the first corner and at the bottom of the hill – so he had to improvise. He pushed past in the slow Omega, the looping, better than 180-degree right-hander that forms the lowest part of the track. It looked like a good move, but as he exited the corner the front slid away, probably because he was carrying

many places at the bottom of the hill. Now there are bumps there and it's dangerous to go to the inside.' It was more difficult starting from sixth this year, he said, than when he'd won from 11th on the grid the previous season.

To pile on the agony, Rossi had to sit and watch every Bridgestone rider except Loris Capirossi hit serious problems – 'Finally!' said Valentino – which turned the race inside out. Three Bridgestone runners who showed at the front in the early laps ran into problems that saw them drop off the pace and circulate together. They were Stoner, Melandri and Hopkins. Their misfortune enabled the slow-starting Michelin runners, Edwards and Hayden, to ride through the group and sort the final rostrum position out between them. Colin Edwards was as puzzled as most people, because he found he was able to lap faster once he'd lost a bit of side grip and the bike became 'more balanced'. John Hopkins said that staying in a group with the other two Bridgestone users, as their lap times fell drastically, was one of the strangest experiences he'd had in racing. Nicky said he could see all three of them were having serious problems with grip as he came through.

The exception to the pattern was Loris Capirossi who, as he habitually does, chose a softer tyre and torquier engine mapping than Stoner and passed both his team-mate and Melandri in one lap to go second, nine laps from the flag. The gap to Pedrosa was over ten seconds and growing but Loris had enough of an advantage over Hayden to be able to give away well over three seconds to the American in the remaining laps and still take second comfortably. It was his best result of the season

Top Pedrosa leads the field down to the Omega on the first lap

Below Stoner, Melandri and Hopkins, a convoy of struggling Bridgestone users

too much lean angle. The crash was as slow as you'll ever see in a Grand Prix, but the handlebar was bent beyond use. Valentino was not happy with de Puniet: 'It's like he rides more to stay in front of me than catch Hopkins.' Rossi also had some interesting views on why it was difficult to overtake: 'On this circuit, where there aren't any straights, everyone's going quicker in the corners on the 800s and there aren't any more places where it's possible to overtake. Last year I made

'ON THIS CIRCUIT, WHERE THERE AREN'T ANY STRAIGHTS, EVERYONE'S GOING QUICKER IN THE CORNERS ON THE 800s AND THERE AREN'T ANY MORE PLACES WHERE IT'S POSSIBLE TO OVERTAKE.'
VALENTINO ROSSI

Right Sylvain Guintoli started from his best grid position of the year so far but crashed out of the race

so far and came as rumours about his future – or lack of it – with Ducati grew ever more persistent.

Hayden was more than happy with consecutive rostrums but was honest enough to give credit to Michelin for the result. He'd had problems early in the race when he thought he might have split an exhaust pipe; a fiddle with the mapping switch didn't make things any better so he turned everything to maximum and pressed on through the field. The World Champion wasn't the only Honda rider looking pleased with his day's work. Melandri had received the new, longer exhaust pipes that had so improved Nicky's life and the Italian was happy, despite the way the race panned out. He also assumed that some new electronics had come with the pipes, and said the bike was immediately easier to ride. Casey Stoner got a good look at Marco's bike, and the Repsol bikes, and reported that the works machinery had much more punch than Team Gresini's.

Yet again Stoner was able to assess his situation and make the best of it. At one point he wasn't even sure he was going to be able to finish the race, because his tyre felt so strange that he was expecting a blow-out. Once it had suffered the first of its rapid performance drops Casey was content to run with, and even be headed by, Melandri – but he made sure he got ahead of Marco a few laps before the flag and then built up a cushion.

Amid all the tyre post-mortems it was easy to overlook the fact that Honda and the pre-season favourite, Pedrosa, had finally won a race under the 800cc formula. The question now was what HRC could do to help their riders on tracks where power matters as much as handling.

Above Dani Pedrosa was untouchable all weekend and won by a record margin

Opposite top After a depressing start to his year, Nicky Hayden made it two rostrums in two races

Opposite bottom Loris Capirossi was the only Bridgestone user to stay competitive all race, and was rewarded with his best result of the season so far

WHAT HAPPENED TO BRIDGESTONE?

Before the 2007 season it was never a total surprise to see Bridgestone tyre users having a tough weekend. Nakano's 200mph Mugello crash sticks in the collective consciousness, but there were races as recently as Donington and Estoril in 2006 when the Japanese company couldn't give its teams competitive tyres. However, seeing the same sort of thing happen, albeit on a smaller scale than some earlier seismic events, was a shock this season. What had happened?

As usual with tyre engineering, which still seems to be as much an art as a science, there is no one single answer. However, it is possible to identify four contributing factors. First, there is the asymmetrical nature of the Sachsenring, with its preponderance of left-handers. Second, the track temperature shot up to well over 50 degrees Centigrade by two o'clock on race day. Third, the track had been partially resurfaced with very abrasive tarmac. And finally, no-one had tested there since the resurfacing had been done. The result was accelerated wear on the left side of Bridgestone's rear slicks. Loris Capirossi's softer tyre was also badly worn but, for reasons no-one can fully explain, he managed to cope better than the others, although finishing 13 seconds behind the winner was hardly any cause for celebration.

The real surprise is that it was Bridgestone who suffered from a change in the weather. Up until then it had been Michelin's tyres, engineered to work in a very narrow spectrum of conditions, which could be expected to react badly when asked to operate outside their comfort zone. Fast forward seven days to the US Grand Prix, at a resurfaced Laguna Seca, and the same thing happened again – only this time the victim was Michelin.

GERMAN GP
SACHSENRING CIRCUIT
ROUND 10
July 15

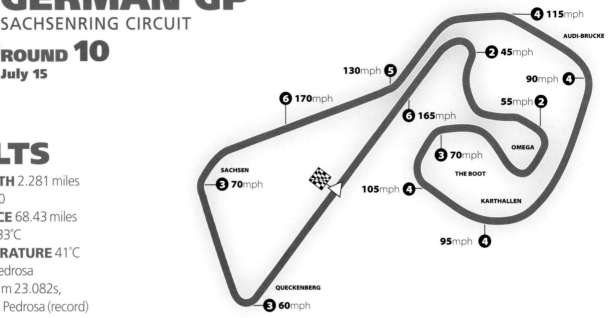

45mph, 90mph, 115mph, 55mph, 130mph, 170mph, 165mph, 70mph, 70mph, 105mph, 95mph, 60mph — AUDI-BRUCKE, OMEGA, THE BOOT, KARTHALLEN, SACHSEN, QUECKENBERG

RACE RESULTS

CIRCUIT LENGTH 2.281 miles
NO. OF LAPS 30
RACE DISTANCE 68.43 miles
WEATHER Dry, 33°C
TRACK TEMPERATURE 41°C
WINNER Dani Pedrosa
FASTEST LAP 1m 23.082s, 98.024mph, Dani Pedrosa (record)
PREVIOUS LAP RECORD 1m 23.355s, 98.456mph, Dani Pedrosa, 2006

QUALIFYING

	Rider	Nationality	Team	Qualifying	Pole +	Gap
1	Stoner	AUS	Ducati Marlboro Team	1m 22.384s		
2	Pedrosa	SPA	Repsol Honda Team	1m 22.388s	0.004s	0.004s
3	Melandri	ITA	Honda Gresini	1m 22.397s	0.013s	0.009s
4	De Puniet	FRA	Kawasaki Racing Team	1m 22.539s	0.155s	0.142s
5	Hopkins	USA	Rizla Suzuki MotoGP	1m 22.561s	0.177s	0.022s
6	Rossi	ITA	Fiat Yamaha Team	1m 22.605s	0.221s	0.044s
7	Capirossi	ITA	Ducati Marlboro Team	1m 22.615s	0.231s	0.010s
8	Barros	BRA	Pramac d'Antin	1m 22.897s	0.513s	0.282s
9	Guintoli	FRA	Dunlop Yamaha Tech 3	1m 22.958s	0.574s	0.061s
10	Nakano	JPN	Konica Minolta Honda	1m 22.969s	0.585s	0.011s
11	Vermeulen	AUS	Rizla Suzuki MotoGP	1m 23.039s	0.655s	0.070s
12	West	AUS	Kawasaki Racing Team	1m 23.056s	0.672s	0.017s
13	Edwards	USA	Fiat Yamaha Team	1m 23.090s	0.706s	0.034s
14	Hayden	USA	Repsol Honda Team	1m 23.151s	0.767s	0.061s
15	Checa	SPA	Honda LCR	1m 23.182s	0.798s	0.031s
16	Hofmann	GER	Pramac d'Antin	1m 23.199s	0.815s	0.017s
17	Fabrizio	ITA	Honda Gresini	1m 23.491s	1.107s	0.292s
18	Tamada	JPN	Dunlop Yamaha Tech 3	1m 23.744s	1.360s	0.253s
19	Roberts K.	USA	Team Roberts	1m 24.209s	1.825s	0.465s

FINISHERS

1 DANI PEDROSA A flag-to-flag win by a record dry-weather margin, lowering his own lap record on the way, was an emphatic way to take his first win in 17 races and Honda's first in the 800cc era. Stoner started from pole and got in front for one corner but, apart from that, the weekend was all about Dani.

2 LORIS CAPIROSSI By far his best race of the season so far and the only Bridgestone runner able to use his tyre as he wanted throughout – he'd chosen a softer rear than the others along with some radical set-up changes he refused to elaborate on. But rumours of his departure from Ducati continued to circulate.

3 NICKY HAYDEN A weekend that started with a crash and progressed through the mother of all blow-ups came good on race day, despite a split exhaust. Realistic enough to credit Michelin for being 'a big reason why I got on the podium today'. It was his fourth consecutive third place at the Sachsenring.

4 COLIN EDWARDS Felt he had 'too much grip' at the start but when he lost a bit of side grip the bike felt better balanced. Came through the field with Hayden and thought he should have made the rostrum, but his best-ever finish at the Sachsenring (from 13th on the grid!) was cause for celebration.

5 CASEY STONER Suffered from a gradual deterioration of tyre performance followed by a 'big drop', but managed the situation cleverly – didn't chase the men in front and concentrated on making sure he beat Melandri and Hopkins. Fifth, said Casey, was 'the maximum I could do', despite the fact that his bike 'was still good enough to win today'.

6 MARCO MELANDRI New exhaust pipes from HRC, probably aided by upgraded engine management electronics, put him on the front row for the first time since Motegi 2006 and he ran at the front on a dry track for the first time this year. Reported much improved throttle response.

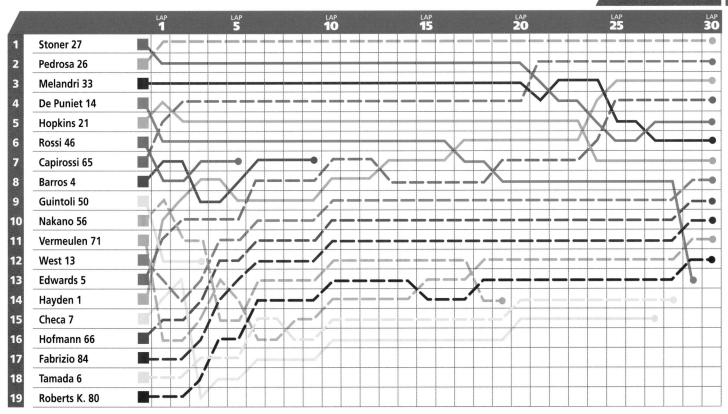

		LAP 1	LAP 5	LAP 10	LAP 15	LAP 20	LAP 25	LAP 30
1	Stoner 27							
2	Pedrosa 26							
3	Melandri 33							
4	De Puniet 14							
5	Hopkins 21							
6	Rossi 46							
7	Capirossi 65							
8	Barros 4							
9	Guintoli 50							
10	Nakano 56							
11	Vermeulen 71							
12	West 13							
13	Edwards 5							
14	Hayden 1							
15	Checa 7							
16	Hofmann 66							
17	Fabrizio 84							
18	Tamada 6							
19	Roberts K. 80							

RACE

	Rider	Motorcycle	Race Time	Time +	Fastest Lap	Average Speed
1	Pedrosa	Honda	41m 53.196s		1m 23.082s	98.024mph
2	Capirossi	Ducati	42m 06.362s	13.166s	1m 23.228s	97.513mph
3	Hayden	Honda	42m 09.967s	16.771s	1m 23.617s	97.734mph
4	Edwards	Yamaha	42m 11.495s	18.299s	1m 23.886s	97.315mph
5	Stoner	Ducati	42m 24.622s	31.426s	1m 23.162s	96.813mph
6	Melandri	Honda	42m 25.113s	31.917s	1m 23.246s	96.795mph
7	Hopkins	Suzuki	42m 26.591s	33.395s	1m 23.456s	96.738mph
8	West	Kawasaki	42m 34.390s	41.194s	1m 23.938s	96.443mph
9	Hofmann	Ducati	42m 36.410s	43.214s	1m 24.087s	96.367mph
10	Fabrizio	Honda	42m 37.655s	44.459s	1m 24.283s	96.319mph
11	Vermeulen	Suzuki	42m 55.090s	1'01.894s	1m 23.884s	95.668mph
12	Roberts K.	Kr212v	43m 03.917s	1'10.721s	1m 25.617s	95.341mph
13	Tamada	Yamaha	42m 48.710s	2 Laps	1m 25.844s	89.512mph
14	Checa	Honda	42m 34.089s	3 Laps	1m 24.148s	86.808mph
15	De Puniet	Kawasaki	41m 46.308s	1 Lap	1m 23.799s	95.017mph
16	Nakano	Honda	28m 40.361s	11 Laps	1m 24.421s	90.692mph
17	Barros	Ducati	12m 41.157s	21 Laps	1m 24.003s	97.097mph
18	Rossi	Yamaha	7m 02.631s	25 Laps	1m 23.529s	97.151mph
19	Guintoli	Yamaha	4m 17.597s	27 Laps	1m 24.683s	95.635mph

CHAMPIONSHIP

	Rider	Team	Points
1	Stoner	Ducati Marlboro Team	196
2	Rossi	Fiat Yamaha Team	164
3	Pedrosa	Repsol Honda Team	144
4	Hopkins	Rizla Suzuki MotoGP	103
5	Melandri	Honda Gresini	97
6	Vermeulen	Rizla Suzuki MotoGP	93
7	Edwards	Fiat Yamaha Team	88
8	Capirossi	Ducati Marlboro Team	77
9	Hayden	Repsol Honda Team	73
10	Barros	Pramac d'Antin	69
11	Hofmann	Pramac d'Antin	60
12	Elias	Honda Gresini	49
13	De Puniet	Kawasaki Racing Team	40
14	Checa	Honda LCR	27
15	Nakano	Konica Minolta Honda	25
16	Tamada	Dunlop Yamaha Tech 3	23
17	West	Kawasaki Racing Team	20
18	Guintoli	Dunlop Yamaha Tech 3	18
19	Roberts K.	Team Roberts	8
20	Fabrizio	Honda Gresini	6
21	Nieto	Kawasaki Racing Team	5
22	Roberts Jr	Team Roberts	4
23	Jacque	Kawasaki Racing Team	4

7 JOHN HOPKINS Described it as 'the strangest race I've ever been in' after running into severe edge grip problems, especially in left-handers; by the end it was 'harder than riding in the rain'. Observers who got a glimpse of his rear tyre in pitlane reported that it was destroyed.

8 ANTHONY WEST In only his third MotoGP race he coped with a near-crash while following Edwards through the field, then dealt with the tyre wear issues for his second top-ten finish.

9 ALEX HOFMANN Raced despite a bizarre accident the day after the Dutch TT when a friend closed a car boot on his right hand. The injury was bad enough to require an operation to insert metalware – not surprisingly, his race was severely compromised.

10 MICHEL FABRIZIO Racing as a replacement for the injured Elias and achieved his target of a top-ten finish. Described it as 'a real bonus in what has been a hard year'.

11 CHRIS VERMEULEN A clutch problem caused a jump-start, for which he had to serve a ride-through penalty. Then got his head down and picked up a few places before running into the same tyre issues as the other Bridgestone users.

12 KURTIS ROBERTS A third successive points-scoring race, although Kurtis 'just hung in there and did what we could do really and let everyone fall off around us and ended up getting 12th'. The team hoped to have the new chassis ready for the US GP the following weekend.

13 MAKOTO TAMADA Pitted early to change his rear tyre in the hope of curing the chatter that afflicted his bike all through practice and qualifying. The team were not impressed.

14 CARLOS CHECA Crashed when he lost the front on the final corner of the third lap but got the bike back to the pits for repairs and went out again to score a couple of points.

NON-FINISHERS

RANDY DE PUNIET A tough weekend: had a big crash in qualifying half-way round a lap that was looking good enough for pole, then forced to retire from eighth place a couple of laps from the flag when his fuel pump failed.

SHINYA NAKANO Retired with engine problems with 11 laps to go. Unlike Hayden's practice spectacular, this breakdown did not involve bits of hot metal all over the track.

ALEX BARROS Hurt his right hand on Friday when he crashed on the fastest part of the track, catching it underneath his sliding Ducati. That injury, and tyre problems, probably contributed to his crash in the race. Fortunately didn't do any further damage to the hand.

VALENTINO ROSSI Lost the chance to take useful points off Stoner by crashing early on after passing de Puniet in the Omega. Unable to get past the Frenchman at the usual places, Vale tried the unconventional and ended up in the dirt. It was a slow crash but the handlebars were bent when the bike hit the gravel trap.

SYLVAIN GUINTOLI Crashed, probably as a result of the engine seizing up. Doubly disappointing as he'd qualified ninth in his – and Dunlop's – best position of the year.

NON-STARTER

TONI ELIAS Recuperating from the broken femur suffered at Assen.

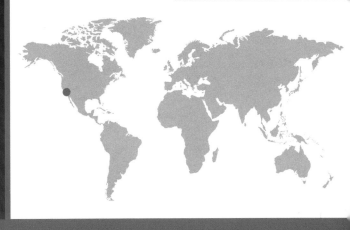

NEW WORLD ORDER

Stoner dominated like never before, as the home challenge hit the deck on the first lap, and Michelin suffered

Up until this Laguna Seca race Casey Stoner thought his win in Turkey was the best of his short MotoGP career. A few weeks later, after he'd secured the world title, he reconsidered and nominated this American race as his best. The common factor in both victories was that Stoner led every lap, but in the States he took things to a new level by being fastest in every free practice session, setting pole position, being fastest in Sunday morning warm-up and then breaking the lap record. It was the sort of display in which the previous Aussie World Champion, Mick Doohan, used to take such grim delight. It also persuaded Casey to admit for the first time that the title might now be a realistic prospect.

Certainly it was difficult to imagine anyone challenging Stoner after Rossi and Pedrosa finished fourth and fifth, respectively 30 and 35 seconds behind him, leaving Valentino the small matter of 44 points adrift in the championship table. Colin Edwards was asked what had happened and replied, 'When did you last see Valentino finish 30 seconds behind the leader?' In other words it was the tyres again, and Rossi himself was heard to say, 'At least I was first Michelin.' That 30-second margin would be brought up more than once later in the season as some Michelin riders sought to abandon ship or justify the one-make tyre proposal.

American hopes for a Hayden three-peat (that's the word they used) were dashed at the second corner of the race. Having been pushed out wide, Nicky was cutting back in and had a coming-together with John Hopkins. The Suzuki rider fell, Hayden somehow managed to stay on but he soon found his brake line

Above Chaz Davies, in his first MotoGP race, shadows Nicky Hayden mid-race

Right John Hopkins had a lonely and frustrating race after his first corner get-off

Opposite Despite being unable to walk, Marco Melandri was able to pass Rossi and take the final rostrum position

had been damaged. Hopkins got back to the pits and came out to do lap times which indicated he could have been in the top three.

That incident took two of Stoner's likely challengers out of the race – although Nicky later said he'd have been in trouble with the tyres – and it was left to Chris

Vermeulen on the other Suzuki to take up the chase. He got past the fast-starting Pedrosa at the end of lap three and set about closing the gap to Stoner. Chris held on for a few laps, even taking a few fractions of a second out of the Ducati's lead, but soon realised that he'd have to settle for his best-ever dry-weather result.

'I thought I was catching him, I must have been kidding myself,' said Vermeulen, although Casey did admit that it was 'difficult pulling away from Chris. I had to stay concentrated.'

The hero of the race was Marco Melandri, who took third off Pedrosa at half-distance and held on despite what was later revealed to be a broken ankle. At the time Marco thought it had merely been dislocated in a nasty incident in Saturday morning free practice. He had glanced off Kurtis Roberts, who was dawdling out of the second corner, and was then speared off into the gravel trap and tumbled at high speed into the air fence. The Italian rider is no stranger to painful injuries, but this one was bad enough for him to sit out warm-up in the hope of saving himself for the race. Even after painkilling injections to enable him to change gear he wasn't sure he'd be able to go the distance and he later described seeing the chequered flag as 'one of the best days of my life'. Given that he held off Rossi in the closing stages, as well as coping with what even Marco called 'a lot of pain', it is difficult to over-praise his ride.

Roberts escaped the disciplinary action over Melandri's crash that most observers were expecting. Rossi was particularly scathing on the subject, saying Kurtis should have been fined, and then dismissing him as 'someone who finishes 13th in Superstock'. That comment also referred to John Hopkins's $2000 Race Direction fine for losing his temper with Carlos Checa and aiming a kick at the Spaniard after being blocked in qualifying. Again, most people's sympathy was with Hopper. Sylvain Guintoli escaped a fine too, after his out-of-control move at the top of the Corkscrew inflicted a horrible injury on Alex Hofmann's left hand in the first five minutes of the very first session.

There was time for the d'Antin team to find a replacement rider and the AMA paddock, at Laguna for two American Championship races, was the obvious place to look. Ben Bostrom's name came up, but his Yamaha employers weren't keen on the idea. IRTA's Mike Trimby then suggested Chaz Davies. The young Brit had plenty of 125 and 250cc GP experience and was going well on a private R6 in the AMA Supersport class. With all of half an hour's notice, Chaz didn't look out of his depth in practice and qualifying, but in the race he really impressed. He was lining up Carlos Checa, who'd gestured at him in practice, for a pass when he had the problem with his rear sprocket that sent him into the pits. He came out to do a 1m 23.7s lap – a personal best that was better than that of six others and only 0.05s slower than Edwards's best lap of the race. Even more impressively, he did the time right at the end of the race. Ducati's management were suitably pleased.

Another MotoGP debutant who impressed everyone was Nicky Hayden's younger brother, Roger Lee. He and his temporary Kawasaki team-mates all finished in the top ten and Hayden was the fastest of the three in free practice. It was enough for Ducati to offer Davies a two-day test at Mugello and for there to be talk of a second Hayden in the MotoGP paddock before long. Team-managers also had a chance to take a good look at Ben Spies, Suzuki's AMA Superbike Champion, who was being linked with a third Suzuki for MotoGP in 2009.

The third Laguna Seca MotoGP race didn't deliver the Nicky Hayden hat-trick the enthusiastic crowd had been hoping for, but they certainly got to see a performance worthy of a World Champion.

Above Roger Lee Hayden (Kawasaki 95) in the midfield dice that kept the crowd entertained

Below Fastest in every session and leading at the end of every lap, it was Stoner's most dominant win yet

Opposite Chris Vermeulen goes well at Laguna, just as he used to do in World Superbike

'I THOUGHT I WAS CATCHING HIM, I MUST HAVE BEEN KIDDING MYSELF'
CHRIS VERMEULEN

ER

By common consent this US GP was a better organised event than the previous two. However, one very serious incident raised some pertinent questions – the accident in the opening minutes of the first practice session when Sylvain Guintoli rammed Alex Hofmann at the top of the Corkscrew. Hofmann's left hand was badly injured – probably by the Yamaha's brake adjuster. It looked like he'd been shot, said one witness. Hofmann was obviously suffering extreme pain, and also realised the severity of what had happened. However, he was left at the side of the track for twenty minutes until the red flag was shown to enable an ambulance to get to him. There is no access road at Laguna. Alex had to grab a marshal's radio and scream into it for 'someone to get me out of here'.

Race Direction were unaware of the situation. They were told by local personnel in communication with the corner that Hofmann was on his way to the medical centre. Race Director Paul Butler described the delay as 'absolutely scandalous' and apologised to the German rider.

The victim himself appeared in the press centre later in the weekend, after noted sports surgeon Dr Arthur Ting had operated on him, to lambast both Guintoli and the circuit's delay in recovering him. At the time it was not known if he would regain feeling in his hand, so he was contemplating a career-ending injury. The only good thing, he said, was that he had kept his hand off the ground so the risk of infection was minimised. Fortunately, Hofmann was able to ride again six weeks later. It could have been so much worse.

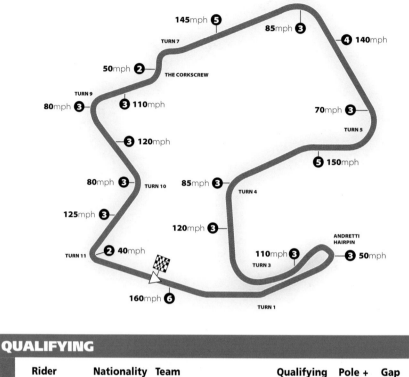

UNITED STATES GP

LAGUNA SECA

ROUND 11
July 22

RACE RESULTS

CIRCUIT LENGTH 2.243 miles
NO. OF LAPS 32
RACE DISTANCE 71.776 miles
WEATHER Dry, 30°C
TRACK TEMPERATURE 46°C
WINNER Casey Stoner
FASTEST LAP 1m 22.542s, 97.833mph, Casey Stoner (record)
PREVIOUS LAP RECORD 1m 23.333s, 96.846mph, Dani Pedrosa, 2006

QUALIFYING

	Rider	Nationality	Team	Qualifying	Pole +	Gap
1	Stoner	AUS	Ducati Team	1m 22.292s		
2	Pedrosa	SPA	Repsol Honda Team	1m 22.501s	0.209s	0.209s
3	Vermeulen	AUS	Rizla Suzuki MotoGP	1m 22.590s	0.298s	0.089s
4	Hayden N.	USA	Repsol Honda Team	1m 22.624s	0.332s	0.034s
5	Rossi	ITA	Fiat Yamaha Team	1m 22.683s	0.391s	0.059s
6	Capirossi	ITA	Ducati Team	1m 22.914s	0.622s	0.231s
7	Hopkins	USA	Rizla Suzuki MotoGP	1m 22.933s	0.641s	0.019s
8	Edwards	USA	Fiat Yamaha Team	1m 22.943s	0.651s	0.010s
9	Nakano	JPN	Konica Minolta Honda	1m 23.006s	0.714s	0.063s
10	Melandri	ITA	Honda Gresini	1m 23.018s	0.726s	0.012s
11	Tamada	JPN	Dunlop Yamaha Tech 3	1m 23.036s	0.744s	0.018s
12	West	AUS	Kawasaki Racing Team	1m 23.091s	0.799s	0.055s
13	De Puniet	FRA	Kawasaki Racing Team	1m 23.113s	0.821s	0.022s
14	Guintoli	FRA	Dunlop Yamaha Tech 3	1m 23.207s	0.915s	0.094s
15	Checa	SPA	Honda Gresini	1m 23.263s	0.971s	0.056s
16	Hayden R.	USA	Kawasaki Racing Team	1m 23.425s	1.133s	0.162s
17	Barros	BRA	Pramac d'Antin	1m 23.557s	1.265s	0.132s
18	Roberts K.	USA	Team Roberts	1m 23.662s	1.370s	0.105s
19	Duhamel	CAN	Honda Gresini	1m 23.923s	1.631s	0.261s
20	Davies	GBR	Pramac d'Antin	1m 24.098s	1.806s	0.175s

FINISHERS

1 CASEY STONER Domination in the style of fellow-countryman Doohan – fastest in every session, in the lead after four corners and never headed, victory by ten seconds, setting the fastest lap. No wonder Casey described it as 'my best racing weekend ever' – and it got even better when his Ducati contract was extended by two years.

2 CHRIS VERMEULEN First dry-weather podium in MotoGP, his third of the season, and some compensation for the mechanical problem that robbed him of a rostrum here in 2006. Fast all weekend, started off the front row and was never out of the top three. Put some mid-race pressure on Stoner, but then couldn't up his pace.

3 MARCO MELANDRI Even by the standards of this tough character a rostrum here was a minor miracle. A practice incident with Roberts left him with a badly swollen ankle and he had to be carried into the post-race press conference. Back in Europe it was discovered the ankle was broken.

4 VALENTINO ROSSI Lucky to escape without injury from a big crash in practice and resigned to his fate in the race. First Michelin man home but, as he pointed out afterwards, he couldn't match Stoner's race lap times on qualifiers or keep up with the injured Melandri.

5 DANI PEDROSA Not happy about his inability to compete, despite a front-row start and winning the week before.

Overtaken by Rossi, Melandri and Vermeulen and found he couldn't follow any of them. Suffered from major chatter from the rear tyre that got worse as the race went on.

6 RANDY DE PUNIET It didn't look good after qualifying 13th, but a change of suspension settings and front tyre for warm-up showed the team the way to go. Got a good start that put him up to ninth, then ran a controlled race to score his first points since Donington.

7 ANTHONY WEST One place better than his German GP result and his third top ten in just four races, this time at a track he'd never seen before, continued his more than impressive start in MotoGP. Had no idea of his race position and had to ask the crew where he'd finished.

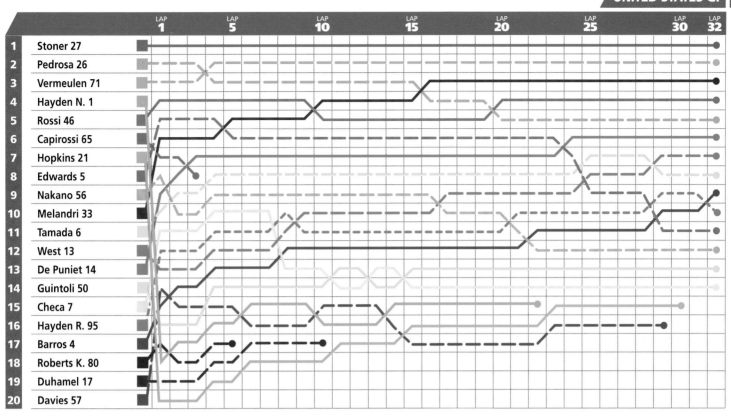

		LAP 1	LAP 5	LAP 10	LAP 15	LAP 20	LAP 25	LAP 30	LAP 32
1	Stoner 27								
2	Pedrosa 26								
3	Vermeulen 71								
4	Hayden N. 1								
5	Rossi 46								
6	Capirossi 65								
7	Hopkins 21								
8	Edwards 5								
9	Nakano 56								
10	Melandri 33								
11	Tamada 6								
12	West 13								
13	De Puniet 14								
14	Guintoli 50								
15	Checa 7								
16	Hayden R. 95								
17	Barros 4								
18	Roberts K. 80								
19	Duhamel 17								
20	Davies 57								

RACE

	Rider	Motorcycle	Race Time	Time +	Fastest Lap	Average Speed
1	Stoner	Ducati	44m 20.325s		1m 22.542s	97.135mph
2	Vermeulen	Suzuki	44m 30.190s	9.865s	1m 22.636s	96.776mph
3	Melandri	Honda	44m 45.966s	25.641s	1m 23.140s	96.208mph
4	Rossi	Yamaha	44m 50.989s	30.664s	1m 23.375s	96.028mph
5	Pedrosa	Honda	44m 55.947s	35.622s	1m 23.339s	95.851mph
6	De Puniet	Kawasaki	44m 58.631s	38.306s	1m 23.607s	95.756mph
7	West	Kawasaki	45m 01.747s	41.422s	1m 23.486s	95.646mph
8	Tamada	Yamaha	45m 02.680s	42.355s	1m 23.661s	95.612mph
9	Barros	Ducati	45m 03.845s	43.520s	1m 23.628s	95.571mph
10	Hayden R.	Kawasaki	45m 04.045s	43.720s	1m 23.615s	95.564mph
11	Edwards	Yamaha	45m 07.701s	47.376s	1m 23.725s	95.435mph
12	Nakano	Honda	45m 13.173s	52.848s	1m 23.695s	95.243mph
13	Guintoli	Yamaha	45m 18.735s	58.410s	1m 23.846s	95.048mph
14	Checa	Honda	45m 35.691s	1m 15.366s	1m 24.228s	94.459mph
15	Hopkins	Suzuki	45m 35.595s	2 Laps	1m 22.848s	88.558mph
16	Davies	Ducati	44m 34.640s	3 Laps	1m 23.781s	87.557mph
	Hayden N.	Honda	31m 49.864s	10 Laps	1m 24.710s	93.021mph
	Duhamel	Honda	14m 29.711s	22 Laps	1m 25.580s	92.850mph
	Roberts K.	Kr212v	7m 16.822s	27 Laps	1m 24.896s	92.433mph
	Capirossi	Ducati	4m 21.970s	29 Laps	1m 24.479s	92.476mph

CHAMPIONSHIP

	Rider	Team	Points
1	Stoner	Ducati Team	221
2	Rossi	Fiat Yamaha Team	177
3	Pedrosa	Repsol Honda Team	155
4	Vermeulen	Rizla Suzuki MotoGP	113
5	Melandri	Honda Gresini	113
6	Hopkins	Rizla Suzuki MotoGP	104
7	Edwards	Fiat Yamaha Team	93
8	Capirossi	Ducati Team	77
9	Barros	Pramac d'Antin	76
10	Hayden	Repsol Honda Team	73
11	Hofmann	Pramac d'Antin	60
12	De Puniet	Kawasaki Racing Team	50
13	Elias	Honda Gresini	49
14	Tamada	Dunlop Yamaha Tech 3	31
15	Checa	Honda LCR	29
16	West	Kawasaki Racing Team	29
17	Nakano	Konica Minolta Honda	29
18	Guintoli	Dunlop Yamaha Tech 3	21
19	Roberts K.	Team Roberts	8
20	Hayden R.	Kawasaki Racing Team	6
21	Fabrizio	Honda Gresini	6
22	Nieto	Kawasaki Racing Team	5
23	Jacque	Kawasaki Racing Team	4
24	Roberts Jr	Team Roberts	4

8 MAKOTO TAMADA Best race of the season, and not just the result but the way it happened. No problems with the Dunlops, which stayed consistent for the whole distance – he was particularly impressed with the rear slick.

9 ALEX BARROS Still suffering from his German crashes on a circuit where there is no chance to rest: a top-ten finish was no mean achievement. His injured hand meant braking, normally his strong point, was compromised. Used his experience to pass Roger Hayden on the last corner.

10 ROGER LEE HAYDEN A great first MotoGP ride as a wild-card entry on a third Kawasaki. First American across the line, having impressed everyone with both his speed and application.

11 COLIN EDWARDS A thoroughly disappointing race with a bike that never worked all weekend – the problem summed up by the words 'no grip'– and whatever the crew did, times stayed the same. Only turned competitive laps in the morning sessions when track temperatures were lower.

12 SHINYA NAKANO Qualified well and looked competitive in the first half of the race, getting as high as eighth before chatter set in at mid-distance.

13 SYLVAIN GUINTOLI Extremely disappointed not to cash in at a circuit where the Dunlops worked well – should have been in the top ten with his team-mate. Made a hash of the start, then tangled with Roberts and dropped to last.

Made more mistakes while dicing with Checa.

14 CARLOS CHECA Suffered from the same problems as the other Michelin men, with the added complication of a new chassis. No feedback from the rear was the main reason he couldn't get involved with the second group's fight for a top-ten finish.

15 JOHN HOPKINS On the floor at the first turn after colliding with Nicky Hayden. Got back to the pits for repairs and came out again to score one point, two laps down on the leaders. Distraught after the race.

16 CHAZ DAVIES Recruited on Friday lunchtime to replace Hofmann. Impressed everyone with his pace in the race. Damaged the rear sprocket when he ran

off at the Corkscrew and had to pit for a replacement. A noteworthy MotoGP debut under the most difficult circumstances.

NON-FINISHERS

NICKY HAYDEN Damaged his brake line when he came together with Hopkins on the first lap. Circulated at reduced pace hoping to score a point or two, but pulled in when the leaders lapped him.

MIGUEL DUHAMEL Replaced Elias at the insistence of American Honda in what looked like a thank-you for his sterling service. Had a nasty crash in Sunday morning warm-up and never got his head right for the race so pulled out.

KURTIS ROBERTS The new chassis finally arrived and improved the bike's behaviour significantly, but engine-braking problems put him out of the race.

LORIS CAPIROSSI The bike stuck in second gear after the gear lever return spring broke. Did not look happy when he got back to the pits.

NON-STARTERS

ALEX HOFMANN Suffered a severe injury to his left hand when he was rammed by Guintoli at the top of the Corkscrew early in the first practice session.

TONI ELIAS Still recovering from the broken femur sustained at Assen.

CZECH REPUBLIC GP
AUTOMOTODROM BRNO
ROUND **12**
August 19

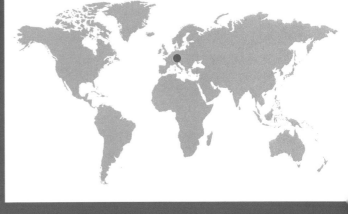

JUST LIKE MICK

Another weekend of total domination by Casey Stoner and Ducati; John Hopkins came second, his best-ever MotoGP result

At Brno Casey Stoner picked up where he'd left off in the USA, never for one second giving the opposition the idea they were in with a chance. He started from pole for the third successive race – a maiden pole for both Ducati and Bridgestone in the Czech Republic – although he didn't quite manage to be fastest in every session because Sylvain Guintoli was quickest on Friday. The Frenchman took advantage of the fact that Dunlop aren't covered by the 31-tyre allocation rule because they've not won a GP in the preceding two seasons: he put a qualifier on at the end of second free practice and went two-tenths faster than Stoner.

The young Aussie's feat in heading every session and every lap at Laguna Seca had reminded everyone of Mick Doohan, as did Casey's reaction to being relegated to second on Friday. He was all for stomping down pitlane to tell Guintoli to take things seriously and not play up to the TV cameras. Mighty Mick would have been proud.

The single most impressive aspect of Stoner's season so far had been his lack of mistakes. Even under race-long pressure from Valentino Rossi he'd shown no signs of cracking, while if he got away from the field he was just as capable of running at lap-record pace on his own. In qualifying he showed another facet of this imperturbability. Early in the session his bike developed a fault with its rear brake, which necessitated the Ducati crew changing the whole hydraulic system. Like most racers, Casey prefers to ride one of his two ostensibly identical machines. Rather than go out on his second bike he sat calmly in the pits on three occasions, losing half the session, while his mechanics made the necessary

'HE DIDN'T MAKE A
MISTAKE ALL WEEKEND.'
JOHN HOPKINS

adjustments to his preferred machine. Despite missing thirty minutes of this practice session he still set pole by over a quarter of a second.

Hopkins summed up Casey's race while commenting on his own second place, the best of his MotoGP career. The Suzuki rider said that after ten laps he gave up, but quickly qualified this by explaining that he gave up pressing to try and catch the runaway winner. 'He didn't make a mistake all weekend,' said Hopper. Well, discounting his crash at the end of qualifying, neither did John. It's just that the combination of Casey, Bridgestone tyres and the Ducati is currently unbeatable if they get everything right. Hopkins got up to second from the second row of the grid, just as he'd hoped to, passing both Repsol Hondas to try and latch on to Stoner – as he'd done in China when Stoner and Valentino Rossi were his 'ticket to a breakaway'. It is to the Aussie's credit that he pushed 'the front and rear to the limit' for so many laps before deciding that second place wasn't such a bad idea.

Nicky Hayden's fortunes continued to improve, as did Honda's. There were rumours of a new frame and a new engine, although Nicky maintained his first front-row start as World Champion was down to a big change to the front forks. His crew, however, reported that he used a frame with some revised stiffness ratios, while the motor had certainly grown a new oil cooler in the chin of the fairing. After being top Honda in qualifying for the first time this season, the American raced to third, his third rostrum in four races, and declared himself happy with his weekend's work. Nicky was close to the leaders after pushing past Pedrosa on the second

Left John Hopkins looks even happier with his second place than Casey Stoner does with another start-to-finish win

Below The fight for fifth kept the crowd entertained

Top Hopkins pressured Stoner in the opening laps but the Aussie was never headed

Top Hopkins pressured Stoner in the opening laps but the Aussie was never headed

Below Sylvain Guintoli was fast all weekend and only lost out on ninth place in the last three laps

lap and thought things were 'looking pretty. Then I got to the straight and realised I was dreaming.'

Nevertheless, he seemed happy with his weekend, unlike Pedrosa, who couldn't make his hard-front/soft-rear tyre combination work early in the race. Even when he did get the rubber up to temperature he couldn't close the gap to his team-mate. Third and fourth places for Michelin suggested some sort of parity had been restored in the tyre wars, but Carmelo Ezpeleta raised for the first time the possibility of MotoGP becoming a one-make tyre championship. Dorna's CEO told the tyre companies to sort out the regulations between themselves, or else.

The picture of Michelin's weekend, though, was distorted by Rossi's lacklustre race to seventh place. He pleaded lack of traction from Friday onwards, but observers as well qualified as Loris Reggiani said they'd never seen him ride so slowly – the ex-racer said that from the side of the track he couldn't spot any machinery problems. Valentino spent the race dicing with Vermeulen and Capirossi, whom he lost out to, and he only just held off Randy de Puniet's late charge. As the first three positions never changed after lap one, this was the dice that held the attention of the record crowd of over 140,000. Brno is always a popular event, but this time attendance was boosted by an estimated 30,000 Hungarian fans who had come along to support 125cc World Championship contender Gabor Talmacsi.

To show that Friday was no fluke, Guintoli spent most of the race harassing Alex Barros for ninth place before his rear Dunlop went off seriously in the closing laps. The Frenchman, the only rookie in the 2007 MotoGP field, was continuing to impress all observers. With motorcycle racing's usual lack of justice it now looked as if there would be no place for him in Yamaha's line-up for 2008. Thankfully, though, it looked as if Sylvain would be able to find a home at d'Antin Ducati next year.

Most teams were staying on after the race for important tests. Yamaha had a pneumatic-valve engine in the truck to evaluate. 'We're not going to give Casey and Ducati the start we gave them this year again,' said Jerry Burgess, obviously with an eye on 2008. It was as near to an admission that the fight for the title was over from such a seasoned competitor.

THE TAX MAN

Valentino Rossi's self-imposed purdah over race weekend meant he avoided having to answer any questions about his tax affairs. The Italian authorities had decided that Rossi owed them 112 million Euros in back tax, mainly on the grounds that his self-imposed exile in London was not genuine. The allegations had been front-page news in every paper in Italy for a week, and it's a measure of Valentino's status at home that a video message he recorded in London was broadcast on the country's main channel. Usually, that sort of message to the nation is only delivered by prime ministers or presidents.

The fiscal police have previously gone after icons like the skier Alberto Tomba and opera star Luciano Pavarotti in their fight against the tax evasion that is endemic in Italian society – they once famously and publicly confiscated the footballer Diego Maradona's collection of Rolex watches in lieu of payment. This was not a threat that Rossi could laugh off or ignore – and maybe what was more worrying for him was that not all the Italian media or the public appeared to be on his side. Editorials lamented the fall from grace of a golden child. Even the Catholic church got involved.

Rossi's decision not to give his usual afternoon briefings apparently did not include the mandatory front-row press conference, but as he qualified sixth it didn't become an issue. The question everyone would have wanted to ask was whether he was able to keep his mind on the job in hand. In the absence of an opinion from the man himself, the vast majority of the paddock decided that he couldn't, and that he didn't race to his full potential – hardly surprising with that sort of tax demand hanging over his head.

Above It's not often that you don't notice Valentino Rossi at a Grand Prix, but he hardly made an impact on the 2007 Czech race

Below Rossi had to work hard in the closing laps to hold off Randy de Puniet

CZECH REPUBLIC GP
AUTOMOTODROM BRNO

ROUND 12
August 19

RACE RESULTS

CIRCUIT LENGTH 3.357 miles
NO. OF LAPS 22
RACE DISTANCE 73.854 miles
WEATHER Dry, 25°C
TRACK TEMPERATURE 32°C
WINNER Casey Stoner
FASTEST LAP 1m 58.301s, 102.160mph, Casey Stoner
PREVIOUS LAP RECORD 1m 58.157s, 102.228mph, Loris Capirossi, 2006 (record)

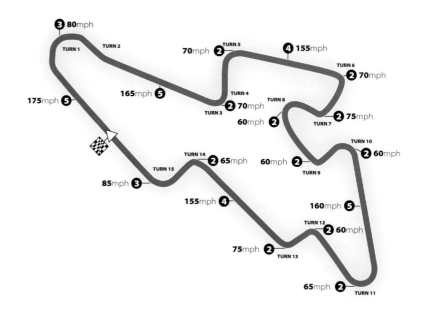

QUALIFYING

	Rider	Nationality	Team	Qualifying	Pole +	Gap
1	Stoner	AUS	Ducati Marlboro Team	1m 56.884s		
2	Hayden	USA	Repsol Honda Team	1m 57.164s	0.280s	0.280s
3	Pedrosa	SPA	Repsol Honda Team	1m 57.179s	0.295s	0.015s
4	Hopkins	USA	Rizla Suzuki MotoGP	1m 57.567s	0.683s	0.388s
5	De Puniet	FRA	Kawasaki Racing Team	1m 57.599s	0.715s	0.032s
6	Rossi	ITA	Fiat Yamaha Team	1m 57.640s	0.756s	0.041s
7	Capirossi	ITA	Ducati Marlboro Team	1m 57.665s	0.781s	0.025s
8	Vermeulen	AUS	Rizla Suzuki MotoGP	1m 57.699s	0.815s	0.034s
9	Edwards	USA	Fiat Yamaha Team	1m 57.702s	0.818s	0.003s
10	Guintoli	FRA	Dunlop Yamaha Tech 3	1m 57.732s	0.848s	0.030s
11	Nakano	JPN	Konica Minolta Honda	1m 57.969s	1.085s	0.237s
12	Checa	SPA	Honda LCR	1m 58.143s	1.259s	0.174s
13	Barros	BRA	Pramac d'Antin	1m 58.204s	1.320s	0.061s
14	Elias	SPA	Honda Gresini	1m 58.264s	1.380s	0.060s
15	Tamada	JPN	Dunlop Yamaha Tech 3	1m 58.399s	1.515s	0.135s
16	West	AUS	Kawasaki Racing Team	1m 59.386s	2.502s	0.987s
17	Roberts K.	USA	Team Roberts	1m 59.446s	2.562s	0.060s
18	Silva	SPA	Pramac d'Antin	1m 59.721s	2.837s	0.275s

FINISHERS

1 CASEY STONER Another faultless weekend. There was an inevitability about the way he got the holeshot from pole, then pulled steadily away once Hopkins's challenge faded slightly. His seventh win of the year extended his championship lead to 60 points.

2 JOHN HOPKINS Best result in MotoGP: got up to second from his second-row start within the first few corners, then charged after Stoner. Pushed as hard as he dared for ten laps before deciding that second was a good idea.

3 NICKY HAYDEN Did all he could, but after forcing past his team-mate on the second lap it took him just two or three corners to realise he wasn't going to catch the men in front. Cagey about which of the new parts available to him he did use.

4 DANI PEDROSA Not happy, walking straight through his pit after the race. Had to go with a hard rear tyre, not his normal choice, and it took six laps to get up to temperature, by which time the leaders had gone. Had to be content with closing in on Rossi's second place in the points table.

5 CHRIS VERMEULEN Boxed in at the start, lucky to avoid Edwards's crash, then got past de Puniet, Capirossi and Rossi, none of whom are easy to pass – the Ducati's speed made Loris particularly tough. Consolidated fourth place in the championship.

6 LORIS CAPIROSSI Chose the same type of tyre construction that'd taken him to victory a year ago, but it didn't work with the 800 as it had with the 990. Corner entry was the biggest problem and he took a few risks, particularly in the last corner.

7 VALENTINO ROSSI Didn't even have the solace of being first Michelin user across the line. Never found a set-up he liked, suffered a sudden drop in tyre performance in the race, lost every dice in which he was involved and only just fended off de Puniet in the closing laps.

8 RANDY DE PUNIET Enjoyed a four-man dice for much of the race but regretted his problems in qualifying which kept him off the front row. Spent

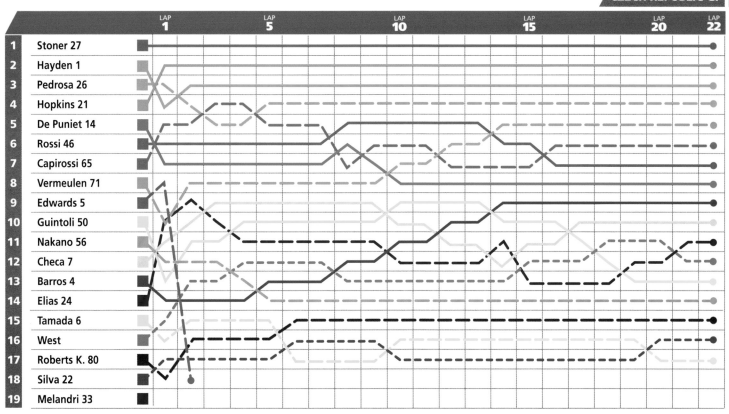

		LAP 1	LAP 5	LAP 10	LAP 15	LAP 20	LAP 22
1	Stoner 27						
2	Hayden 1						
3	Pedrosa 26						
4	Hopkins 21						
5	De Puniet 14						
6	Rossi 46						
7	Capirossi 65						
8	Vermeulen 71						
9	Edwards 5						
10	Guintoli 50						
11	Nakano 56						
12	Checa 7						
13	Barros 4						
14	Elias 24						
15	Tamada 6						
16	West						
17	Roberts K. 80						
18	Silva 22						
19	Melandri 33						

RACE

	Rider	Motorcycle	Race Time	Time +	Fastest Lap	Average Speed
1	Stoner	Ducati	43m 45.810s		1m 58.301s	101.262mph
2	Hopkins	Suzuki	43m 53.713s	7.903s	1m 58.306s	100.958mph
3	Hayden	Honda	43m 58.910s	13.100s	1m 58.714s	100.760mph
4	Pedrosa	Honda	44m 01.610s	15.800s	1m 58.964s	100.657mph
5	Vermeulen	Suzuki	44m 03.113s	17.303s	1m 59.399s	100.600mph
6	Capirossi	Ducati	44m 05.173s	19.363s	1m 59.016s	100.522mph
7	Rossi	Yamaha	44m 08.295s	22.485s	1m 59.221s	100.402mph
8	De Puniet	Kawasaki	44m 08.883s	23.073s	1m 59.329s	100.380mph
9	Barros	Ducati	44m 18.102s	32.292s	1m 59.930s	100.033mph
10	Checa	Honda	44m 20.963s	35.153s	1m 59.894s	99.930mph
11	Elias	Honda	44m 23.558s	37.748s	2m 00.128s	99.828mph
12	West	Kawasaki	44m 24.060s	38.250s	2m 00.017s	99.810mph
13	Guintoli	Yamaha	44m 29.504s	43.694s	1m 59.771s	99.605mph
14	Nakano	Honda	44m 42.879s	57.069s	2m 00.450s	99.109mph
15	Roberts K.	Kr212v	44m 55.413s	1m 09.603s	2m 00.952s	98.647mph
16	Silva	Ducati	45m 07.220s	1m 21.410s	2m 00.919s	98.218mph
17	Tamada	Yamaha	45m 11.614s	1m 25.804s	2m 00.999s	98.059mph
18	Edwards	Yamaha	5m 25.074s	20 Laps	2m 06.884s	74.360mph

CHAMPIONSHIP

	Rider	Team	Points
1	Stoner	Ducati Marlboro Team	246
2	Rossi	Fiat Yamaha Team	186
3	Pedrosa	Repsol Honda Team	168
4	Vermeulen	Rizla Suzuki MotoGP	124
5	Hopkins	Rizla Suzuki MotoGP	124
6	Melandri	Honda Gresini	113
7	Edwards	Fiat Yamaha Team	93
8	Hayden	Repsol Honda Team	89
9	Capirossi	Ducati Marlboro Team	87
10	Barros	Pramac d'Antin	83
11	Hofmann	Pramac d'Antin	60
12	De Puniet	Kawasaki Racing Team	58
13	Elias	Honda Gresini	54
14	Checa	Honda LCR	35
15	West	Kawasaki Racing Team	33
16	Tamada	Dunlop Yamaha Tech 3	31
17	Nakano	Konica Minolta Honda	31
18	Guintoli	Dunlop Yamaha Tech 3	24
19	Roberts K.	Team Roberts	9
20	Hayden R.	Kawasaki Racing Team	6
21	Fabrizio	Honda Gresini	6
22	Nieto	Kawasaki Racing Team	5
23	Jacque	Kawasaki Racing Team	4
24	Roberts Jr	Team Roberts	4

the last few laps waiting for Rossi to make a mistake, 'which characteristically he didn't'.

9 ALEX BARROS Hampered by his starting position (13th) and being caught behind slower riders in the opening laps. That meant his tyres took too long to get up to temperature and he couldn't attack as he wanted.

10 CARLOS CHECA Happier than he'd been all season thanks to the exhaust system and associated modifications HRC handed out to their satellite teams. Enjoyed the fight with Guintoli and Elias.

11 TONI ELIAS Carried the Team Gresini banner alone just 51 days after breaking his femur at Assen. Put in a

typically gritty performance in the group battling for ninth place, despite the physical nature of the Brno circuit.

12 ANTHONY WEST Kawasakis never seem to like the Brno track and it took Ant all of practice and half the race to feel comfortable. His biggest race problem was wheelspin on corner exits; in practice it was that he was slower on his qualifiers than on race tyres.

13 SYLVAIN GUINTOLI Enlivened the first day of free practice by topping the timing sheets thanks to a Dunlop qualifier. Led the dice for ninth at mid-distance but suffered a severe drop in rear grip just three laps from the flag.

14 SHINYA NAKANO Happy with the new pipes and engine modifications which made the engine much smoother, but still suffered from front-end chatter. Tried a hard front tyre but that only postponed the problem, so he couldn't push hard once the race was a few laps old.

15 KURTIS ROBERTS Bogged the bike down getting off the line and then spent too long fighting with Silva and Tamada to be able to get to Nakano. The Team KR bike did not get the new pipes or engine modifications handed out to the Honda satellite teams.

16 IVAN SILVA The d'Antin team's Spanish Championship rider replaced Hofmann. Silva's contract specifies he will

be the first-choice replacement if either of the regular MotoGP riders is unable to take part, so there was no second chance for Chaz Davies to shine.

17 MAKOTO TAMADA Picked a different tyre from his team-mate after it seemed to work in warm-up, but found out very quickly in the race that he had no grip.

NON-FINISHERS

COLIN EDWARDS An uncharacteristic crash put him out of the race when he lost the front early in the second lap.

NON-FINISHERS

MARCO MELANDRI Was going to race, despite discovering he'd broken his ankle at Laguna, but then suffered sudden and severe pain in his neck in first free practice. Initial diagnosis was a trapped nerve, further investigation found a herniated disc.

ALEX HOFMANN Not fully recovered from the hand injury suffered at Laguna Seca. Replaced by Ivan Silva.

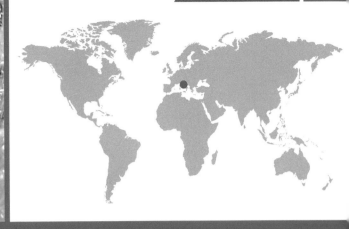

HOME WIN

It was meant to be a homecoming celebration for Valentino Rossi, but instead the revised Misano track hosted Ducati's first MotoGP victory on Italian tarmac

If you were looking for an image to sum up Valentino Rossi's season, you could do no better than rewind to the end of qualifying at Misano. The Doctor had set fastest time on his second qualifying tyre and thought he had done enough to be on pole. He was rolling back to the pits, waving to the crowd, when he realised something was going on. Glancing over his shoulder to check one of the giant screens around the track, he saw Casey Stoner on the way to his fourth successive pole position. A TV camera looking straight down the track pictured a tiny Valentino looking back at an enormous on-screen Stoner with the red-backed graphics clearly showing the Australian's ominous progress. It was the first inkling that, for once, Rossi was not going to get it all his own way at home – he had yet to be beaten on a MotoGP bike in Italy.

This was the first time the Grand Prix regulars had visited Misano since the accident fourteen years previously which ended the career of Wayne Rainey. The return was doubtless driven by the need for a second Italian race, and where better than the track just ten miles from Tavullia, home town of Valentino Rossi himself. Of course, some updating was necessary and for reasons that escaped most people the direction of the track was reversed from anticlockwise to clockwise; maybe it was a desire not to race on the tarmac that had so grievously injured Rainey. What used to be three left-handers through which riders accelerated onto the back straight – Misano's unique feature that separated the men from the also-rans – are now three ever-tightening rights through which it is all but impossible to overtake.

No advantage, then, to the ex-World Superbike Championship contenders who had raced at the old Misano. 'It's just that I know where to park my motorhome,' said Chris Vermeulen. There was one man who had raced on the revised track, though: Anthony West. Kawasaki's new recruit had been in the Yamaha World Supersport team for three races and had won here three months previously. As usual for a circuit new to Grand Prix, extra practice was scheduled. However, a thunderstorm of Old Testament proportions wiped out most of Friday's track time and flooded two corners. The water was as high as the top of the Armco barrier on the inside of the left-hander at Quercia. General opinion was that it would be impossible to have the track in a fit state by Saturday morning, but ready it was and there were no problems with grip.

Valentino may have been disappointed to miss out on pole, but second place gave him his first front-row start since Donington Park. To the surprise of most of the paddock, Fiat Yamaha brought a new iteration of the pneumatic-valve motor they'd tested after Brno. Even more surprisingly, they elected to race it. Rossi reported that, as might be expected, it allowed him to use a few more revs and made a difference to acceleration in the higher gears. As ultimate top speed is not a consideration at Misano it was doubly surprising that the new engine was used. It is difficult to think of anything less likely for that great pragmatist Jerry Burgess to do than indulge in experimentation in the middle of a season. Assuming Jerry had a say in the decision, it had to be taken as further evidence of

Top Three flag-to-flag wins in a row, all from pole position: the Championship was now looking a distinct possibility

Right Yes, it really was that dark on Friday afternoon. The Rizla Suzuki crew contemplate building an ark

Opposite There was history-making for Suzuki too, their first double rostrum of the four-stroke era

Top Misano's first turn is now a right-hander – Stoner leads the way on lap one

Below Dani Pedrosa vents his anger at a slightly defensive looking Randy de Puniet after the first-lap crash

a tacit admission that the championship was out of reach and that testing for the 2008 season was regarded as more important than winning races in 2007. In the event, it neither won nor put in much testing time. Early in the fifth lap Rossi rolled to a halt after feeling his motor tighten up. There was no smoke, which lends credence to the team's later statement that it was nothing to do with the new valve

system. 'It could have happened to any four-stroke engine,' said team director, Davide Brivio. The lack of a smoke screen suggests a crankshaft bearing failure but that could, of course, have been down to the extra revs allowed by the pneumatic valves.

By then two other contenders were also out of the race. On the first lap Randy de Puniet got into Turn 2 way too fast, appeared to try and use a lot of rear brake

WHY PNEUMATIC VALVES?

The Misano rostrum was the first to be populated entirely by motorcycles with pneumatic-valve operation – there wasn't a valve spring in sight. Yamaha's adoption of pneumatic valves leaves Honda as the only manufacturer still using conventional metal springs. This technology is not new – F1 has been using it for years, and Aprilia introduced it to MotoGP in 2002 – but the new-for-2007 800cc motors rev high enough to be at the limit of conventional coil-spring technology. At around 17,000rpm metal springs stop being able to keep the valves in contact with their cam lobes and they 'float'. Ducati get around this with Desmodromic operation (positive opening and closing of the valves with two sets of cams, one for each operation). Suzuki introduced pneumatic valves for 2006, Kawasaki started using them this season and, as well as Aprilia, KTM utilised them when their V4 motor was used by Team Roberts.

Pneumatic operation uses a small volume of nitrogen at 10–15 bar as a spring to close the valve. Think of it like a balloon or a polythene mineral water bottle with its lid on: squeeze it and it compresses (the cam opening the valve); let go and it springs back into shape (pushing the valve closed). Of course this sort of system is not leak proof, so there is a small on-board reservoir of nitrogen at around 200 bar to keep the valves topped up. This needs a complicated system of valves and pressure lines, and it was failures in their set-up that are thought to have caused Suzuki's disastrous rash of breakdowns at the Qatar GP of 2006. Current F1 engines rev to around 20,000rpm so there shouldn't be any reliability problems in MotoGP engines.

It looks as if Yamaha have brought their planned introduction of pneumatic-valve technology forward to try to counter Ducati's unforeseen power advantage. The question now is what Honda will do to get their V4 up to speed.

to scrub of some speed, but only caused the back end to come round. The Kawasaki's rear wheel took Dani Pedrosa's front out from under him and Nicky Hayden, who'd made a hash of his front-row start, took to the gravel trap to avoid the resultant chaos. Which left the two Suzukis chasing the fast-disappearing Stoner, and that's the way a largely uneventful race finished, with Chris Vermeulen getting the better of his team-mate and Suzuki putting two men on the rostrum for the first time in MotoGP.

Stoner's victory made him the only man other than Rossi to win three MotoGP races on the bounce and, even more impressively, the first to lead every single lap of three consecutive races. The only other GP Ducati had won on home tarmac was Bruno Spaggiari's victory in the 125cc race at Monza in 1958, so the factory reacted with understandable delight at making history on a track just an hour's drive from their Bologna factory. One aspect of the win seemed especially to delight engine designer Filippo Preziosi: both Ducatis ran out of petrol on the slow-down lap. That, he said, was the level of accuracy to which Ducati engineers work.

Misano's Grand Prix was meant to be an event where Rossi's real home fans could worship their idol. There was never any danger of his tax affairs overshadowing anything here, because Valentino retains unquestioning loyalty in the area in which he grew up. His yellow-clad fan club marched in from Tavullia on race morning like a latter-day legion, but by 3 o'clock in the afternoon the Italians doing the cheering were wearing the red of Bologna.

SAN MARINO GP
MISANO WORLD CIRCUIT

ROUND 13
September 2

RACE RESULTS

CIRCUIT LENGTH 2.597 miles
NO. OF LAPS 28
RACE DISTANCE 72.725 miles
WEATHER Dry, 26°C
TRACK TEMPERATURE 42°C
WINNER Casey Stoner
FASTEST LAP 1m 34.649s,
98.790mph, Casey Stoner (record)

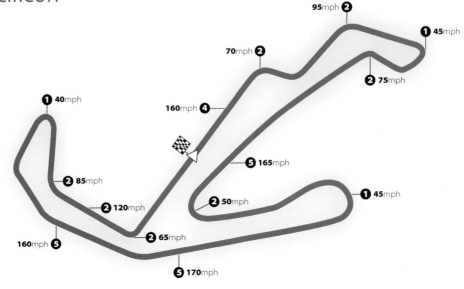

QUALIFYING

	Rider	Nationality	Team	Qualifying	Pole +	Gap
1	Stoner	AUS	Ducati Marlboro Team	1m 33.918s		
2	Rossi	ITA	Fiat Yamaha Team	1m 34.094s	0.176s	0.176s
3	Hayden	USA	Repsol Honda Team	1m 34.469s	0.551s	0.375s
4	De Puniet	FRA	Kawasaki Racing Team	1m 34.506s	0.588s	0.037s
5	Hopkins	USA	Rizla Suzuki MotoGP	1m 34.536s	0.618s	0.030s
6	Pedrosa	SPA	Repsol Honda Team	1m 34.580s	0.662s	0.044s
7	Checa	SPA	Honda LCR	1m 34.628s	0.710s	0.048s
8	Vermeulen	AUS	Rizla Suzuki MotoGP	1m 34.717s	0.799s	0.089s
9	Edwards	USA	Fiat Yamaha Team	1m 34.768s	0.850s	0.051s
10	West	AUS	Kawasaki Racing Team	1m 34.939s	1.021s	0.171s
11	Guintoli	FRA	Dunlop Yamaha Tech 3	1m 35.202s	1.284s	0.263s
12	Melandri	ITA	Honda Gresini	1m 35.236s	1.318s	0.034s
13	Capirossi	ITA	Ducati Marlboro Team	1m 35.283s	1.365s	0.047s
14	Nakano	JPN	Konica Minolta	1m 35.389s	1.471s	0.106s
15	Elias	SPA	Honda Gresini	1m 35.632s	1.714s	0.243s
16	Tamada	JPN	Dunlop Yamaha Tech 3	1m 35.865s	1.947s	0.233s
17	Barros	BRA	Pramac d'Antin	1m 35.897s	1.979s	0.032s
18	Roberts K.	USA	Team Roberts	1m 36.605s	2.687s	0.708s
19	Hofmann	GER	Pramac d'Antin	1m 36.659s	2.741s	0.054s

FINISHERS

1 CASEY STONER Another faultless win from pole, setting fastest lap at half-distance as he refused to allow an extremely persistent Vermeulen within range. Wouldn't talk about the title, but with a lead of 85 points it was possible for him to take it next time out. The team was more excited about Ducati's first-ever MotoGP win on Italian soil.

2 CHRIS VERMEULEN Did himself a huge favour by getting a good start from the third row and missing the big crash. Had to pass his team-mate and Rossi before he could try and catch Stoner. Got within a second but felt he'd already used the best of his tyres.

3 JOHN HOPKINS Had a big front-end slide in the fast right early on, then almost lost his left knee-slider – he tried to re-attach it on the back straight – but refused to use that as an excuse. 'I really didn't have anything for them,' he said, referring to the two men in front of him.

4 MARCO MELANDRI His ability to absorb physical punishment and come back stronger continues to amaze. Had a massive crash in free practice after putting his rear wheel on the Astroturf in the third of three fast right-handers. Started the race well, disposing of West and Edwards, then held his rhythm before pushing in the closing laps to stay clear of Capirossi.

5 LORIS CAPIROSSI Had real problems getting the bike turned for the slow corners in practice, but a set-up gamble for warm-up found the cure. Made another move in the same direction for the race and was relieved to be able to compete. Happier with fifth than might've been expected.

6 CARLOS CHECA Fast all through practice. First Honda and first Michelin in the race, able to put pressure on Capirossi past half-distance before he felt his front tyre pushing and decided to settle for sixth.

7 TONI ELIAS Finished in pain from the femur he broke at Assen. Misano is a physical circuit and he really suffered in the second half of the race, but another brave and skilful performance from a man who, unlike much of the grid, had yet to sign a contract for 2008.

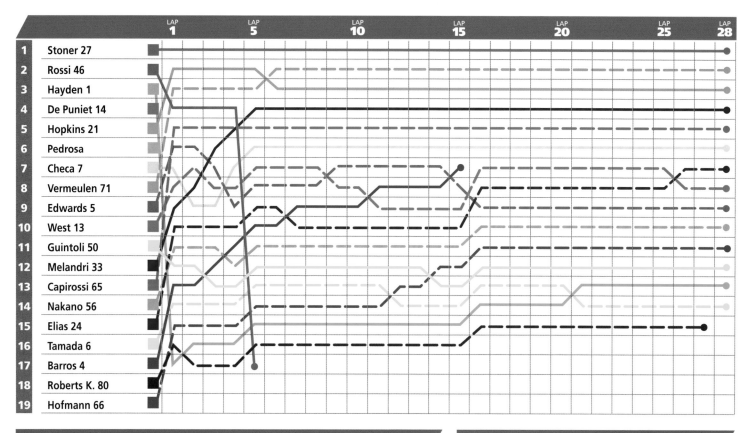

			LAP 1	LAP 5	LAP 10	LAP 15	LAP 20	LAP 25	LAP 28
1	Stoner 27								
2	Rossi 46								
3	Hayden 1								
4	De Puniet 14								
5	Hopkins 21								
6	Pedrosa								
7	Checa 7								
8	Vermeulen 71								
9	Edwards 5								
10	West 13								
11	Guintoli 50								
12	Melandri 33								
13	Capirossi 65								
14	Nakano 56								
15	Elias 24								
16	Tamada 6								
17	Barros 4								
18	Roberts K. 80								
19	Hofmann 66								

RACE

	Rider	Motorcycle	Race Time	Time +	Fastest Lap	Average Speed
1	Stoner	Ducati	44m 34.720s		1m 34.649s	97.528mph
2	Vermeulen	Suzuki	44m 39.571s	4.851s	1m 34.709s	97.243mph
3	Hopkins	Suzuki	44m 50.722s	16.002s	1m 34.945s	97.591mph
4	Melandri	Honda	44m 57.457s	22.737s	1m 35.572s	97.200mph
5	Capirossi	Ducati	44m 59.507s	24.787s	1m 35.652s	96.081mph
6	Checa	Honda	45m 09.706s	34.986s	1m 35.846s	96.494mph
7	Elias	Honda	45m 15.616s	40.896s	1m 36.222s	96.155mph
8	West	Kawasaki	45m 16.494s	41.774s	1m 36.246s	96.105mph
9	Edwards	Yamaha	45m 21.866s	47.146s	1m 35.717s	96.799mph
10	Nakano	Honda	45m 23.528s	48.808s	1m 36.334s	96.705mph
11	Hofmann	Ducati	45m 24.019s	49.299s	1m 36.461s	96.677mph
12	Guintoli	Yamaha	45m 43.896s	1m 09.176s	1m 36.560s	95.556mph
13	Hayden	Honda	45m 55.144s	1m 20.424s	1m 36.706s	95.929mph
14	Tamada	Yamaha	46m 08.943s	1m 34.223s	1m 36.645s	94.167mph
	Roberts K.	Kr212v	45m 14.795s	1 Lap	1m 37.020s	92.659mph
	Barros	Ducati	24m 17.361s	13 Laps	1m 36.053s	96.882mph
	Rossi	Yamaha	8m 58.083s	23 Laps	1m 35.225s	86.829mph
	De Puniet	Kawasaki				
	Pedrosa	Honda				

CHAMPIONSHIP

	Rider	Team	Points
1	Stoner	Ducati Marlboro Team	271
2	Rossi	Fiat Yamaha Team	186
3	Pedrosa	Kawasaki Racing Team	168
4	Vermeulen	Rizla Suzuki MotoGP	144
5	Hopkins	Rizla Suzuki MotoGP	140
6	Melandri	Honda Gresini	126
7	Edwards	Fiat Yamaha Team	100
8	Capirossi	Ducati Marlboro Team	98
9	Hayden	Repsol Honda Team	92
10	Barros	Pramac d'Antin	83
11	Hofmann	Pramac d'Antin	65
12	Elias	Honda Gresini	63
13	De Puniet	Kawasaki Racing Team	58
14	Checa	Honda LCR	45
15	West	Kawasaki Racing Team	41
16	Nakano	Konica Minolta Honda	37
17	Tamada	Dunlop Yamaha Tech 3	33
18	Guintoli	Dunlop Yamaha Tech 3	28
19	Roberts K.	Team Roberts	10
20	Hayden R.	Kawasaki Racing Team	6
21	Fabrizio	Honda Gresini	6
22	Nieto	Kawasaki Racing Team	5
23	Jacque	Kawasaki Racing Team	4
24	Roberts Jr.	Team Roberts	4

8 ANTHONY WEST Almost a replay of his Brno race. Despite quite big problems on some parts of the track was able to fight with a much more experienced group of riders and only succumbed to Elias three laps from the flag.

9 COLIN EDWARDS Missed the crash but was then on the receiving end of a couple of tough moves from Checa which put him to the back of the group. Got back past West only to run into serious lack of grip on the left side of his rear tyre, making the left-hand flicks in the fast changes of direction decidedly scary.

10 SHINYA NAKANO Happier than he'd been for a while with his joint best result of the year so far. Came out of the mêlée at Turn 2 better than most and was putting in his best laps of the weekend at half-distance. Pushed at the end to close on Edwards but lost his rhythm, was passed by Hofmann but managed to get him back before the flag.

11 ALEX HOFMANN First race since his horrific hand injury at Laguna Seca, and struggled under heavy braking at the end after he'd passed Nakano. Not surprisingly described it as 'One of the most physically difficult races I've had in my life.'

12 SYLVAIN GUINTOLI A replay of Brno: good pace in qualifying but couldn't find a Dunlop rear tyre with the endurance to go the distance. No problems for 12 laps but then the tyre's performance dropped off suddenly and seriously. Did not enjoy the last part of the race.

13 NICKY HAYDEN Wasted his second front-row start of the year and became a victim of the de Puniet-instigated fracas at Turn 2. Had to run into the gravel to avoid running over the Frenchman, which took a lump out of his rear slick getting back on track. All he could then do was circulate for a few points.

14 MAKOTO TAMADA Reported the same problems as his team-mate – no problems for 12 laps, then rear-tyre performance dropped off though stayed constant until a few laps from the flag, when there was another step down.

15 KURTIS ROBERTS Had the same problem as at Brno, with the bike bogging off the line, so started with the launch control switched off. Didn't get away cleanly, then ran off track after clipping Hofmann in the aftermath of the Turn 2 incident. Only stayed out because there was a point to be had.

NON-FINISHERS

ALEX BARROS Started way back in 17th but had worked his way up to seventh when an electrical problem stopped him just after half-distance. Was sure he could have got sixth or even fifth.

VALENTINO ROSSI Decided to race a new version of the pneumatic-valve engine first used at the Brno test and later reported he'd just got his tyres working when he felt the engine tighten as he braked hard on lap five. The lack of any smoke would seem to indicate subsequent rumours of a seized crank may have been correct.

DANI PEDROSA The innocent victim of someone else's first-lap crash for the second time this season when he was collected by de Puniet's crashing Kawasaki in the second corner.

RANDY DE PUNIET Appeared to ask the impossible of his rear tyre in the first left-hander as he went up the inside of the pack. Lost the back end, his bike slid out from under him, he skittled Pedrosa and scattered the pack. Lucky not to be injured.

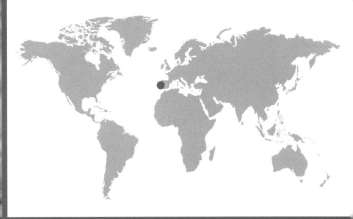

ACTION STATIONS

It might be the slowest track on the calendar, but Estoril staged another thriller as Rossi staved off the inevitable

For the first time, Casey Stoner was in a position to win the World Championship. It would need Valentino Rossi to have another disastrous weekend, but stranger things have happened this season. Instead Rossi, Yamaha and Michelin remembered how they used to work together and came out on top in a thrilling encounter. Valentino had to overcome a spirited Dani Pedrosa, who hadn't been on the podium since winning in Germany – and, amazingly, had never made it to the rostrum at Estoril in any class.

As well as reminding all and sundry of his talent, Dani also showed he could outbrake people. The Portuguese track may be slow, but MotoGP bikes still reach 200mph on the main straight at the end of which they have to get round an almost right-angled first-gear corner. That requires a lot of upper-body strength and, not surprisingly, given Dani's slight build, this was regarded as an area in which he was suspect. At Le Mans he'd already almost quashed the notion that he couldn't ride in the wet; now he outbraked both Stoner and Rossi at Turn 1. When Valentino went to repay the compliment he found he'd outbraked himself – all of which should put paid to the idea that Dani Pedrosa is weak on the brakes.

It didn't look as if Michelin were having any problems either. At this track twelve months previously Rossi had complained about his tyres publicly for the first time, after an unexpected overnight temperature drop compromised their grip, and his relationship with the company had been strained ever since. This time there were no such problems. Nicky Hayden set pole and the fastest lap while his fellow Michelin users, Rossi and Pedrosa, were first and second in the race.

For the first time this year, however, Casey Stoner had to deal with a problem with his bike. He was leading on lap five when he found himself without engine braking on the way into corners. Worse, it was an intermittent fault. It dropped him back to third and nearly into the clutches of Hayden, who had got the better of a frenetic set-to with Melandri. The World Champion gave a graphic and entertaining post-race description of being on the outside of Marco going round Turn 3, with his crash helmet right next to the Italian's exhaust and having to tell himself to ignore the noise and hang on to make sure he was on the inside for the following left-hander.

It took Stoner a big chunk of the middle of the race to work out how to cope with his problem and adjust his braking markers. By then Nicky had run into his own problems so Casey got on with the job of closing up on Rossi and Pedrosa. In the event there wasn't quite enough time left, but he was less than 1.5 seconds behind them at the flag. The young Aussie wouldn't say that he'd have won without his slipper-clutch difficulty but he did allow that, before the start, the least he had expected was to be fighting for the lead. As we've come to expect from Stoner, he was distinctly displeased with himself for taking so long to work out how to ride round the trouble: one more similarity to Mick Doohan's gritty attitude.

That left Rossi and Pedrosa to fight it out for the win. When Stoner's early lead evaporated Pedrosa led for three laps until Rossi went past on the brakes for Turn 1. Eight laps later the Spanish rider was back in front, although he realised it was a risky tactic that

'I WAS ABLE TO KEEP IN THE SLIPSTREAM OF THE HONDA AND DUCATI'
VALENTINO ROSSI

would let Valentino see where he was strongest and where he might be vulnerable. Dani knew that Stoner and Hayden were closing and thought Rossi 'was not pushing at 100 per cent', so he took to the front and the gap back to the Ducati, in third, increased from half a second to over 2.25 seconds in four laps. Casey

did close the gap in the last seven laps, but Pedrosa's push had made sure Stoner wasn't in contention for the win.

Dani later said he'd really wanted to wait for the last two laps to attack Rossi. Valentino was thinking the same way – and just to show that he was back to

his old form, he went for it with three laps to go, only to outbrake himself at Turn 1 and let Pedrosa back through. Rossi made a pass at the end of the back straight stick next time round, but had to put in 1m 37s laps for the final two, having been cruising at 1m 38s since lap 20 of the 28.

Valentino Rossi's reaction to the win told everyone what they needed to know– it was like watching the teenage 125 rider again – and unalloyed delight and some serious milking of the crowd's applause followed his victory. He said later that, coming out of the final corner, all he could think about was that this was where he'd lost the title twelve months previously, and it wasn't going to happen again. During the race Valentino claimed he wondered if he was dreaming, unused as he was to being able to stay with Stoner and Pedrosa's bikes this season. An exaggeration, maybe, but both lap times and top speeds suggested there was little between the top three bikes. Neither were there any difficulties with Yamaha's pneumatic-valve engine, which didn't give a problem all weekend. Dani Pedrosa seemed just as happy, saying he was pleased with the progress the bike had made and that he had enjoyed it 'after three races with no fun'.

The Doctor certainly looked like he'd had fun. Asked how it felt to win after such a long time, nearly three months, he replied that it was like having sex again after a long break: 'The men understand me well!' On a more dignified note, Valentino dedicated his win to the memory of Colin McRae. He described the Scot, who had died in a helicopter crash the previous day, as one of his idols and 'the Kevin Schwantz of rally cars'.

Opposite There were dices all down the field; Alex Barros looked to be winning this one before his engine broke

Below There didn't appear to be much to choose between the performance of the factory Ducati, the Repsol Hondas and Rossi's Yamaha

RED BULL ROOKIES

The inaugural Red Bull Rookies Cup, run over eight rounds alongside the European rounds of MotoGP, produced a French champion. A balanced blend of intelligence and talent won the 17-year-old Johann Zarco the series with one race still to go. Estoril was his third and most impressive victory of the season as he fought off a strong challenge from American Cameron Beaubier and British rider Matthew Hoyle. His main championship rival, Italian Lorenzo Savadori, struggled for straight-line speed and could do no better than tenth.

Brought up in Antibes in the south of France, Zarco used his home's proximity to Italy and the higher level of competition there to broaden his race experience. He started racing minimotos in 2004, finishing second in 2005 in the Senior Mini European Championship, and came second again a year later in the European Open Championship. He also gained full-size race-bike experience in Italy's Challenge Honda, finishing 12th in the championship in 2006 after missing one round.

Far from being just a one-dimensional racer, Johann reluctantly admits to doing OK at school. In fact he is overall top of his class. 'I like mathematics and am better at Italian than English' – an obvious spin-off from his racing trips to Italy.

Zarco barely put a foot wrong all season in the Rookies Cup and might never have been off the rostrum had he not been knocked off on the last lap in Holland. He took a firm grip on the championship when he dominated the Czech round at Brno where arch-rival Savadori was taken out in a multi-bike accident. 'I loved Brno, the long fast corners, that was something new and very interesting, not easy to get right. It was also a lucky race for me because Lorenzo did not score. I think my best race, though, was Estoril, because it was such a hard race all the way with Cameron and Matt, two really good riders.'

The Rookies race-identical KTM 125s are prepared by the factory. For 2008 there will be a Rookies Cup in the USA as well as in Europe. Zarco will be considered for a place in the MotoGP Academy, or he may well go straight to 125 GPs.

PORTUGUESE GP
ESTORIL

ROUND 14
September 16

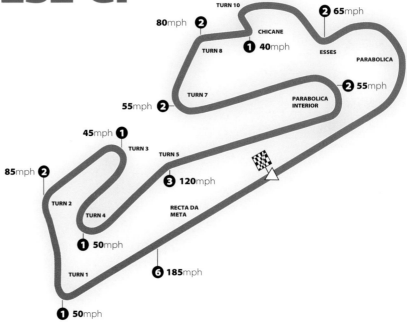

RACE RESULTS

CIRCUIT LENGTH 2.599 miles
NO. OF LAPS 28
RACE DISTANCE 72.772 miles
WEATHER Dry, 28°C
TRACK TEMPERATURE 34°C
WINNER Valentino Rossi
FASTEST LAP 1m 37.493s,
95.954mph, Nicky Hayden (record)
PREVIOUS LAP RECORD 1m 37.914s,
95.484mph, Kenny Roberts Jr, 2006

QUALIFYING

	Rider	Nationality	Team	Qualifying	Pole +	Gap
1	Hayden	USA	Repsol Honda Team	1m 36.301s		
2	Stoner	AUS	Ducati Marlboro Team	1m 36.341s	0.040s	0.040s
3	Rossi	ITA	Fiat Yamaha Team	1m 36.576s	0.275s	0.235s
4	Tamada	JPN	Dunlop Yamaha Tech 3	1m 36.736s	0.435s	0.160s
5	Pedrosa	SPA	Repsol Honda Team	1m 36.829s	0.528s	0.093s
6	Edwards	USA	Fiat Yamaha Team	1m 36.904s	0.603s	0.075s
7	Melandri	ITA	Honda Gresini	1m 37.157s	0.856s	0.253s
8	Guintoli	FRA	Dunlop Yamaha Tech 3	1m 37.189s	0.888s	0.032s
9	Elias	SPA	Honda Gresini	1m 37.246s	0.945s	0.057s
10	Hopkins	USA	Rizla Suzuki MotoGP	1m 37.280s	0.979s	0.034s
11	Checa	SPA	Honda LCR	1m 37.296s	0.995s	0.016s
12	Vermeulen	AUS	Rizla Suzuki MotoGP	1m 37.365s	1.064s	0.069s
13	Nakano	JPN	Konica Minolta Honda	1m 37.530s	1.229s	0.165s
14	Barros	BRA	Pramac d'Antin	1m 37.550s	1.249s	0.020s
15	Capirossi	ITA	Ducati Marlboro Team	1m 37.733s	1.432s	0.183s
16	West	AUS	Kawasaki Racing Team	1m 37.885s	1.584s	0.152s
17	Hofmann	GER	Pramac d'Antin	1m 37.959s	1.658s	0.074s
18	De Puniet	FRA	Kawasaki Racing Team	1m 38.271s	1.970s	0.312s
19	Roberts K.	USA	Team Roberts	1m 39.017s	2.716s	0.746s

FINISHERS

1 VALENTINO ROSSI The pneumatic-valve engine and a new design of Michelin front tyre helped him to his first podium since victory at Assen five races ago. Had to fight off a persistent Pedrosa to get there, and only made the final, crucial pass on the penultimate lap.

2 DANI PEDROSA Back on the podium for the first time since his win in Germany. Happy to be competitive again and managed to look pleased with second place. Pushed Rossi all the way but couldn't match his pace on the last lap.

3 CASEY STONER Handicapped by an intermittent and unpredictable slipper-clutch fault that gave him a false neutral going into corners – took him most of the race to deal with it, then he was no longer in touch with the leading duo. Annoyed with himself for not solving the problem more quickly.

4 NICKY HAYDEN Pole position and fastest lap but no rostrum. Got the best of a frantic set-to with Melandri before closing on Stoner, but lost touch when distracted by Barros's blow-up. Had given his tyres a hard time early in the race and had to settle for fourth.

5 MARCO MELANDRI Involved in two good scraps, first with Hayden, then with Hopkins. The chatter that afflicted him in practice came back in the race. That, and

selecting a rear tyre that was too hard for race-day conditions, stopped him getting involved in the fight at the front.

6 JOHN HOPKINS A difficult weekend. His worst qualifying of the year so far was followed by a race where, unusually, he never figured in the fight for a rostrum spot. Only got past Melandri for a couple of corners, but at least retook fourth position in the championship from his team-mate.

7 CARLOS CHECA Carved past Elias, Edwards and West in the opening laps to go from 11th on the grid to eighth on lap four. Took another two laps to get past Tamada's Yamaha but too far behind the leading group to make further progress. Given better qualifying reckoned he could have raced with Melandri and Hopkins.

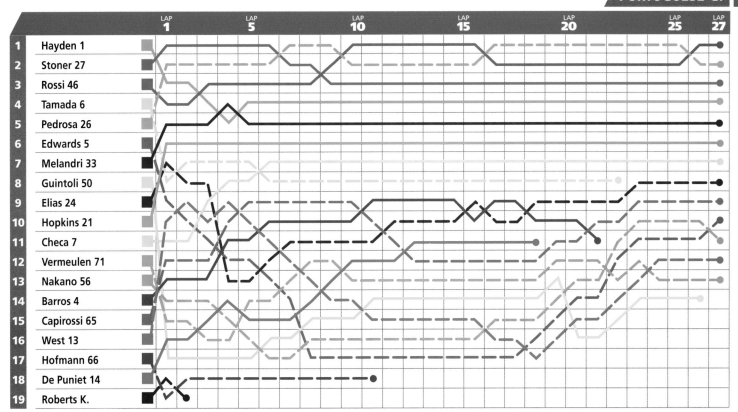

		LAP 1	LAP 5	LAP 10	LAP 15	LAP 20	LAP 25	LAP 27
1	Hayden 1							
2	Stoner 27							
3	Rossi 46							
4	Tamada 6							
5	Pedrosa 26							
6	Edwards 5							
7	Melandri 33							
8	Guintoli 50							
9	Elias 24							
10	Hopkins 21							
11	Checa 7							
12	Vermeulen 71							
13	Nakano 56							
14	Barros 4							
15	Capirossi 65							
16	West 13							
17	Hofmann 66							
18	De Puniet 14							
19	Roberts K.							

RACE

	Rider	Motorcycle	Race Time	Time +	Fastest Lap	Average Speed
1	Rossi	Yamaha	45m 49.911s		1m 37.508s	95.252mph
2	Pedrosa	Honda	45m 50.086s	0.175s	1m 37.671s	95.246mph
3	Stoner	Ducati	45m 51.388s	1.477s	1m 37.600s	95.201mph
4	Hayden	Honda	46m 02.862s	12.951s	1m 37.493s	94.806mph
5	Melandri	Honda	46m 07.254s	17.343s	1m 38.006s	94.655mph
6	Hopkins	Suzuki	46m 08.768s	18.857s	1m 37.831s	94.604mph
7	Checa	Honda	46m 21.435s	31.524s	1m 38.286s	94.173mph
8	Elias	Honda	46m 30.446s	40.535s	1m 38.870s	94.869mph
9	Capirossi	Ducati	46m 33.018s	43.107s	1m 38.833s	93.782mph
10	Edwards	Yamaha	46m 34.585s	44.674s	1m 38.650s	93.730mph
11	Nakano	Honda	46m 35.314s	45.403s	1m 39.016s	93.705mph
12	West	Kawasaki	46m 44.473s	54.562s	1m 39.179s	93.399mph
13	Vermeulen	Suzuki	46m 49.913s	1m 00.002s	1m 39.013s	93.218mph
14	Guintoli	Yamaha	46m 57.523s	1 Lap	1m 38.997s	89.646mph
	Tamada	Yamaha	38m 04.958s	5 Laps	1m 38.523s	94.164mph
	Barros	Ducati	36m 37.792s	6 Laps	1m 38.979s	93.642mph
	De Puniet	Kawasaki	31m 36.089s	9 Laps	1m 38.718s	93.741mph
	Hofmann	Ducati	18m 41.437s	17 Laps	1m 39.468s	91.760mph
	Roberts K.	Kr212v	3m 47.574s	26 Laps	1m 49.703s	82.213mph

CHAMPIONSHIP

	Rider	Team	Points
1	Stoner	Ducati Marlboro Team	287
2	Rossi	Fiat Yamaha Team	211
3	Pedrosa	Repsol Honda Team	188
4	Hopkins	Rizla Suzuki MotoGP	150
5	Vermeulen	Rizla Suzuki MotoGP	147
6	Melandri	Honda Gresini	137
7	Edwards	Fiat Yamaha Team	106
8	Capirossi	Ducati Marlboro Team	105
9	Hayden	Repsol Honda Team	105
10	Barros	Pramac d'Antin	83
11	Elias	Honda Gresini	71
12	Hofmann	Pramac d'Antin	65
13	De Puniet	Kawasaki Racing Team	58
14	Checa	Honda LCR	54
15	West	Kawasaki Racing Team	45
16	Nakano	Konica Minolta Honda	42
17	Tamada	Dunlop Yamaha Tech 3	33
18	Guintoli	Dunlop Yamaha Tech 3	30
19	Roberts K.	Team Roberts	10
20	Hayden R.	Kawasaki Racing Team	6
21	Fabrizio	Honda Gresini	6
22	Nieto	Kawasaki Racing Team	5
23	Jacque	Kawasaki Racing Team	4
24	Roberts Jr.	Team Roberts	4

8 TONI ELIAS The previous season's winner was the victim of a very tough move by Checa while lying eighth, after which he rejoined the track in 13th. Did well to fight back, although still not fit enough to make the most of a circuit he likes.

9 LORIS CAPIROSSI Only got into the top ten late in the race thanks to other people's misfortunes, and never got near a set-up he was happy with all weekend. Worst result since Jerez, where he'd had the excuse of his son's imminent birth to distract him.

10 COLIN EDWARDS A bad weekend at a track where he's always gone well. Had three of the new tyre designs in his allocation – was he being used as the test mule again? – only to find that two of them didn't work. The last one was fine in right-handers, but estimated he lost a half-second a lap in the two left-handers.

11 SHINYA NAKANO Things were looking distinctly better in free practice thanks to improved feeling from his Michelins, but then a crash in the qualifying hour knocked his confidence. Never got off the back of the pack after being boxed in at the first corner.

12 ANTHONY WEST Happy for the first few laps, getting as high as ninth, then hit problems with the front sliding going into corners. Tried to compensate by using the rear more, but that just resulted in a lot of spinning at the back.

13 CHRIS VERMEULEN What a contrast to the preceding race at Misano. No solution to severe chatter all through practice and, like his team-mate, found the Suzuki not best suited to the track. A bit of progress in the race, but the bike developed 'a strange vibration' and he 'went backwards', so felt lucky to rescue three points from an awful weekend.

14 SYLVAIN GUINTOLI Very happy with best-ever qualifying (eighth) but not with the race. Had to cope with serious chatter from the off which got so bad he was forced to pit for a new rear after coming very close to crashing. Went out again because there were points on offer.

NON-FINISHERS

MAKOTO TAMADA Qualified fourth, the best grid spot for a Dunlop rider since McCoy in 2002, the first year of MotoGP. Has always gone well at Estoril and was running in eighth and pressuring Checa when he crashed just five laps from the flag.

ALEX BARROS Put out by a mechanical problem for the second race running. This time it was a smoky engine failure that stopped the Brazilian while he was behind Elias.

RANDY DE PUNIET Looked to be redeeming dreadful qualifying (18th) on Sunday. Second fastest in warm-up and heading for the top ten in the race when his motor failed eight laps from home when he was in 11th place.

ALEX HOFMANN Had to start from pitlane after finding a problem with his number-one bike on the sighting lap. Running at the back of the field when he pulled in on lap 12 citing 'lack of motivation': team-manager Luis d'Antin took this as grounds for dismissal, and Alex was sacked.

KURTIS ROBERTS Eliminated after two laps by a clutch that started slipping half-way round the first lap. 'It wasn't because of the extra power we put in it,' said Kenny Roberts Snr.

MAKING HISTORY

Casey Stoner took the title with his worst result of the year, Capirossi's win made Ducati's day and tyres became the subject of the moment

At the start of the weekend the situation was quite simple: Stoner had to beat Rossi to become World Champion, no matter what anyone else did. After Casey's worst practice and qualifying of the year it looked as if he might have to wait for his home Grand Prix in Phillip Island, with all the extra stress that would entail. But race day dawned damp and cold at Motegi, and everyone's calculations were thrown into disarray as the flag-to-flag racing rule came into play for the first time on a track that went from wet to dry.

It already looked as if the formbook had been thrown out the window. On a track where Bridgestone users had won from pole for the past three seasons, the front row was completely Michelin; and pole-man Dani Pedrosa looked like the odds-on favourite. He even made the pace early on when all the riders were on fully treaded wet tyres, but as the track started to dry the whole field was presented with a completely new problem. When is the best time to come in and swap your wet bike for a dry set-up? In previous races where bikes have been swapped it has always been because rain has hit a dry track, with subsequent analysis showing that the timing of the change didn't really affect the outcome. Not this time.

It took six laps for the track to start drying, by which time Pedrosa, West, Stoner and Melandri had all led the race. Unfortunately for Ant West he had jumped the start, and his was the first of several hard-luck stories. The next phase was the most confusing of the race. If a rider swapped bikes early the track was not yet dry enough for him to take advantage and turn faster lap times than the guys still out on wets. It was noticeable that the leaders did not come in immediately – and also very noticeable that the Michelin wets of Rossi and Pedrosa were dealing

with the conditions better than the Bridgestones of Melandri and Stoner. The French tyre users closed down a five-second gap in half-a-dozen laps, at which point the two Bridgestone men dived up pit lane to change bikes. Rossi stayed out for one more lap, leading the field, but when he came in Pedrosa stayed out. It was too much for Dani's rear tyre: he crashed at the end of the next lap.

Changing bikes costs around 20 seconds but by now – 15 laps into the race – riders on dry set-ups were lapping six or seven seconds quicker than those who had persevered with their wets. The turning point had been lap ten so, with hindsight, it was the men who pitted around lap nine who had made the best choice. They turned out to be the eventual rostrum finishers, Capirossi, de Puniet and Elias, plus the real surprise of the race, Sylvain Guintoli. The Yamaha Tech 3 rider had changed his bike on lap seven, Elias and de Puniet on lap eight, and Capirossi on lap nine. Rossi had waited until the 15th lap to come in. He should have come out of the change losing his 19-second advantage over (then sixth-placed) Capirossi, but little else. Instead, he ran into the problem that ruined most of the Michelin runners' chances.

After the race, Nicky Hayden was watching a TV replay of Rossi waggling his handlebars and looking over the screen at his front tyre. 'See,' he said to his dad, Earl, 'that's what I thought, I thought I'd got a flat tyre.' In fact he, like Rossi, did not have enough heat in the front tyre in the early laps on the dry bike. Valentino then ran on at the right-hander at the end of the back straight and promptly pulled into the pits again, convinced he had a problem. On his next out-lap he ran across the gravel trap at the same corner. It was the moment when he knew the title was gone.

Top It was going so well for the Michelin men, like Hayden; then it rained

Below Sylvain Guintoli came within an ace of giving Dunlop a rostrum

Opposite De Puniet got his first rostrum in MotoGP and Kawasaki's first of the season

'SYLVAIN – AND HE'S TRYING TO OVERTAKE ME ON EVERY CORNER!'
TONI ELIAS

Top Toni Elias charged through to third place, just two months after his horrible Assen accident

Below Loris Capirossi sprints to his dry bike after nine laps on his wet bike; his timing turned out to be perfect

There was the expected criticism of Michelin afterwards, but this time the tyre men didn't take it lying down. They pointed out that Rossi's crew took off and replaced the tyre warmers three times, and that the pit lane had still been wet when some early changers, like Hayden, went back out. Most dry bikes on Michelins were fitted with cut slicks, namely rubber from the 31-tyre allocation modified with a hot soldering iron to give a tread pattern. As the tyres were chosen when Sunday temperatures were supposed to be much higher, it was difficult to get them up to their working range. The first Michelin user home was Nicky Hayden, in ninth place.

There was nearly a Dunlop rider on the rostrum. Sylvain Guintoli changed to cut slicks front and rear on lap seven, but spent an extra ten seconds in the pits waiting for the tyre warmers to be removed as he hadn't signalled to his crew that he was coming in. He then ripped through the field, setting a succession of fastest laps, and even managed to pass Elias for third and hold on to the place for about a hundred metres. Toni had seen the unexpected name 'Guintoli' and '+0.1' on his board. He looked over his shoulder and saw 'Sylvain – and he is trying to overtake me on every corner!' Elias had more rubber left, but he had to set the fastest lap of the race on the penultimate time round to hold on to his place. Would it have made a difference if Guintoli had signalled his crew and pitted a lap later? Probably not, because he would almost certainly have lost most of that ten seconds doing another high-risk lap on his worn-out wets.

All of which left Stoner in an unaccustomed sixth place, keeping his concentration up by chasing Marco Melandri, but crossing the line to become the second-youngest World Champion after Freddie Spencer, and the first to take the crown in the premier class on a non-Japanese bike since MV Agusta and Phil Read in 1974. The utterly dominating manner of Casey Stoner's success left most of the paddock in shock and significant sections of it in denial, blaming everything from their tyres to the ability of Ducati's electronics to perform miracles. The truth is, the whole package – rider, tyres, bike – worked at full potential all season but, as Rossi has proved in the past and Ducati team-manager Livio Suppo constantly reminded anyone who'd listen, the most important factor in that equation is 'Rider! Rider! Rider!'

ONE TYRE RULE: Pt 1

All the mutterings about Casey Stoner's supposed advantage came to a head at Motegi when Dorna CEO Carmelo Ezpeleta announced that he would be tabling a suggestion that MotoGP move to a solus tyre supplier in 2008. It was difficult to find anybody who would go on record as thinking this was a good idea, and Ezpeleta himself had never been in favour. So how come he felt it necessary to suggest it to the Grand Prix Commission?

It goes back to the Safety Commission meeting at Laguna when Carmelo was asked what he intended to do about 'the show'. He reacted angrily to the suggestion that the new tyre regulation should be altered so soon after it had been introduced, but two days later Rossi was 30 seconds behind the winner. That figure was quoted ceaselessly over the summer as the pressure on Ezpeleta intensified. His proposal mentioned 'certain factories' being unable to get the results they were capable of because of their tyres. Most paddock politicians translated that as Valentino Rossi and Dani Pedrosa wanting to switch from Michelin to Bridgestone.

Italian and Spanish TV audiences are fundamental to the commercial health of the series, so that 30 seconds will have scared quite a few people. Both riders were willing to say in public that they wanted Bridgestones, but they certainly didn't say they wanted a one-tyre rule. There is a difference between getting what you want and everyone else getting it as well. The issue was due to be settled by the Malaysian GP.

Above Valentino Rossi, Jerry Burgess and their Michelin man: not a happy relationship this season

Below The old Loris Capirossi was back: big grin, lots of aggression, and very, very fast

JAPANESE GP
TWIN-RING MOTEGI

ROUND 15
September 19

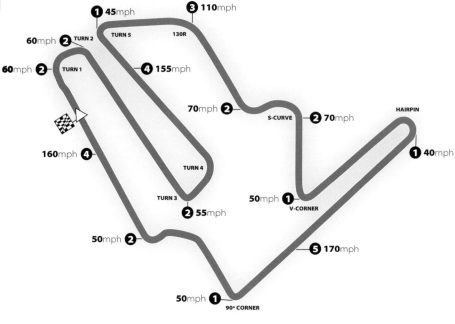

- **1** 45mph
- **3** 110mph
- TURN 5
- 130R
- **2** 60mph TURN 2
- **2** 60mph TURN 1
- **4** 155mph
- **2** 70mph
- S-CURVE
- **2** 70mph
- HAIRPIN
- **4** 160mph
- **1** 40mph
- TURN 4
- **50**mph **1**
- V-CORNER
- TURN 3
- **2** 55mph
- **5** 170mph
- **2** 50mph
- **1** 50mph
- 90° CORNER

RACE RESULTS

CIRCUIT LENGTH 2.983 miles
NO. OF LAPS 24
RACE DISTANCE 71.597 miles
WEATHER Wet/Dry, 21°C
TRACK TEMPERATURE 24°C
WINNER Loris Capirossi
FASTEST LAP 1m 50.718s, 96.998mph, Toni Elias
PREVIOUS LAP RECORD 1m 47.288s, 100.099mph, Valentino Rossi, 2006

QUALIFYING

	Rider	Nationality	Team	Qualifying	Pole +	Gap
1	Pedrosa	SPA	Repsol Honda Team	1m 45.864s		
2	Rossi	ITA	Fiat Yamaha Team	1m 46.255s	0.391s	0.391s
3	Hayden	USA	Repsol Honda Team	1m 46.575s	0.711s	0.320s
4	De Puniet	FRA	Kawasaki Racing Team	1m 46.643s	0.779s	0.068s
5	Elias	SPA	Honda Gresini	1m 46.804s	0.940s	0.161s
6	West	AUS	Kawasaki Racing Team	1m 46.912s	1.048s	0.108s
7	Edwards	USA	Fiat Yamaha Team	1m 46.997s	1.133s	0.085s
8	Capirossi	ITA	Ducati Marlboro Team	1m 47.047s	1.183s	0.050s
9	Stoner	AUS	Ducati Marlboro Team	1m 47.121s	1.257s	0.074s
10	Melandri	ITA	Honda Gresini	1m 47.136s	1.272s	0.015s
11	Hopkins	USA	Rizla Suzuki MotoGP	1m 47.163s	1.299s	0.027s
12	Nakano	JPN	Konica Minolta Honda	1m 47.295s	1.431s	0.132s
13	Akiyoshi	JPN	Rizla Suzuki MotoGP	1m 47.316s	1.452s	0.021s
14	Checa	SPA	Honda LCR	1m 47.334s	1.470s	0.018s
15	Barros	BRA	Pramac d'Antin	1m 47.367s	1.503s	0.033s
16	Tamada	JPN	Dunlop Yamaha Tech 3	1m 47.714s	1.850s	0.347s
17	Vermeulen	AUS	Rizla Suzuki MotoGP	1m 47.914s	2.050s	0.200s
18	Guintoli	FRA	Dunlop Yamaha Tech 3	1m 48.085s	2.221s	0.171s
19	Yanagawa	JPN	Kawasaki Racing Team	1m 48.569s	2.705s	0.484s
20	Ito	JPN	Pramac d'Antin	1m 49.548s	3.684s	0.979s
21	Roberts K.	USA	Team Roberts	1m 50.035s	4.171s	0.487s

FINISHERS

1 LORIS CAPIROSSI Totally altered his usual set-up, then took a risk by changing bikes early and it paid off. Found himself in front when he came out of the pits and in two laps had a ten-second lead. A man of his experience wasn't going to throw away his third consecutive win at Motegi from that position.

2 RANDY DE PUNIET First rostrum in MotoGP and the team's first of the 800cc era. Despite two trips into the gravel on his hard rain tyres and dropping from eighth to 13th when he changed bikes, he persevered and found himself behind the Ducati eight laps from the flag. Also Bridgestone's best qualifier.

3 TONI ELIAS Back on the rostrum just six races after breaking his femur at Assen – a tough couple of months, he called it. Made a mistake at the start, dropping back to tenth on lap three, but came in early which turned out to be 'perfect timing and the perfect strategy'. Set the fastest lap fending off Guintoli.

4 SYLVAIN GUINTOLI Set fastest lap after fastest lap as he harassed Elias to try for a rostrum finish, but still by far his and Dunlop's best result in MotoGP. Lost time at the bike change as his team didn't know he was coming in, but regained it on the first flying lap on dry tyres.

5 MARCO MELANDRI Led for a third of the race and was one of the last to come in when the team eventually signalled him. Took a lap or two to understand his

dry bike and then made a mistake which cost him a couple of places. Got the better of Stoner in the closing stages.

6 CASEY STONER His worst race from his worst qualifying position of the year – but he did have the consolation of being crowned World Champion! Lost time on his wet bike as the track dried, then had a problem with his dry bike's steering damper. Tried to block out thoughts of the title in the final laps by concentrating on racing Melandri.

7 ANTHONY WEST An eventful race. Equalled his best finish despite having to take a ride-through penalty for jumping the start, and his flier from the second row let him lead a MotoGP race for the first time. Then he had problems at the bike change, which he'd never done before, and stalled.

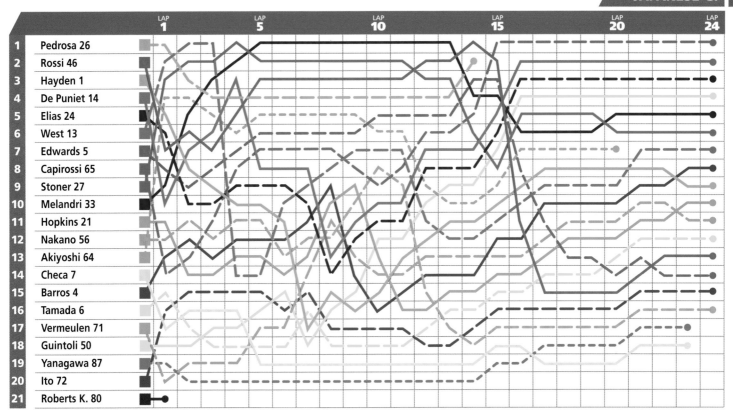

		LAP 1	LAP 5	LAP 10	LAP 15	LAP 20	LAP 24
1	Pedrosa 26						
2	Rossi 46						
3	Hayden 1						
4	De Puniet 14						
5	Elias 24						
6	West 13						
7	Edwards 5						
8	Capirossi 65						
9	Stoner 27						
10	Melandri 33						
11	Hopkins 21						
12	Nakano 56						
13	Akiyoshi 64						
14	Checa 7						
15	Barros 4						
16	Tamada 6						
17	Vermeulen 71						
18	Guintoli 50						
19	Yanagawa 87						
20	Ito 72						
21	Roberts K. 80						

RACE

	Rider	Motorcycle	Race Time	Time +	Fastest Lap	Average Speed
1	Capirossi	Ducati	47m 05.484s		1m 51.146s	91.222mph
2	De Puniet	Kawasaki	47m 16.337s	10.853s	1m 50.806s	90.873mph
3	Elias	Honda	47m 17.010s	11.526s	1m 50.718s	90.851mph
4	Guintoli	Yamaha	47m 17.676s	12.192s	1m 50.758s	90.830mph
5	Melandri	Honda	47m 34.053s	28.569s	1m 51.002s	90.309mph
6	Stoner	Ducati	47m 36.663s	31.179s	1m 51.235s	90.226mph
7	West	Kawasaki	47m 55.485s	50.001s	1m 51.499s	89.636mph
8	Barros	Ducati	47m 57.827s	52.343s	1m 51.316s	89.563mph
9	Hayden	Honda	47m 59.113s	53.629s	1m 52.840s	89.523mph
10	Hopkins	Suzuki	48m 05.199s	59.715s	1m 51.254s	89.334mph
11	Vermeulen	Suzuki	48m 08.288s	1m 02.804s	1m 52.270s	89.238mph
12	Tamada	Yamaha	48m 14.797s	1m 09.313s	1m 52.857s	89.038mph
13	Rossi	Yamaha	48m 15.183s	1m 09.699s	1m 51.153s	89.026mph
14	Edwards	Yamaha	48m 17.219s	1m 11.735s	1m 51.574s	88.963mph
15	Ito	Ducati	48m 17.774s	1m 12.290s	1m 51.977s	88.946mph
16	Nakano	Honda	48m 38.463s	1m 32.979s	1m 54.182s	88.316mph
17	Yanagawa	Kawasaki	47m 34.190s	1 Lap	1m 52.477s	86.542mph
18	Checa	Honda	48m 03.727s	1 Lap	1m 56.124s	85.656mph
	Akiyoshi	Suzuki	40m 07.818s	4 Laps	1m52.195s	89.205mph
	Pedrosa	Honda	28m 09.647s	10 Laps	1m 58.519s	88.984mph
	Roberts K.	Kr212v	2m 47.984s	23 Laps		

CHAMPIONSHIP

	Rider	Team	Points
1	Stoner	Ducati Marlboro Team	297
2	Rossi	Fiat Yamaha Team	214
3	Pedrosa	Repsol Honda Team	188
4	Hopkins	Rizla Suzuki MotoGP	156
5	Vermeulen	Rizla Suzuki MotoGP	152
6	Melandri	Honda Gresini	148
7	Capirossi	Ducati Marlboro Team	130
8	Hayden	Repsol Honda Team	112
9	Edwards	Fiat Yamaha Team	108
10	Barros	Pramac d'Antin	91
11	Elias	Honda Gresini	87
12	De Puniet	Kawasaki Racing Team	78
13	Hofmann	Pramac d'Antin	65
14	West	Kawasaki Racing Team	54
15	Checa	Honda LCR	54
16	Guintoli	Dunlop Yamaha Tech 3	43
17	Nakano	Konica Minolta Honda	42
18	Tamada	Dunlop Yamaha Tech 3	37
19	Roberts K.	Team Roberts	10
20	Hayden R.	Kawasaki Racing Team	6
21	Fabrizio	Honda Gresini	6
22	Nieto	Kawasaki Racing Team	5
23	Roberts Jr.	Team Roberts	4
24	Jacque	Kawasaki Racing Team	4
25	Ito	Pramac d'Antin	1

8 ALEX BARROS Reported the front of his bike as 'perfect' but had real problems with the rear. Made stealthy progress in the second half of the race but couldn't close on West.

9 NICKY HAYDEN The fact that he was the first Michelin rider home speaks volumes. His wet tyres lasted six laps and his cut slicks then took several laps to warm up. Made a point of stopping on the slow-down lap to congratulate Stoner: 'Just a bit of respect.'

10 JOHN HOPKINS Motegi is not a track where his main weapon of corner speed can be used. Qualified outside the top ten for the first time this year, ran off track on his dry bike and also encountered what he coyly called 'a few mechanical problems'.

11 CHRIS VERMEULEN Like his teammate, started from his lowest grid position of the year. Compounded the problem by stalling on the grid and was nearly a minute behind the leader at the end of lap one. Eleventh place from that position didn't seem too bad.

12 MAKOTO TAMADA Started on soft rain tyres, which proved to be the wrong choice, and then stayed out too long before changing to his dry bike.

13 VALENTINO ROSSI Fastest on the drying track and pitted to change his bike from the lead, despite a bad start. Came back out with only Capirossi in front of him. That's when things went wrong: his cut slicks wouldn't get up to working temperature, convincing him he had a flat front tyre and sending him back into the pits.

14 COLIN EDWARDS Was looking good in third place when he changed bikes, then ran into the same problems with his front cut slick as his teammate. Nearly followed Vale back to the pit garage.

15 SHINICHI ITO Bridgestone's veteran tyre tester rode the second d'Antin bike in place of the sacked Hofmann (Chaz Davies wasn't fit due to complications with an arm injury sustained testing the factory Ducati). Ito's long absence from top-level racing showed, but so did his experience in bringing the bike home in the points.

16 SHINYA NAKANO Encouraged to stay out on the drying track as his wet Michelins stood up to the conditions well. Inside the top ten when he changed bikes, but his hard-compound slicks never got up to temperature and he dropped through the field.

17 AKIRA YANAGAWA Given a wild-card entry as a reward for development work on the ZX-RR which he debuted during the first MotoGP season, in 2002, at what was then called the Pacific GP. Changed bikes early due to a rear brake problem, teetering round on the still wet track, but put in some respectable lap times during the closing stages.

18 CARLOS CHECA Came in early to change his bike and had to wait as the crew hadn't had time to change the settings on his spare. Went out on a slick rather than the planned treaded front and lost a sackful of time before the track dried.

NON-FINISHERS

KOUSUKE AKIYOSHI Suzuki's wild card was quickest of their three riders but unfortunately blew his motor while lying in an impressive seventh place.

DANI PEDROSA Fastest all through practice and qualifying. High-sided out of second place on lap 15 while still on wet tyres. Fortunately, worries over a suspected broken bone in his left foot turned out to be unfounded.

KURTIS ROBERTS Suffered an extreme version of the problems that afflicted all Michelin users, finding himself going sideways on his wets. Thought he had an oil leak, and his cut slicks wouldn't work on the still wet track.

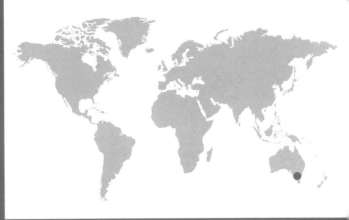

WELCOME HOME

Casey Stoner gave a record crowd and Ducati exactly what they wanted: a home win, and the Constructors' and Team Championships

It was exactly what Casey Stoner wanted, an event he could relish. With the world title safely secured three weeks previously in Japan, he enjoyed a public reception in Melbourne and yet another start-to-finish victory, was thrilled to win by a large margin and was really delighted at being on the rostrum. Sometimes Casey doesn't look as if he is enjoying himself, even when he's won, but on the podium at Phillip Island he was grinning from ear to ear, soaking up the sight and sound of the Aussie fans covering the front straight and bellowing out the national anthem in his honour. 'I've never felt anything like it,' he said afterwards.

In previous seasons his home circuit has not been kind to him: he'd only been on the rostrum once before, back in 2004 when he was a 125 rider. That fact could serve as a metaphor for Stoner's whole year – the memory of the struggle of earlier seasons obliterated by total domination of a championship in the manner of his heroes Mick Doohan and even Valentino Rossi. Not bad for a rider who wouldn't turn 22 for another two days. It wasn't an easy weekend, though. He was on the floor twice in practice as he forced his Ducati to the top of the time sheets for every session except qualifying, when Michelin users Pedrosa and Rossi were able to get more out of their qualifiers than Casey could from his Bridgestones.

There were, though, just a few hints that the opposition was gathering its forces to make sure that Stoner does not dominate next season in the way he has managed to do this year. There was the welcome sight of Nicky Hayden, shadowing the new World Champion and looking comfortable for the first nine laps. Honda had certainly found more power in

'I'VE NEVER FELT ANYTHING LIKE IT'
CASEY STONER

Top The fight for second early on; Nicky Hayden leads Valentino Rossi and Loris Capirossi

Below Fiat-Yamaha ran a special livery to celebrate the relaunch of the Abarth tuning brand

Opposite Nicky Hayden saw his best chance of a win all season disappear when his Honda dropped a valve

recent races (although only for its factory bikes), but the most significant factor may well turn out to be the new 16-inch Michelin rear tyre Nicky was using. Hayden later reported that he was happy following Casey's pace and didn't have any worries about tyre conservation.

The pair were taking time out of third-placed Rossi when, on lap ten, Hayden's lap time dropped from 1m 31s to low 1m 32s circuits. A lap later Valentino was past but still nearly three seconds adrift of Stoner. The Honda's motor had dropped a valve but somehow the American managed to get back in the 1m 31s groove, with the engine effectively running on three cylinders, before it stopped on the 13th lap. Not surprisingly Nicky wasn't at all happy to see the chance he'd been waiting for all season disappear, because he was sure he would at least have had the chance to challenge Casey in the final laps. Hayden could cope with losing the title, but what he'd feared was going through a year as defending champion and never winning. The number-one plate can truly be a heavy burden.

As Stoner continued with his exhibition at the front, his team-mate Loris Capirossi was embroiled in a frantic set-to with Marco Melandri. Gauge just how brutal it was by the fact that Loris, a man not afraid of banging handlebars, opined afterwards that Marco was 'a little bit too aggressive'. Pot and kettle comparisons aside, once free of the Gresini Honda man's attentions Capirossi ripped across a 1.5-second gap in a couple of laps on to the back wheel of Rossi, who had just been relegated to third by Pedrosa. Loris caught the Yamaha at Turn 1, drove underneath

and immediately passed Dani at Turn 2. If there were a competition for move of the year, that daring manoeuvre would probably have won it.

Rossi got back past Pedrosa immediately, although it might not have been so easy to pass the pole-setter if the Spanish rider had been on his favoured bike. That he was not was down to a bizarre accident after the end of warm-up: when Dani went to do his practice start something went wrong and the Honda instantaneously flipped over backwards in front of a startled John Hopkins. It looked as if the launch-control software either hadn't been engaged or had malfunctioned, although the HRC people were talking about a clutch problem.

All Ducati's opposition had altered their bikes considerably, in both chassis and engine departments, as they attempted to match the performance of the red bikes from Bologna. It had been part of Stoner's implacable response to questions about his machinery that it hadn't changed since he first sat on it, although he did get a new attenuated fairing to cope with the gales that howl in off the Bass Strait; he had found it hard-going in the comparatively mild cross-winds of Assen earlier in the season. Ironically, Honda brought Nicky Hayden the wider fairing he'd been asking for all year to the one circuit where he definitely didn't need it.

Yamaha also decided against racing their pneumatic-valve engine, probably because of doubts about reliability over race distance. The Fiat team ran another special livery, this time to publicise the rebirth of the Abarth tuning brand, which Rossi topped off with a new helmet design inspired by Aboriginal designs. Yamaha's artistic efforts were eclipsed, however, by Chris Vermeulen's tribute to Barry Sheene. The Australian's GSV-R was in the livery of the 1974 RG500, Suzuki and Sheene's first 500 GP winner, his leathers were period and his helmet in Sheene-replica paint. Unfortunately, Suzuki and Kawasaki both had flashbacks to the 990 days when their bikes were obviously second best to the Hondas and Ducatis. No-one could say exactly why. Mechanical traction? Power delivery characteristics at high revs and high wheel speeds? Suzuki would be back at Phillip Island in November, testing to try and eliminate this weak spot.

The Desmosedici's unchanging nature through the season proved just how right Ducati had got their bike, and how well Stoner had ridden it. At the World Champion's homecoming celebration Japan Inc were reduced to also-rans as Ducati followed up their World Championship-clinching win in Motegi with a one-two finish that secured the Constructors' title for the factory and the Team trophy for their works team. It was the small matter of 34 years since a European factory and its rider had triumphed in any of these categories.

Left Casey Stoner was lucky to escape uninjured from this crash in practice. He put his rear tyre off the drying line on a damp track and this was the result

Opposite Chris Vermeulen and his Suzuki dressed as Barry Sheene on a 1974 RG500

NORIFUMI ABE

Japan's 'Legendary Rider' Norifumi Abe died as the result of a traffic accident at home in Japan one week before the Australian GP. He was thirty-two years old. Abe's Grand Prix career spanned ten years, from the wildest of wild card rides at Suzuka in 1994 through three wins on 500s to the four-stroke era. His last GP was in 2004 after which he rode in World Superbike before returning home to compete in the All-Japan Championship. His best championship position was fifth in 1996 when he won his home GP at Suzuka.

It was the circuit where he made that wild card ride in '94. At eighteen years old the youngest ever All-Japan 500 Champion, a title he won at the first attempt, he harried – and shocked – Mick Doohan and Kevin Schwantz all race long before crashing at the turn one just three laps from the flag. It was a young Valentino Rossi's favourite race, he used to watch his tape of it every morning, only going to school once Abe had fallen. Rossi's first racing nickname, Rossifumi, was a tribute to Abe.

After that breathtaking debut on a Honda, Abe was tempted away to Yamaha by the Kenny Roberts team and it was for that factory that Norick raced for the rest of his career. Norick's other wins came in one of the best finishes you could hope to see, at Rio in 1999, and to the delight of the home crowd he won the Japanese GP again in 2000. He also finished second four times and third ten times.

At home, Abe will be remembered primarily as the first Japanese rider to win the 500cc Japanese Grand Prix. It was for that race, rather than his wild card in '94, that he was known as The Legendary Rider.

Above Norifumi 'Norick' Abe at the 1994 Japanese Grand Prix at Suzuka where he burst onto the world stage with the most astonishing wild-card ride ever seen

AUSTRALIAN GP
PHILLIP ISLAND

ROUND 16
October 14

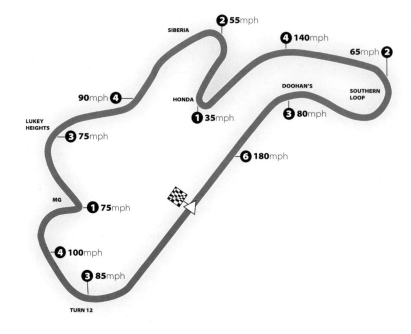

Circuit map labels:
- 55mph – SIBERIA
- 140mph
- 65mph
- 90mph
- HONDA – DOOHAN'S – SOUTHERN LOOP
- 35mph
- 80mph
- LUKEY HEIGHTS – 75mph
- 180mph
- MG – 75mph
- 100mph
- 85mph
- TURN 12

RACE RESULTS

CIRCUIT LENGTH 2.760 miles
NO. OF LAPS 27
RACE DISTANCE 74.620 miles
WEATHER Dry, 20°C
TRACK TEMPERATURE 31°C
WINNER Casey Stoner
FASTEST LAP 1m 30.801s, 109.580mph, Valentino Rossi
PREVIOUS LAP RECORD 1m 29.337s, 111.129mph, Hicky Hayden, 2005

QUALIFYING

	Rider	Nationality	Team	Qualifying	Pole +	Gap
1	Pedrosa	SPA	Repsol Honda Team	1m 29.201s		
2	Rossi	ITA	Fiat Yamaha Team	1m 29.419s	0.218s	0.218s
3	Stoner	AUS	Ducati Marlboro Team	1m 29.816s	0.615s	0.397s
4	Hayden	USA	Repsol Honda Team	1m 29.932s	0.731s	0.116s
5	Capirossi	ITA	Ducati Marlboro Team	1m 30.090s	0.889s	0.158s
6	De Puniet	FRA	Kawasaki Racing Team	1m 30.110s	0.909s	0.020s
7	Barros	BRA	Pramac d'Antin	1m 30.325s	1.124s	0.215s
8	Nakano	JPN	Konica Minolta Honda	1m 30.612s	1.411s	0.287s
9	Guintoli	FRA	Dunlop Yamaha Tech 3	1m 30.621s	1.420s	0.009s
10	West	AUS	Kawasaki Racing Team	1m 30.649s	1.448s	0.028s
11	Edwards	USA	Fiat Yamaha Team	1m 30.676s	1.475s	0.027s
12	Melandri	ITA	Honda Gresini	1m 31.078s	1.877s	0.402s
13	Checa	SPA	Honda LCR	1m 31.203s	2.002s	0.125s
14	Hopkins	USA	Rizla Suzuki MotoGP	1m 31.386s	2.185s	0.183s
15	Tamada	JPN	Dunlop Yamaha Tech 3	1m 31.595s	2.394s	0.209s
16	Vermeulen	AUS	Rizla Suzuki MotoGP	1m 31.810s	2.609s	0.215s
17	Davies	GBR	Pramac d'Antin	1m 32.043s	2.842s	0.233s
18	Elias	SPA	Honda Gresini	1m 32.442s	3.241s	0.399s
19	Roberts K.	USA	Team Roberts	1m 32.948s	3.747s	0.506s

FINISHERS

1 CASEY STONER The perfect homecoming, with a start-to-finish victory in front of a record crowd, most of whom seemed to gather in front of the podium to salute their new hero. He'd arrived at his home race with the crown already won, so could relax and enjoy the whole event.

2 LORIS CAPIROSSI Got involved in a hectic scrap with Melandri that lasted for two-thirds of the race, then took Pedrosa and Rossi in successive corners to secure second and Ducati's first one-two finish of the season.

3 VALENTINO ROSSI Lost touch with the leaders when he made a mistake coming onto the straight first time round, then set fastest lap getting back past Pedrosa. Couldn't match the Ducatis' pace when he lost some grip late on but was happy to stand on the Phillip Island podium for the tenth year in a row.

4 DANI PEDROSA Started from his first pole at Phillip Island, a circuit that's not been kind to him before, but couldn't use his number-one bike because it'd looped when he tried a practice start after warm-up. Rear grip dropped off significantly in the last ten laps, preventing him fighting for a rostrum place.

5 ALEX BARROS His best qualifying of the year, followed by a strong race. Used a hard rear tyre but afterwards thought he might have achieved a better pace with a medium.

6 RANDY DE PUNIET Another bad start from a good grid slot and a mistake put him back in 11th on lap two, then made four good passes to take a comfortable sixth and hold off Hopkins to the flag. It was Kawasaki's best-ever finish in the top class at Phillip Island.

7 JOHN HOPKINS Not a bad result from a woeful 14th in qualifying. Got one of his customary rapid starts and was up to eighth at the end of the first lap, then latched on to De Puniet and used him as a 'wind break'. Gained points on his rivals for fourth in the championship.

8 CHRIS VERMEULEN Like his team-mate suffered from lowly qualifying (16th) but rescued the weekend on race day. Came out on top of a four-man dice with Checa, West and Edwards, taking the American on the last lap.

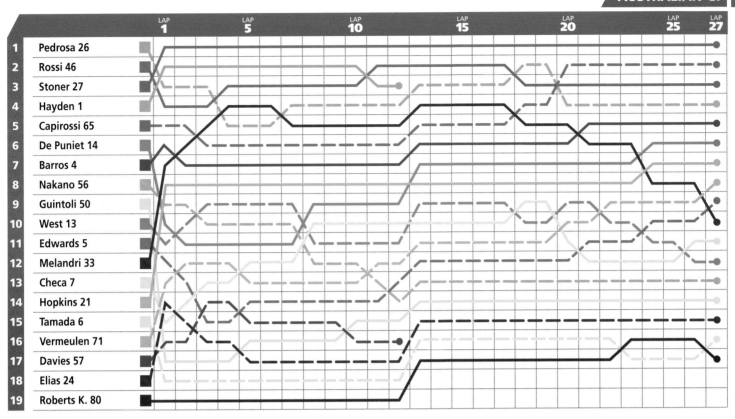

		LAP 1	LAP 5	LAP 10	LAP 15	LAP 20	LAP 25	LAP 27
1	Pedrosa 26							
2	Rossi 46							
3	Stoner 27							
4	Hayden 1							
5	Capirossi 65							
6	De Puniet 14							
7	Barros 4							
8	Nakano 56							
9	Guintoli 50							
10	West 13							
11	Edwards 5							
12	Melandri 33							
13	Checa 7							
14	Hopkins 21							
15	Tamada 6							
16	Vermeulen 71							
17	Davies 57							
18	Elias 24							
19	Roberts K. 80							

RACE

	Rider	Motorcycle	Race Time	Time +	Fastest Lap	Average Speed
1	Stoner	Ducati	41m 12.244s		1m 30.871s	108.425mph
2	Capirossi	Ducati	41m 19.007s	6.763s	1m 31.073s	108.129mph
3	Rossi	Yamaha	41m 22.282s	10.038s	1m 30.801s	107.987mph
4	Pedrosa	Honda	41m 23.907s	11.663s	1m 30.956s	107.916mph
5	Barros	Ducati	41m 31.719s	19.475s	1m 31.364s	107.577mph
6	De Puniet	Kawasaki	41m 39.557s	27.313s	1m 31.572s	107.240mph
7	Hopkins	Suzuki	41m 41.487s	29.243s	1m 31.719s	107.158mph
8	Vermeulen	Suzuki	41m 47.077s	34.833s	1m 31.920s	106.919mph
9	Edwards	Yamaha	41m 47.317s	35.073s	1m 31.987s	106.908mph
10	Melandri	Honda	41m 49.215s	36.971s	1m 30.806s	106.828mph
11	Checa	Honda	41m 49.965s	37.721s	1m 31.751s	106.796mph
12	West	Kawasaki	41m 50.670s	38.426s	1m 31.871s	106.766mph
13	Nakano	Honda	41m 59.674s	47.430s	1m 32.043s	106.384mph
14	Guintoli	Yamaha	42m 06.568s	54.324s	1m 32.479s	106.094mph
15	Elias	Honda	42m 22.715s	1m 10.471s	1m 32.492s	105.420mph
16	Tamada	Yamaha	42m 25.148s	1m 12.904s	1m 33.373s	105.319mph
17	Roberts K.	Kr212v	42m 25.264s	1m 13.020s	1m 33.594s	105.314mph
18	Hayden	Honda	18m 22.054s	15 laps	1m 30.816s	108.102mph
19	Davies	Ducati	18m 45.841s	14 laps	1m 32.302s	104.818mph

CHAMPIONSHIP

	Rider	Team	Points
1	Stoner	Ducati Marlboro Team	322
2	Rossi	Fiat Yamaha Team	230
3	Pedrosa	Repsol Honda Team	201
4	Hopkins	Rizla Suzuki MotoGP	165
5	Vermeulen	Rizla Suzuki MotoGP	160
6	Melandri	Honda Gresini	154
7	Capirossi	Ducati Marlboro Team	150
8	Edwards	Fiat Yamaha Team	115
9	Hayden	Repsol Honda Team	112
10	Barros	Pramac d'Antin	102
11	Elias	Honda Gresini	88
12	De Puniet	Kawasaki Racing Team	88
13	Hofmann	Pramac d'Antin	65
14	Checa	Honda LCR	59
15	West	Kawasaki Racing Team	58
16	Guintoli	Dunlop Yamaha Tech 3	45
17	Nakano	Konica Minolta Honda	45
18	Tamada	Dunlop Yamaha Tech 3	37
19	Roberts K.	Team Roberts	10
20	Hayden R.	Kawasaki Racing Team	6
21	Fabrizio	Honda Gresini	6
22	Nieto	Kawasaki Racing Team	5
23	Jacque	Kawasaki Racing Team	4
24	Roberts Jr	Team Roberts	4
25	Ito	Pramac d'Antin	1

9 COLIN EDWARDS Couldn't find a setting in practice so made drastic changes for race day and managed to do a faster lap time than he'd done in qualifying. Took him a while to learn the bike which, along with a major moment at the end of the first lap, meant he lost places early on.

10 MARCO MELANDRI Looked like a rostrum certainty early on and set the second-best lap of the race, but a technical problem saw him lose five places in the last ten laps. Went with medium-hard tyres against the advice of Bridgestone to try and make up for lack of feeling, and paid the price.

11 CARLOS CHECA Very fast early on but suffered from the perennial turn-in problem on fast corners and lack of pace on the big straight. Content that he got the best result possible.

12 ANTHONY WEST Another learning experience. Used up his rear tyre, especially the left side, pushing early on so had nothing left in the final laps, dropping to the back of an entertaining dice.

13 SHINYA NAKANO A third-row grid spot for the first time since the second round and a promising opening to the race were negated by the old bugbear of chatter at the front when braking for the two slow corners, Honda and MG.

14 SYLVAIN GUINTOLI His race was dictated by his tyres, which took three or four laps to get up to temperature. Then managed to gain a few places but their performance dropped off and it was a matter of hanging on for a couple of points.

15 TONI ELIAS A weekend to forget: next to last in qualifying, then suffered front tyre troubles from the start of the race and electronics problems from half-distance.

16 MAKOTO TAMADA Very happy with his bike's settings and the front tyre but severe problems with the rear Dunlop – not at full lean but in the transitions going into the corner and straightening up coming out. Corner-entry speed was severely compromised.

17 KURTIS ROBERTS Another tough race, not helped by the weather being awful throughout practice plus he hadn't been to Phillip Island for ten years. Lost out to Tamada on the last lap.

NON-FINISHERS

NICKY HAYDEN The hard-luck story of the weekend, when he saw his best chance of a win with the number-one plate disappear. Going really well on Michelin's new 16-inch rear and shadowing Stoner when his engine lost power, then stopped two laps later. The diagnosis was a dropped valve.

CHAZ DAVIES For five laps thought he was on the best bike he'd ever ridden, then the medium rear tyre started sliding. Eventually put out of the race by a problem with the fly-by-wire electronics.

MALAYSIAN GP

SEPANG INTERNATIONAL CIRCUIT

ROUND **17**

October 21

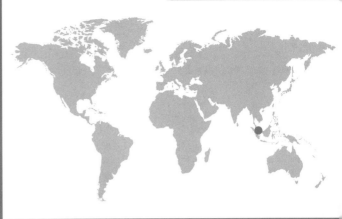

HOT STUFF

Casey Stoner and Ducati beat a new opponent – the weather – as the World Champion continued to break records

Casey Stoner didn't quite lead every inch of this race – Dani Pedrosa got in front for a few yards going into the final corner of the first lap – but the champion improvised a new line and drove past the Honda, never to be headed again. That's not to say he didn't have problems. The Malaysian weather had changed from the overcast and oppressive humidity of practice to just plain hot for race day. Twenty-one laps of Sepang is never easy, and most riders make use of 'camelback' drink holders in the race and iced towels on the grid.

Extreme conditions can produce phases in a race where the riders are only too glad to hold position and avoid extra exertion. Looking at the lap chart it would seem that this is exactly what happened. However, a lap-by-lap analysis showed that while the only changes in the top four all race long involved Melandri working his way from fourth to second, the gaps between riders oscillated in a very atypical fashion. Stoner never got a chance to take the breather he was looking for, as the temperature and humidity took their toll. Every time Casey looked to reduce his effort just a touch his pit board told him Marco Melandri was closing and he had to redouble his efforts. A couple of big moments with the front end didn't help, forcing the Aussie into altering his corner entry. It was not, he said afterwards, an easy race, and he'd found it difficult to maintain the necessary level of concentration. He even admitted to being a bit woozy on the slow-down lap and the rostrum – it really was that hot.

Melandri had a self-inflicted problem, for when he went to adjust his drinks tube on the warm-up lap he

For once Marco Melandri
didn't have any problems with
his tyres or his bike: the result
was a storming second place

only succeeded in pulling it out. It spent the first two laps spraying water on the inside of his visor when he braked, and the rest of the race flapping about in the slipstream. For once, Marco had no complaints about his machinery – quite the reverse. Despite the necessary hard braking efforts at the end of the two long straights there was no sign of the chatter that had afflicted the Gresini Honda for most of the year. Unlike the previous weekend, in Australia, Marco was also upbeat about his tyres, saying his only problem was which one of his excellent selection to choose. Amazingly, his third spot on the grid was only his second front-row start of the season, while his second place in the race gave him what was – quite unbelievably – his first-ever rostrum finish in any class at Sepang.

Dani Pedrosa also had a few nice surprises. He didn't expect his tyres to last the distance so he pressed like a demon in the early laps, hoping to make a break and then manage the situation as best he could in the closing stages. Early on he held second until, like Stoner, he had a couple of front-end slides when pressing hard and Melandri came past. However, there was no drop-off in tyre performance and grip, so Dani was able to keep the impressive de Puniet at bay and ended the race much happier with third place than might have been expected. His result may well have had something to do with the noticeable improvement in his Honda's pace over the last few races. It may have been no coincidence, either, that the new MD of HRC, Kosuke Yasutake, was in attendance to announce that the 2008

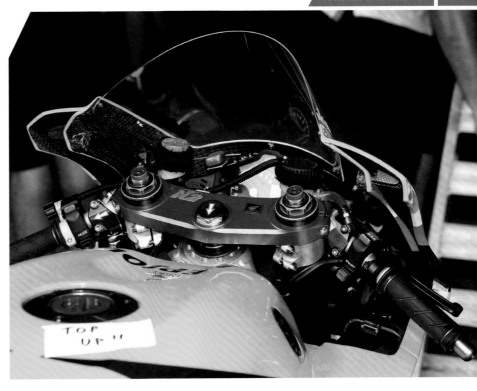

'RIDER, ENGINE AND TYRES MUST ALL BE AT 100 PER CENT'
JERRY BURGESS

Above Nicky Hayden finally got to use the wider fairing he'd been asking for all year

Below Nobu Aoki heading for points on the prototype of the 2008 Suzuki

Above Chaz Davies was back on the d'Antin Ducati

Below Story of the race – Rossi shadowing the front four

RC212V would be tested the day after Valencia and that it would have a new chassis and a new motor. It had taken them a while, but HRC were finally showing signs of being serious about hunting down Ducati.

Valentino Rossi wasn't so sure that Yamaha were

doing quite as well. In the race he turned lap times as fast as anyone except Casey, and made up a lot of ground on the front men in the early laps, but he struggled through practice and qualifying, unable to find any grip in the inconsistent conditions. It looked like he

might have been able to disguise the problem with his qualifying tyres, but a mistake on his second set meant he started from the back of the third row. If there is one thing that the change to the 800cc formula has highlighted it's that you can't give the opposition any advantage and hope to win. Jerry Burgess summed it up neatly: 'Rider, engine and tyres must all be at 100 per cent.' On these bikes, rider talent cannot overcome a lack of grip or horsepower, as used to happen with the old 990s. Sure, Rossi was fast once his Michelins had warmed up, and his crew had as usual cured a lot of his problems overnight, but he gave the leaders too much of a start.

Valentino put in a strong performance during the race, but on Friday and Saturday he had seemed out of sorts. It had become clear that the proposed one-tyre rule was dead in the water but that Rossi was, in all probability, going to get the Bridgestone tyres he so wanted. Now he wondered aloud if Yamaha needed to build a V4 to be more competitive and made the same sort of 'they must try harder' statements he'd been aiming at Michelin all year. He clearly didn't enjoy the press's questioning and decided to hold his post-race briefing in the open, in front of the Fiat team's office in the paddock. The autograph hunters enjoyed it.

While most of the paddock was preoccupied with the tyre debate, and who was manipulating whom and to what end, Casey Stoner marched on, breaking records as he went. This was his tenth win of the year. Only Doohan, Agostini and Rossi have managed more in a season. And there was still one more race to go.

CASEY BY NUMBERS

Casey Stoner's victory in Malaysia moved him above Eddie Lawson and Wayne Rainey in the list of riders with the best win rates in the modern era of motorcycle racing. This is the only way to judge riders who have competed in widely varying numbers of races and is simply the number of wins they have had taken as a percentage of the number of races they competed in. As usual, the modern era is deemed to have started in 1975, the first season that a two-stroke motorcycle won the 500cc championship (it was a Yamaha, ridden by Giacomo Agostini). The vast majority of Ago's wins were on the MV Agusta four-stroke, so he does not figure in these calculations.

The list is headed by Valentino Rossi, who has a win rate of 47.3% despite his comparative lack of success this year. At the end of the 2006 season his rate was over 50%. No-one else has got near that sort of strike rate. Mick Doohan, who competed in 137 GPs to Rossi's 131 (and counting), had a win rate of 39.4%, and is second on the list. Third is Kenny Roberts Snr with 37.9%, Freddie Spencer is fourth with 32.3%. The win in Sepang gave Casey a win rate of over 30% and put him above Rainey. His win a week previosuly in Phillip Island had taken him above Eddie Lawson.

At this stage in his career, Stoner had competed in only 33 GPs, so even one win is going to alter his win rate by a percentage point or two. However, the fact that the rest of the names in the top ten are Kevin Schwantz, Barry Sheene and Wayne Gardner shows just what an exceptional year he's had. Remember, he didn't win one race in his debut season 2006.

This was also Casey's tenth win of the year. The only men to make double figures in a single season are Mick Doohan, Giacomo Agostini and Valentino Rossi. More evidence that Casey's year hasn't just been good, it's been exceptional. If he's achieved these marks in just two seasons, what will he do over a career that will span at least the rest of the decade?

MALAYSIAN GP
SEPANG INTERNATIONAL CIRCUIT

ROUND 17
October 21

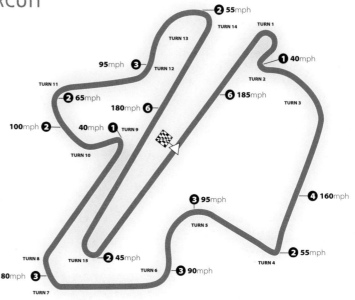

RACE RESULTS

CIRCUIT LENGTH 3.447 miles
NO. OF LAPS 21
RACE DISTANCE 72.394 miles
WEATHER Dry, 32°C
TRACK TEMPERATURE 38°C
WINNER Casey Stoner
FASTEST LAP 2m 02.108s, 101.640mph, Casey Stoner
PREVIOUS LAP RECORD 2m 01.731s, 101.696mph, Valentino Rossi, 2005

QUALIFYING

	Rider	Nationality	Team	Qualifying	Pole +	Gap
1	Pedrosa	SPA	Repsol Honda Team	2m 01.877s		
2	Stoner	AUS	Ducati Marlboro Team	2m 01.918s	0.041s	0.041s
3	Melandri	ITA	Honda Gresini	2m 01.944s	0.067s	0.026s
4	De Puniet	FRA	Kawasaki Racing Team	2m 02.107s	0.230s	0.163s
5	West	AUS	Kawasaki Racing Team	2m 02.202s	0.325s	0.095s
6	Hayden	USA	Repsol Honda Team	2m 02.225s	0.348s	0.023s
7	Vermeulen	AUS	Rizla Suzuki MotoGP	2m 02.301s	0.424s	0.076s
8	Elias	SPA	Honda Gresini	2m 02.432s	0.555s	0.131s
9	Rossi	ITA	Fiat Yamaha Team	2m 02.466s	0.589s	0.034s
10	Hopkins	USA	Rizla Suzuki MotoGP	2m 02.697s	0.820s	0.231s
11	Capirossi	ITA	Ducati Marlboro Team	2m 02.708s	0.831s	0.011s
12	Barros	BRA	Pramac d'Antin	2m 03.022s	1.145s	0.314s
13	Edwards	USA	Fiat Yamaha Team	2m 03.040s	1.163s	0.018s
14	Nakano	JPN	Konica Minolta Honda	2m 03.233s	1.356s	0.193s
15	Guintoli	FRA	Dunlop Yamaha Tech 3	2m 03.408s	1.531s	0.175s
16	Checa	SPA	Honda LCR	2m 03.525s	1.648s	0.117s
17	Davies	GBR	Pramac d'Antin	2m 04.197s	2.320s	0.672s
18	Tamada	JPN	Dunlop Yamaha Tech 3	2m 04.314s	2.437s	0.117s
19	Aoki	JPN	Rizla Suzuki MotoGP	2m 04.604s	3.727s	0.290s
20	Roberts K.	USA	Team Roberts	2m 05.404s	3.527s	0.800s

FINISHERS

1 CASEY STONER Tenth win of the season, but this time he was headed, if only for one corner. His only difficulties after that came courtesy of the conditions – temperatures well into the thirties and high humidity – and for once he found it hard to concentrate.

2 MARCO MELANDRI Delighted for once with both his bike and his tyres, keeping the pressure on Stoner throughout the race and beating the factory Honda on his satellite team machine. Overtook the Suzukis to go fourth in the championship.

3 DANI PEDROSA Started from his third consecutive pole position, expecting his tyres' performance to drop off in the closing laps, and was pleasantly surprised when they stayed with him. Both the Honda and the Michelins looked very competitive.

4 RANDY DE PUNIET Fast all weekend and very happy with his best start of the year – his only good one in 17 races, he said. Held third for a while, and was less than a second behind Pedrosa towards the flag, but a few moments on the brakes made him settle for fourth.

5 VALENTINO ROSSI A much better race than fifth place would suggest: he set the second-best lap of the day and did more overtaking than anyone. Distracted by the tyre debate, however, and never got going properly in practice or qualifying so his race was compromised by a third-row starting position.

6 TONI ELIAS A great comeback from the disappointment of Phillip Island and a boost in time for Valencia. Good qualifying, got the better of the Suzukis in the opening laps, then hung on in the heat to make it a very good day for Honda Gresini.

7 CHRIS VERMEULEN Had to work out how to cope with some vibration under acceleration in the early laps, then got involved in a race-long fight with his team-mate. Like Phillip Island, Team Suzuki finished lower than they'd come to expect.

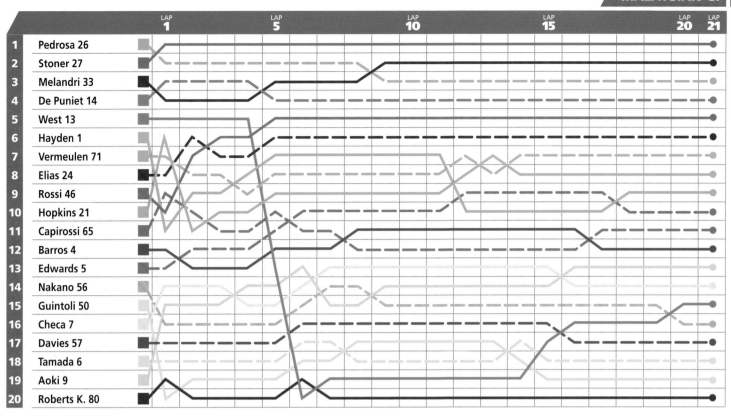

	1	Pedrosa 26
	2	Stoner 27
	3	Melandri 33
	4	De Puniet 14
	5	West 13
	6	Hayden 1
	7	Vermeulen 71
	8	Elias 24
	9	Rossi 46
	10	Hopkins 21
	11	Capirossi 65
	12	Barros 4
	13	Edwards 5
	14	Nakano 56
	15	Guintoli 50
	16	Checa 7
	17	Davies 57
	18	Tamada 6
	19	Aoki 9
	20	Roberts K. 80

RACE

	Rider	Motorcycle	Race Time	Time +	Fastest Lap	Average Speed
1	Stoner	Ducati	43m 04.405s		2m 02.108s	100.621mph
2	Melandri	Honda	43m 06.106s	1.701s	2m 02.330s	100.555mph
3	Pedrosa	Honda	43m 06.731s	2.236s	2m 02.487s	100.530mph
4	De Puniet	Kawasaki	43m 08.170s	3.765s	2m 02.503s	100.475mph
5	Rossi	Yamaha	43m 09.178s	4.773s	2m 02.303s	100.435mph
6	Elias	Honda	43m 22.072s	17.667s	2m 02.738s	99.938mph
7	Vermeulen	Suzuki	43m 25.355s	20.950s	2m 03.023s	99.812mph
8	Hopkins	Suzuki	43m 26.603s	22.198s	2m 03.112s	99.764mph
9	Hayden	Honda	43m 26.855s	22.450s	2m 02.349s	99.754mph
10	Edwards	Yamaha	43m 34.151s	29.746s	2m 03.013s	99.476mph
11	Capirossi	Ducati	43m 39.328s	34.923s	2m 03.398s	99.279mph
12	Barros	Ducati	43m 40.072s	35.667s	2m 03.421s	99.251mph
13	Aoki	Suzuki	43m 48.518s	44.113s	2m 03.975s	98.932mph
14	Checa	Honda	43m 48.891s	44.486s	2m 04.154s	98.918mph
15	West	Kawasaki	43m 54.063s	49.658s	2m 03.046s	98.724mph
16	Nakano	Honda	43m 56.131s	51.726s	2m 04.580s	98.646mph
17	Davies	Ducati	44m 03.310s	58.905s	2m 04.866s	98.378mph
18	Tamada	Yamaha	44m 04.001s	59.596s	2m 04.728s	98.353mph
19	Guintoli	Yamaha	44m 27.524s	1m 23.119s	2m 04.828s	97.486mph
20	Roberts K.	Kr212v	44m 55.365s	1m 50.960s	2m 05.251s	96.479mph

CHAMPIONSHIP

	Rider	Team	Points
1	Stoner	Ducati Marlboro Team	347
2	Rossi	Fiat Yamaha Team	241
3	Pedrosa	Repsol Honda Team	217
4	Melandri	Honda Gresini	174
5	Hopkins	Rizla Suzuki MotoGP	173
6	Vermeulen	Rizla Suzuki MotoGP	169
7	Capirossi	Ducati Marlboro Team	155
8	Edwards	Fiat Yamaha Team	121
9	Hayden	Repsol Honda Team	119
10	Barros	Pramac d'Antin	106
11	De Puniet	Kawasaki Racing Team	101
12	Elias	Honda Gresini	98
13	Hofmann	Pramac d'Antin	65
14	Checa	Honda LCR	61
15	West	Kawasaki Racing Team	59
16	Guintoli	Dunlop Yamaha Tech 3	45
17	Nakano	Konica Minolta Honda	45
18	Tamada	Dunlop Yamaha Tech 3	37
19	Roberts K.	Team Roberts	10
20	Hayden R.	Kawasaki Racing Team	6
21	Fabrizio	Honda Gresini	6
22	Nieto	Kawasaki Racing Team	5
23	Jacque	Kawasaki Racing Team	4
24	Roberts Jr.	Team Roberts	4
25	Aoki	Pramac d'Antin	3
26	Ito	Pramac d'Antin	1

8 JOHN HOPKINS Started better than his team-mate but ran off track on the second lap. Two laps later he was on Vermeulen's tail and they spent the rest of the race having their own private dice. Hopper tried a last-lap attack but the Aussie held him off.

9 NICKY HAYDEN Made a mess of the start and then found himself 'in the wrong place at the wrong time' everywhere on the first lap, which dropped him to 11th. Got back up to sixth, again using Michelin's new 16-inch rear, before spearing off track trying to pass Elias, which put him down to tenth. Good lap times to the flag, though.

10 COLIN EDWARDS Closed on the Suzukis after a bad start but couldn't get close enough to try a pass. Had been ill earlier in the week, which probably explained why he started feeling light-headed and spent the last few laps in a blur.

11 LORIS CAPIROSSI After two outings where he'd looked like the old Loris, he reverted to his form of the first half of the season and spent the race fighting with Barros, on the satellite Ducati. And this is a circuit he really likes.

12 ALEX BARROS Not at all happy with his race: the motor was well down on performance at the start of the race, and the tyres didn't work as expected either.

13 NOBUATSU AOKI Suzuki's test rider debuted the 2008 GSV-R800 and was happy with the way it performed after his team solved a number of minor problems in practice. Not a bad result for a shakedown race.

14 CARLOS CHECA Another tough race, although Sunday was better than he expected. Never found a good set-up in practice but was able to run consistent laps in the race.

15 ANTHONY WEST The best qualifying in his short MotoGP career – fifth – was wasted when he lined up on the wrong grid slot and was called in for a ride-through penalty while lying fifth. Did well to come back from 20th to maintain his record of scoring points in every race he's contested.

16 SHINYA NAKANO Another weekend plagued with front-end chatter. Lost out on the final point two laps from the end, then earned his team-manager's disapproval by throwing a hissy fit in the pit garage.

17 CHAZ DAVIES Depressed after not being able to run with the Checa group and fight for some points. Looking forward to Valencia, where he had his best result in 250s, a fifth in 2004.

18 MAKOTO TAMADA For the first time this season neither Tech 3 Yamaha rider scored a point. Makoto thought he'd found a set-up in warm-up but never had any grip in the race.

19 SYLVAIN GUINTOLI Thought he had a good set-up and tyres for the race and blamed himself for the result. 'I blew it from the very beginning, I pushed really hard but I was making too many mistakes.'

20 KURTIS ROBERTS Ran off track early on, then spent the rest of the race experimenting with settings. Did his fastest lap of the weekend with the traction control switched off.

VALENCIAN GP

CIRCUITO RICARDO TORMO

ROUND 18

November 4

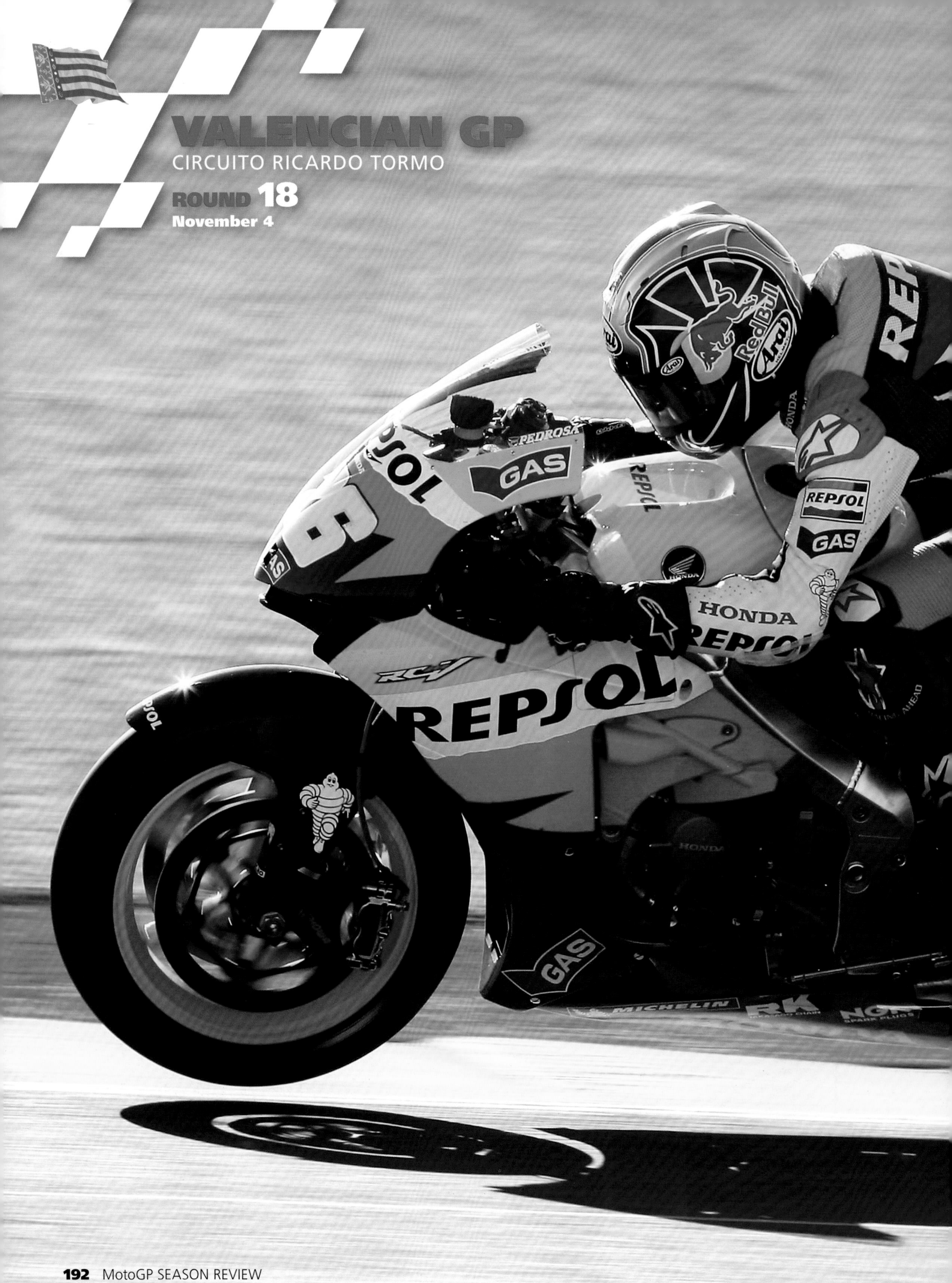

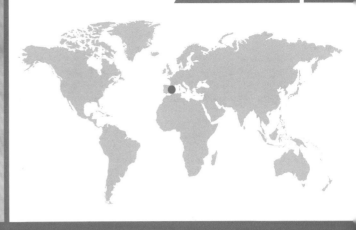

BREAKING THE PATTERN

If the final race of 2007 was an indicator of what's going to happen in 2008, the Pedrosa–Honda–Michelin combination is going to give Stoner, Ducati and Bridgestone a hard time next year

It all looked settled. Stoner had won and Rossi needed a single point to keep hold of second in the championship. The only real fight looked to be for fourth place, with Melandri and Hopkins a mere point apart and Vermeulen just four points further back. Given that Ducati took their first-ever one–two finish here in 2006, everyone expected another masterclass from Casey Stoner. Even Pedrosa's fourth consecutive pole position, the first time a Honda rider has achieved that since Rossi in '02, didn't seriously alter expectations.

What changed things was Valentino Rossi's crash early in qualifying. Turn 1 at Valencia, named after local hero 'Aspar' Martinez, is a lightly cambered right-angled left, but it's easy to run wide as the camber flattens rapidly. Valentino caught the first slide, but the Yamaha tank-slapped viciously twice more before he was thrown down the track. Rossi was obviously hurt and the bike was wrecked. The damage was remarkably similar to Vale's Assen crash last season – minor breaks in the right hand, little finger and forearm. 'He hasn't got the pain threshold of a Wayne Gardner or a Mick Doohan,' said a blasé Jerry Burgess, 'but I think he'll be alright.' And he was.

Again, the similarity to the events of Assen was striking. Valentino started from low down on the grid, took a few laps to work out how to ride with his injuries, and then started to ghost through the backmarkers. When he got up to 14th he must have thought, 'Perfect! My job is done.' Then, two laps later, came his second engine failure of the year during a race.

To make matters worse for Rossi, Dani Pedrosa had

Above John Hopkins on his way to third in front of the usual massive Valencia crowd

Below Is yours there? Just some of the 15,502 names on the Team KR bike

Opposite top Rossi signing autographs with strapped wrist; and cruising to a halt in the race

Opposite Dani on a mission

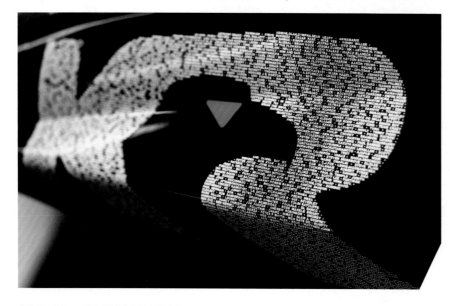

disposed of early leader Casey Stoner, and by the 18th lap, when the Yamaha broke down, he was leading by 1.5 seconds. The Spanish rider was working hard; in fact if he'd been painted red it might have been Stoner in the lead. Dani has spent the year bitterly disappointed at not having the material to contend for wins, let alone the title, and he now unleashed all that pent-up frustration in front of over 132,500 Spanish fans. Watching the Repsol Honda bouncing off the kerbs, sliding both wheels and being wrenched upright coming out of slow corners, it was difficult to remember that this was a rider who was supposed to be a clinical perfectionist with a smooth riding style derived from his days in 125s and 250s.

The new World Champion was matter of fact about

being beaten, congratulating Dani and saying he was never in as good shape as he'd looked through practice. He could stay with the Honda, but never get back the fractions of a second that Pedrosa took out of him on most laps. Casey declared himself 'reasonably happy' and was sure that he'd 'got the most out of the bike'.

The twists and turns of the Ricardo Tormo track make this the longest race of the year, at nearly 47 minutes. Pedrosa and Stoner were at the maximum for every second. Both men were surprised at the number of 1m 32s laps they could do. 'I didn't think I could have such a race,' said Dani. 'I was just thinking of the public, I had to win here.' The difference between the two, according to Casey, was that he made a couple of mistakes while Dani rode a 'faultless' race.

The man in third place was a massive 15 seconds back. After an initial skirmish with Nicky Hayden, John Hopkins marked his last race for Suzuki with his fourth podium of the year, which was also enough to take fourth place in the championship away from Marco Melandri. Dani Pedrosa didn't know he had made it to second overall until he got back to *parc fermé*. With characteristic understatement he said it was 'a nice surprise'. The Fiat Yamaha team were considerably less happy. Not only had their rider lost the runner-up position in the title race, but the squad dropped from second to fourth in the teams' championship, not just behind Repsol Honda but also Rizla Suzuki. Valentino Rossi then added to Yamaha's discomfort by criticising them loudly and publicly. He was particularly unamused at going through the injections – 'no fun' – that enabled him to race, then finding he couldn't out-drag Makoto Tamada's customer Yamaha. Then there was the final straw of the breakdown: 'I

'I DESERVED TO SCORE THREE OR FOUR POINTS; FOR SURE I DIDN'T LOOSE SECOND PLACE, YAMAHA DID.'
VALENTINO ROSSI

ONE TYRE RULE: Pt 2

After all the posturing and politicking in the wake of Dorna CEO Carmelo Ezpeleta's suggestion that MotoGP move to a single tyre supplier, it seemed that, by season's end, most people had got what they wanted.

Valentino Rossi will use Bridgestone tyres in the 2008 season, which is what he has increasingly wanted as his trust in Michelin has evaporated, but the mono-tyre suggestion has been ditched. Rossi's new team-mate, Jorge Lorenzo, will run on Michelins, as will the Tech 3 Yamaha team.

The one man who didn't get what he wanted, however, was Dani Pedrosa, who has been as vocal as Rossi in his demands. HRC's official announcement that they would continue with Michelin mentioned 'mutual respect' and 'our dignity'. That is probably code for what happened after some very high-up people in the Honda Motor Company pointed out that they had been working with Michelin since 1982, and had won 14 titles and 193 races. Honda could not be seen to end a relationship like that because of one difficult season.

If Ezpeleta's intention was to force the tyre companies into agreeing to changes in the new-for-this-season tyre allocation rule, he has succeeded. For the 2008 season each rider will be allowed 40 tyres for the race weekend, an increase of nine. This is seen as a concession by Bridgestone that will allow Michelin runners to be competitive if track temperatures differ markedly from those forecast when the allocation is chosen on the afternoon before practice starts. Only the departure of Dunlop from MotoGP after a spirited couple of years can be regarded as a bad thing for competition among the tyre companies.

Opposite Stoner's Ducati carries the *tricolore* flag livery and the words 'Made in Italy' to celebrate the factory winning the riders', constructors' and teams' championships

Right Double World Superbike Champion James Toseland assessing the task that will face him when he moves to MotoGP in 2008

deserved to score three or four points; for sure I didn't lose second place, Yamaha did.'

Lower down the order there were some emotional scenes as Carlos Checa, Makoto Tamada and Alex Barros said goodbye to MotoGP, and John Hopkins, Randy de Puniet, Marco Melandri, Toni Elias, Sylvain Guintoli, Colin Edwards and Shinya Nakano all said goodbye to their teams. Uncertainty hung over the future of Team Roberts. They had failed to come to an agreement with Honda to supply enough engines for two bikes and will only be back if they can cut a deal with Ducati. To give something back to the fans, Team Roberts came up with a novel idea. By signing up on-line anyone could have their name on the bike – the team's website had to be shut early after 15,502 people signed up to the idea – and notable participants included David Coulthard, the whole Mamola family, and a goodly percentage of the MotoGP media circus, including the author of, and several contributors to, this book. Their names were printed on decals carried on the bike's nose, tail and fairing. Lots of paddock people spent ages looking for theirs.

The 2007 Valencia GP was the 100th MotoGP race. The dominant figure for that century of races has been Valentino Rossi, who has won slightly under half of them, and his celebrity has reached far beyond the sport. This year he has faced more problems than ever before and finished lower in the championship than at any time since his first season in 125s. As MotoGP looks forward to its second century of races, the question occupying the collective consciousness of the paddock was, 'Have we seen the last of Rossi as a winning force?'

VALENCIAN GP
CIRCUITO RICARDO TORMO

ROUND 18
November 4

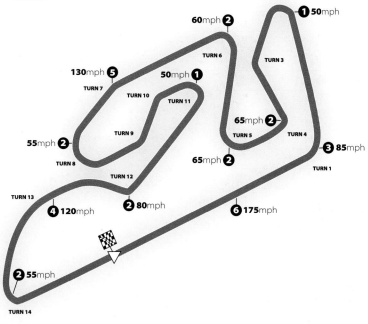

TURN 2
1 50mph
60mph 2
TURN 6
TURN 3
130mph 5
TURN 7
50mph 1
TURN 10
TURN 11
65mph 2
TURN 5
TURN 4
55mph 2
TURN 9
3 85mph
TURN 8
65mph 2
TURN 12
TURN 1
TURN 13
4 120mph
2 80mph
6 175mph
2 55mph
TURN 14

RACE RESULTS

CIRCUIT LENGTH 2.489 miles
NO. OF LAPS 30
RACE DISTANCE 74.657 miles
WEATHER Dry, 19°C
TRACK TEMPERATURE 25°C
WINNER Dani Pedrosa
FASTEST LAP 1m 32.748s, 96.600mph, Dani Pedrosa (record)
PREVIOUS LAP RECORD 1m 32.924s, 96.353mph, Loris Capirossi, 2006

QUALIFYING

	Rider	Nationality	Team	Qualifying	Pole +	Gap
1	Pedrosa	SPA	Repsol Honda Team	1m 31.517s		
2	Stoner	AUS	Ducati Marlboro Team	1m 31.603s	0.086s	0.086s
3	Hayden	USA	Repsol Honda Team	1m 31.903s	0.386s	0.300s
4	De Puniet	FRA	Kawasaki Racing Team	1m 31.963s	0.486s	0.060s
5	Guintoli	FRA	Dunlop Yamaha Tech 3	1m 32.074s	0.557s	0.111s
6	Tamada	JPN	Dunlop Yamaha Tech 3	1m 32.151s	0.634s	0.077s
7	Hopkins	USA	Rizla Suzuki MotoGP	1m 32.165s	0.648s	0.014s
8	Capirossi	ITA	Ducati Marlboro Team	1m 32.261s	0.744s	0.096s
9	Checa	SPA	Honda LCR	1m 32.273s	0.756s	0.012s
10	Melandri	ITA	Honda Gresini	1m 32.367s	0.850s	0.094s
11	Vermeulen	AUS	Rizla Suzuki MotoGP	1m 32.617s	1.100s	0.250s
12	Barros	BRA	Pramac d'Antin	1m 32.714s	1.197s	0.097s
13	Nakano	JPN	Konica Minolta Honda	1m 32.730s	1.213s	0.016s
14	Elias	SPA	Honda Gresini	1m 32.790s	1.273s	0.060s
15	Edwards	USA	Fiat Yamaha Team	1m 33.211s	1.504s	0.231s
16	West	AUS	Kawasaki Racing Team	1m 33.231s	1.714s	0.210s
17	Rossi	ITA	Fiat Yamaha Team	1m 33.290s	1.773s	0.059s
18	Roberts K.	USA	Team Roberts	1m 33.431s	1.914s	0.141s
19	Davies	GBR	Pramac d'Antin	1m 34.436s	2.919s	1.005s

FINISHERS

1 DANI PEDROSA Had to win to overhaul Rossi for second in the championship, and succeeded by hunting down the fast-starting Stoner, then edging away from the Aussie and making no mistakes, despite obviously riding on the limit for the entire distance. The first rider to win in all three classes at Valencia.

2 CASEY STONER Looked like he was running away to another win when he led the first five laps, but had no answer to Pedrosa's charge and his ability to run so many low 1m 33s laps. Seemed quite happy he'd got the best out of the bike on the day.

3 JOHN HOPKINS An emotional farewell to Suzuki with the rostrum he so wanted to achieve in front of his mother, sister, fiancée, family and friends. A good start was followed by a short duel with Hayden and then a lonely race. Confessed to being so emotional in the final laps he found it difficult to keep concentration.

4 MARCO MELANDRI A blinding start from tenth on the grid put him in a gloves-off fight with Hayden, which used up his front tyre, so took very defensive lines later to keep Nicky behind him. Hopkins was too far ahead to catch, enough to lose Marco fourth place in the championship.

5 LORIS CAPIROSSI Another emotional farewell as this was his last race for Ducati. He was the first man to get the Desmosedici on the rostrum, put it on pole and win on it. Described his race as 'not bad and not good' despite the fact his high-lean-angle style worked the tyres very hard.

6 CHRIS VERMEULEN Never had a chance to race team-mate Hopkins and Melandri for fourth in the championship, mainly because of disappointing qualifying. Worked hard to come through from 12th at the end of the first lap, but once he'd been boxed in on the first corner a rostrum was never going to be possible.

7 ALEX BARROS Possibly his last race on the world stage. Looked to be on course for fourth but a front-tyre problem

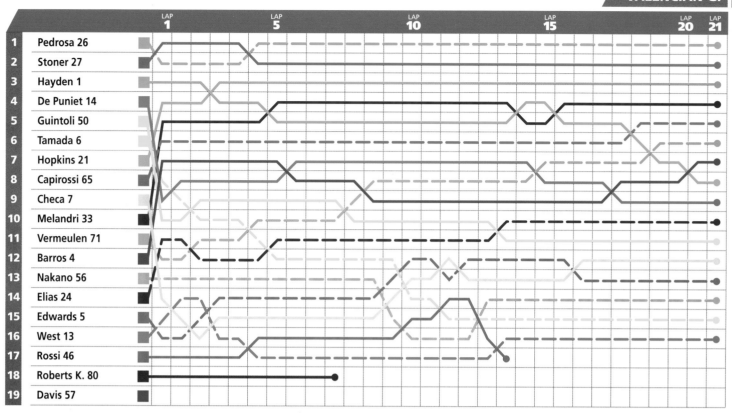

		LAP 1	LAP 5	LAP 10	LAP 15	LAP 20	LAP 21
1	Pedrosa 26						
2	Stoner 27						
3	Hayden 1						
4	De Puniet 14						
5	Guintoli 50						
6	Tamada 6						
7	Hopkins 21						
8	Capirossi 65						
9	Checa 7						
10	Melandri 33						
11	Vermeulen 71						
12	Barros 4						
13	Nakano 56						
14	Elias 24						
15	Edwards 5						
16	West 13						
17	Rossi 46						
18	Roberts K. 80						
19	Davis 57						

RACE

	Rider	Motorcycle	Race Time	Time +	Fastest Lap	Average Speed
1	Pedrosa	Honda	46m 43.533s		1m 32.748s	95.655mph
2	Stoner	Ducati	46m 48.980s	5.447s	1m 32.775s	95.470mph
3	Hopkins	Suzuki	47m 03.937s	20.404s	1m 33.064s	94.965mph
4	Melandri	Honda	47m 08.360s	24.827s	1m 33.244s	94.816mph
5	Capirossi	Ducati	47m 09.337s	25.804s	1m 33.463s	94.783mph
6	Vermeulen	Suzuki	47m 09.395s	25.862s	1m 33.598s	94.781mph
7	Barros	Ducati	47m 13.003s	29.470s	1m 33.347s	94.660mph
8	Hayden	Honda	47m 13.866s	30.333s	1m 33.435s	94.632mph
9	De Puniet	Kawasaki	47m 14.428s	30.895s	1m 33.199s	94.613mph
10	Elias	Honda	47m 14.563s	31.030s	1m 33.811s	94.608mph
11	Guintoli	Yamaha	47m 22.296s	38.763s	1m 33.759s	94.351mph
12	Checa	Honda	47m 26.039s	42.506s	1m 33.913s	94.227mph
13	Edwards	Yamaha	47m 30.105s	46.572s	1m 33.985s	94.092mph
14	Nakano	Honda	47m 33.753s	50.220s	1m 34.137s	93.972mph
15	Tamada	Yamaha	47m 40.412s	56.879s	1m 34.159s	93.753mph
16	West	Kawasaki	47m 58.902s	1m 15.369s	1m 34.802s	93.151mph
17	Rossi	Yamaha	30m 32.477s	11 laps	1m 33.696s	92.685mph
18	Roberts K.	Kr212v	16m 15.099s	20 laps	1m 34.768s	91.674mph

CHAMPIONSHIP

	Rider	Team	Points
1	Stoner	Ducati Marlboro Team	367
2	Pedrosa	Repsol Honda Team	242
3	Rossi	Fiat Yamaha Team	241
4	Hopkins	Rizla Suzuki MotoGP	189
5	Melandri	Honda Gresini	187
6	Vermeulen	Rizla Suzuki MotoGP	179
7	Capirossi	Ducati Marlboro Team	166
8	Hayden	Repsol Honda Team	127
9	Edwards	Fiat Yamaha Team	124
10	Barros	Pramac d'Antin	115
11	De Puniet	Kawasaki Racing Team	108
12	Elias	Honda Gresini	104
13	Hofmann	Pramac d'Antin	65
14	Checa	Honda LCR	65
15	West	Kawasaki Racing Team	59
16	Guintoli	Dunlop Yamaha Tech 3	50
17	Nakano	Konica Minolta Honda	47
18	Tamada	Dunlop Yamaha Tech 3	38
19	Roberts K.	Team Roberts	10
20	Hayden R.	Kawasaki Racing Team	6
21	Fabrizio	Honda Gresini	6
22	Nieto	Kawasaki Racing Team	5
23	Jacque	Kawasaki Racing Team	4
24	Roberts Jr.	Team Roberts	4
25	Aoki	Rizla Suzuki MotoGP	3
26	Ito	Pramac d'Antin	1

slowed him from the sixth lap onwards. An anti-climactic career finale for a man no-one in the paddock has a bad word for.

8 NICKY HAYDEN The 16-inch Michelin rear simply didn't work, and he was reduced to using wet-weather settings to try to get some heat into it, which meant he was spinning all race. The engine-management system leaned the carburation right off in the final laps to make sure he got to the flag; it also meant he lost three places.

9 RANDY DE PUNIET Another trademark bad start from fourth on the grid. Fought back past Barros, Tamada and Capirossi, then ran into problems with his rear tyre: had used a hard

compound expecting an advantage in the second part of the race but instead lost grip on the left side.

10 TONI ELIAS Simply lost all weekend and only got in a good rhythm when the fuel load went down later in the race.

11 SYLVAIN GUINTOLI Blazingly fast in practice on race tyres and quicker in the race itself. Suffered from gradual loss of grip on the left side of the tyre, but no more than expected in the longest race of the year. Proud of his progress during the year, and pointed to the fact he beat Edwards as proof.

12 CARLOS CHECA His final Grand Prix, ridden in severe pain – he spent Friday night in hospital undergoing tests

for what may have been an inflamed appendix. Determined to finish the race to say goodbye to his fans.

13 COLIN EDWARDS Not the way he wanted to say goodbye to the factory team. A weekend plagued by lack of grip.

14 SHINYA NAKANO The race was a microcosm of his whole season as he once again suffered from the lack of feel with the front end his style needs, so couldn't press after mid-distance.

15 MAKOTO TAMADA Enjoyed his last race in MotoGP. Happy with the performance and endurance of his tyres, even though a small drop-off in performance saw him lose contact with the group in front.

16 ANTHONY WEST Another learning experience: thought he had problems with rear grip but in fact wasn't pushing the front hard enough. 'The race for me was terrible and long.'

got worse and worse. A disappointment for the team, who don't know if they will be back next year, and for the 15,502 fans who had their names on the bike's bodywork.

NON-FINISHERS

VALENTINO ROSSI As if the qualifying crash that gave him three cracked bones in his right forearm and hand wasn't bad enough, his engine broke in the race when he was looking comfortable. The breakdown deprived him of the single point he needed to be second in the championship.

KURTIS ROBERTS Retired when a misfire at the bottom of the rev range

NON-STARTER

CHAZ DAVIES Two nasty crashes damaged his right hand badly enough to prevent his third ride on the d'Antin Ducati: the first broke fingertips, the second cracked the scaphoid in his right wrist.

WORLD CHAMPIONSHIP CLASSIFICATION

MotoGP

	Rider	Nation	Motorcycle	QAT	SPA	TUR	CHN	FRA	ITA	CAT	GBR	NED	GER	USA	CZE	RSM	POR	JPN	AUS	MAL	VAL	Points
1	Stoner	AUS	Ducati	25	11	25	25	16	13	25	25	20	11	25	25	25	16	10	25	25	20	367
2	Pedrosa	SPA	Honda	16	20	–	13	13	20	16	8	13	25	11	13	–	20	–	13	16	25	242
3	Rossi	ITA	Yamaha	20	25	6	20	10	25	20	13	25	–	13	9	–	25	3	16	11	–	241
4	Hopkins	USA	Suzuki	13	–	10	16	9	11	13	11	11	9	1	20	16	10	6	9	8	16	189
5	Melandri	ITA	Honda	11	8	11	11	20	7	7	6	6	10	16	–	13	11	11	6	20	13	187
6	Vermeulen	AUS	Suzuki	9	7	5	9	25	8	9	16	–	5	20	11	20	3	5	8	9	10	179
7	Capirossi	ITA	Ducati	–	4	16	10	8	9	10	–	20	–	10	11	7	25	20	5	11	166
8	Hayden	USA	Honda	8	9	9	4	–	6	5	–	16	16	–	16	3	13	7	–	7	8	127
9	Edwards	USA	Yamaha	10	16	–	5	4	4	6	20	10	13	5	–	7	6	2	7	6	3	124
10	Barros	BRA	Ducati	7	5	13	2	–	16	8	9	9	–	7	7	–	–	8	11	4	9	115
11	De Puniet	FRA	Kawasaki	–	3	8	8	–	–	11	10	–	–	10	8	–	–	20	10	13	7	108
12	Elias	SPA	Honda	2	13	20	–	–	10	–	4	–	–	5	9	8	16	1	10	6		104
13	Hofmann	GER	Ducati	5	–	7	7	11	5	3	7	8	7	–	–	5	–	–	–	–	–	65
14	Checa	SPA	Honda	–	10	4	6	–	–	–	5	2	2	6	10	9	–	5	2	4		65
15	West	AUS	Kawasaki	–	–	–	–	–	–	5	7	8	9	4	8	4	9	4	1	–		59
16	Guintoli	FRA	Yamaha	1	1	1	3	6	2	2	–	2	–	3	3	4	2	13	2	-	5	50
17	Nakano	JPN	Honda	6	6	3	–	–	3	1	2	4	–	4	2	6	5	–	3	–	2	47
18	Tamada	JPN	Yamaha	–	2	2	–	7	1	4	1	3	3	8	–	2	–	4	–	–	1	38
19	Roberts K.	USA	Kr212v	–	–	–	–	–	–	–	3	1	4	–	1	1	–	–	–	–	–	10
20	Hayden	ITA	Honda	–	–	–	–	–	–	–	–	–	6	–	–	–	–	–	–	–	–	6
21	Fabrizio	ITA	Honda	–	–	–	–	–	–	–	–	6	–	–	–	–	–	–	–	–	–	6
22	Nieto	SPA	Kawasaki	–	–	–	–	5	–	–	–	–	–	–	–	–	–	–	–	–	–	5
23	Jacque	FRA	Kawasaki	4	–	–	–	–	–	–	–	–	–	–	–	–	–	–	–	–	–	4
24	Roberts Jr.	USA	Kr212v	3	–	–	1	–	–	–	–	–	–	–	–	–	–	–	–	–	–	4
25	Aoki	JPN	Suzuki	–	–	–	–	–	–	–	–	–	–	–	–	–	–	–	–	3	–	3
26	Ito	JPN	Ducati	–	–	–	–	–	–	–	–	–	–	–	–	–	–	1	–	–	–	1

CONSTRUCTOR

	Motorcycle	QAT	SPA	TUR	CHN	FRA	ITA	CAT	GBR	NED	GER	USA	CZE	RSM	POR	JPN	AUS	MAL	VAL	Points
1	Ducati	25	11	25	25	16	16	25	25	20	20	25	25	25	16	25	25	25	20	394
2	Honda	16	20	20	13	20	20	16	8	16	25	16	16	13	20	16	13	20	25	313
3	Yamaha	20	25	6	20	10	25	20	20	25	13	13	9	7	25	13	16	11	5	283
4	Suzuki	13	7	10	16	25	11	13	16	11	9	20	20	20	10	6	9	9	16	241
5	Kawasaki	4	3	8	8	5	–	11	10	7	8	10	8	8	4	20	10	13	7	144
6	Kr212v	3	–	–	1	–	–	–	3	1	4	–	1	1	–	–	–	–	–	14

TEAM

	Team	QAT	SPA	TUR	CHN	FRA	ITA	CAT	GBR	NED	GER	USA	CZE	RSM	POR	JPN	AUS	MAL	VAL	Points
1	Ducati Marlboro Team	25	15	41	35	24	22	35	25	20	31	25	35	36	23	35	45	30	31	533
2	Repsol Honda Team	24	29	9	17	13	26	21	8	29	41	11	29	3	33	7	13	23	33	369
3	Rizla Suzuki Team	22	7	15	25	34	19	22	27	11	14	21	31	36	13	11	17	17	26	368
4	Fiat Yamaha Team	30	41	6	25	14	29	26	33	35	13	18	9	7	31	5	23	17	3	365
5	Honda Gresini	13	21	31	11	20	17	7	10	6	16	16	5	22	19	27	7	30	19	297
6	Pramac d'Antin	12	5	20	9	11	21	11	16	17	7	7	7	5	–	9	11	4	9	181
7	Kawasaki Racing Team	4	3	8	8	5	–	11	15	7	8	19	12	8	4	29	14	14	7	176
8	Dunlop Yamaha Tech 3	1	3	3	3	13	3	6	1	5	3	11	3	6	2	17	2	–	6	88
9	Honda LCR	–	10	4	6	–	–	–	–	5	2	–	6	10	9	–	5	2	4	65
10	Konica Minolta Honda	6	6	3	–	–	3	1	2	4	–	4	2	6	5	–	3	–	2	47
11	Team Roberts	3	–	–	1	–	–	–	3	1	4	–	1	1	–	–	–	–	–	14

2007 MotoGP World Champions

125cc

	Rider	Nation	Points
1	Gabor Talmacsi	HUN	282
2	Hector Faubel	SPA	277
3	Tomoyoshi Koyama	JPN	193
4	Lukas Pesek	CZE	182
5	Mattia Pasini	ITA	174
6	Simone Corsi	ITA	168
7	Sergio Gadea	SPA	160
8	Joan Olive	SPA	131
9	Pol Espargaro	SPA	110
10	Bradley Smith	GBR	101
11	Esteve Rabat	SPA	74
12	Michael Ranseder	AUT	73
13	Randy Krummenacher	SWI	69
14	Sandro Cortese	GER	66
15	Pablo Nieto	SPA	57

250cc

	Rider	Nation	Points
1	Jorge Lorenzo	SPA	312
2	Andrea Dovizioso	ITA	260
3	Alex de Angelis	RSM	235
4	Alvaro Bautista	SPA	181
5	Hector Barbera	SPA	177
6	Hiroshi Aoyama	JPN	160
7	Mika Kallio	FIN	157
8	Thomas Luthi	SWI	133
9	Julian Simon	SPA	123
10	Marco Simoncelli	ITA	97
11	Shuhei Aoyama	JPN	90
12	Yuki Takahashi	JPN	90
13	Roberto Locatelli	ITA	59
14	Fabrizio Lai	ITA	49
15	Aleix Espargaro	SPA	47

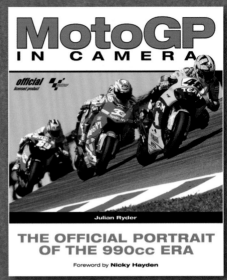

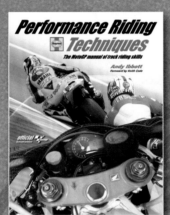

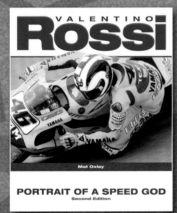
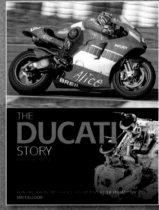
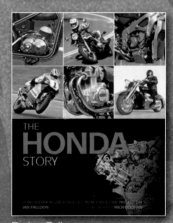
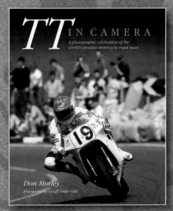

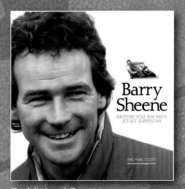

Best Location and Exclusive Privileges

Situated at the heart of the action, either directly above the Pit Lane or in a smart village area, MotoGP VIP VILLAGE puts you as close as you can get to the world's top motorcycle racers.

Privileged Parking, excellent views, race coverage on closed-circuit TV, Pit Lane Walk, Paddock Tour, Service Road Tour and complimentary Official Programme on Sunday.

The MotoGP VIP VILLAGE Game will offer all guests the chance to win the possibility to view races from the pit wall, a service road tour and one of the many licensed MotoGP products.

Best Service and Excellent Cuisine

Hospitality is of the highest quality, from the buffet breakfast in the morning to gourmet lunch and afternoon petit fours, with a complimentary bar all day.

RIDERS FOR HEALTH
BARRY COLEMAN

Ewan McGregor and
Charley Boorman visited
the Mbirikani AID Village
in Kenya, a project
supported by Riders, on
their Long Way Down

ANNUAL REPORT

There was a time when nobody involved in motorcycle racing gave much thought to African ministers of health. It just never came up, really. But times have changed. Just as 500cc two-strokes gave way to 990 four-strokes that in turn became 800s, so the question of how such ministers go about their business has become something worth thinking about. Because these days, motorcycle racing owns a rather important global health agency – it's our very own, home-grown Riders for Health.

Take Dr Paulo Garrido, for instance, minister of health for Mozambique. He is a thin, tall man and he has slightly wild-looking hair. African ministers of health can be rather guarded but Dr Garrido is not. He is often passionate and he has a glint in his eye that betrays a distinct streak of righteous anger. He doesn't like what is going on in Mozambique and what he likes least of all is that he can't bring his ministry's armoury of health services to his rural population. He just can't reach them and it drives him nuts.

We first met at a global health event in New York in 2005, when I was standing in front of a huge window in Jazz at the Lincoln Center explaining why a bright yellow Suzuki was parked in such a context in such a sexy place (well, global health folk, because that's how we are going to get healthcare to the unreached, that's why). Bill Gates, an excellent chap if you are willing to forgive him the software, was among those who came and asked, listened, nodded and moved on.

Garrido was different. He asked and listened and I got the impression his hair stood on end. 'Can you do that in Mozambique?' he asked.

We motorcyclists in global health don't mess about.
'Yes.'
'When can you start?'
Neither do some ministers of health.

We are indeed about to press the launch button. We have done the preliminary work, we are registered as a Mozambiquan non-governmental organisation (has any other sport ever done that?) and Dr Garrido is on the edge of his seat. So are we. Mozambique is a big, important country and one that sets the highest standards for development in Africa. Riders for Health is going to make a big difference to Mozambique, and vice versa.

So, since our last annual report, we added a whole

new country. But don't go away. Don't switch channels. There's more.

In last year's report we dropped all sorts of unexpected names. You can't expect to have that much fun every year, but here's an interesting one. Way back in 1991 we began a programme in Lesotho, a country in southern Africa no-one had ever heard of. They have now. *OK* magazine readers may even remember faintly that that's the country in which Prince Harry did good things in his gap year and the country in which his very own charity, Sentebale, now operates.

But global health workers know it for a much less happy reason: it has the highest HIV/AIDS infection rate in the world. And, if it's possible to imagine, it has even worse problems than that. Since we last worked there Lesotho has become a public health nightmare. And I do not use the word lightly.

Every single country in sub-Saharan Africa has an HIV problem. But there are a number of fateful factors that make Lesotho so much worse. One of them, as ever, is general isolation and distance from medical help. The other, plain and simple, is altitude. Lesotho has mountains.

There are a number of excellent agencies supporting the ministry of health in the fight against HIV. One of them is the Clinton Foundation and another is Partners in Health, who are widely regarded as the rock stars of global health (we, merely, the roadies). Not unreasonably, they reported back to the waiting world that it simply wasn't possible to reach the communities isolated in the mountains. Couldn't be done. And the infection rate in some villages up there is above 50 per cent. They were beyond reach.

Of course, we knew otherwise. Our very own Mohale Moshoeshoe (whose surname bears an uncanny resemblance to that of the founding father, King Moshoeshoe I) ran a

fleet of 47 motorcycles up there for seven years. We know those mountains and we know how to get up there – by motorcycle.

Mohale Moshoeshoe, our operations director, had to demonstrate the point to PiH so we asked them to drive as far up the mountains from their clinic at Ha Nohana as they possibly could. When the driver and the 4WD came to a complete, terminal halt, we got out and pointed to the distant peaks and passes and explained how a motorcycle would get up there and far beyond, time and time again. It was all completely outside their experience, but they believed us.

So, starting in January, we are back in Lesotho. And our principal partner there, the one who is buying the 120 bikes we will need and stumping up the running costs for two years, is none other than our old mate Sir Elton John. The Rocket Man becomes the Bike Man. The Elton John Aids Foundation has done a wonderful job in helping us get to the starting blocks and we will report just before Valencia next year on what a year in Lesotho looks like.

And of course the rest of the work goes on. The Zimbabwe programme, brilliant as ever under new leader Tsitsi Gwese, deals most adeptly with everything that fate throws at them; Gambia is as innovative and professional as ever; and Nigeria has a whole new lease of life under new local management. All spaces to watch. And of course Ewan and Charley and their fabulous team came to look at the AID Village Clinics programme in Kenya, but you know all about that because you watched the film, read the book, saw the chat shows and followed it all the way in *MCN*.

As ever, we are grateful to all our wonderful supporters and we look forward to reporting again at the end of what will almost certainly be an eventfully scary 2008. ∎

Opposite The only way health workers can do their jobs in this sort of terrain is with the help of a motorcycle

Below Mums and toddlers in rural Zimbabwe

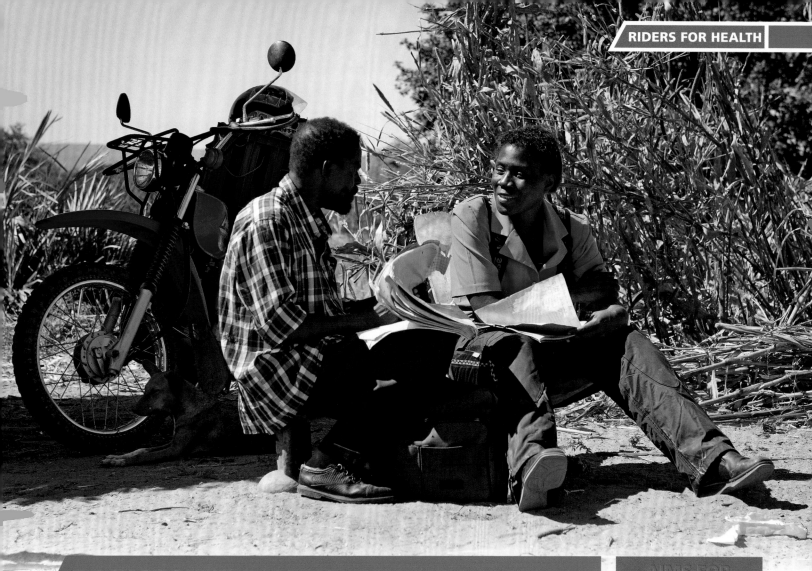

BACKGROUND BY ANDREA COLEMAN

hen Riders for Health began, the notion of systematic management of motorcycles to deliver healthcare and services to rural communities wasn't taken seriously by the development community. But we're motorcyclists and we didn't worry about mixing things up with a little initiative and an innovative solution. And we didn't worry about being different.

With the support of the motorcycle community, we managed to prove our point and today most people acknowledge that the failure to actually reach people in need has been one of the major reasons for the continuation of ill health and poverty in Africa.

We at Riders are very proud to have blossomed from MotoGP. It's the only sport that has given birth to 'something that has the potential to have an impact on the whole of the continent of Africa' (Dr Nils Daulaire, Global Health Council, Washington DC).

And there was something else that was important to Randy, Barry and me when we began Riders for Health. That was to show what great people motorcyclists are and what a wonderful sport we have! We have been very proud of the films of our work made by PBS in the USA (thank you, Brad) and by the BBC (thank you, Suzi).

Our fundraising in MotoGP has increased in 2007. In July, Riders held the first-ever Riders for Health Day at the US GP at Laguna Seca, raising £17,000. We now have events at Jerez, Barcelona, Assen, Sachsenring, Brno and Valencia as well as our own in the UK, the Day of Champions at Donington. For us, all the riders are stars on that day as they all give up their time – 125, 250 and MotoGP riders – to support the work, however busy they are. As if all that wasn't enough, Dorna allows us to auction a pair of tickets on our website for each and every MotoGP race.

With the money that we raise, we are able to support our work in Zimbabwe, the Gambia and Nigeria, and to start new programmes in Kenya and Lesotho. When we visit those programmes and see how hard the Riders staff in Africa are working, the sacrifices and hardships that health workers are enduring and the improvements that are being made with access to clean water (digging bore holes and constructing pumps), improvements in sanitation (building latrines), as a result of delivering immunisation to children, caring for TB patients in their homes, and nutrition for children under five – and much, much more – I know that everyone involved with MotoGP (and our amazing volunteers in the UK, Holland, Germany, Spain and the US) has a reason to be very proud.

The start of 2007 represented a turning point for Riders for Health as an organisation. We have been able to build on the achievements in our field programmes and upon our successes in profile-raising. In September 2006 Riders celebrated a landmark success – ten years as an independent organisation and ten million people reached with regular healthcare. Our Patron, HRH the Princess Royal, took the opportunity to drive home the link between lack of transportation and lack of development, urging the development community to unite in its efforts to make the neglect of rural communities a thing of the past.

Throughout 2007 we have been raising awareness about the important work we do with the support of the motorcycling community at international development conferences, including the Clinton Global Initiative in New York, the Global Philanthropy Forum in San Francisco and the Skoll World Forum in Oxford.

AIMS FOR 2008/2009

To manage a further 1000 motorcycles and a total of 3000 vehicles by 2009.

To increase the number of partners working in healthcare-focused organisations, particularly public health, HIV/AIDS/TB and malaria.

To enable healthcare to reach an additional ten million people, reaching a total of twenty million men, women and children by 2009.

To maintain and enhance the standards set in the Riders system, and to build the vehicle maintenance 'culture' Riders for Health established the International Academy of Vehicle Management (IAVM) in Harare, Zimbabwe, in 2002. Since its launch, over 1000 delegates – men and women – have been trained from across Africa. Bursaries are available for small organisations with limited resources.

To constantly increase support for Riders' staff working in Africa.

WIN

A FABULOUS RIDE WITH RANDY MAMOLA ON THE DUCATI TWO-SEAT MotoGP BIKE

IN ASSOCIATION WITH **RIDERS FOR HEALTH**

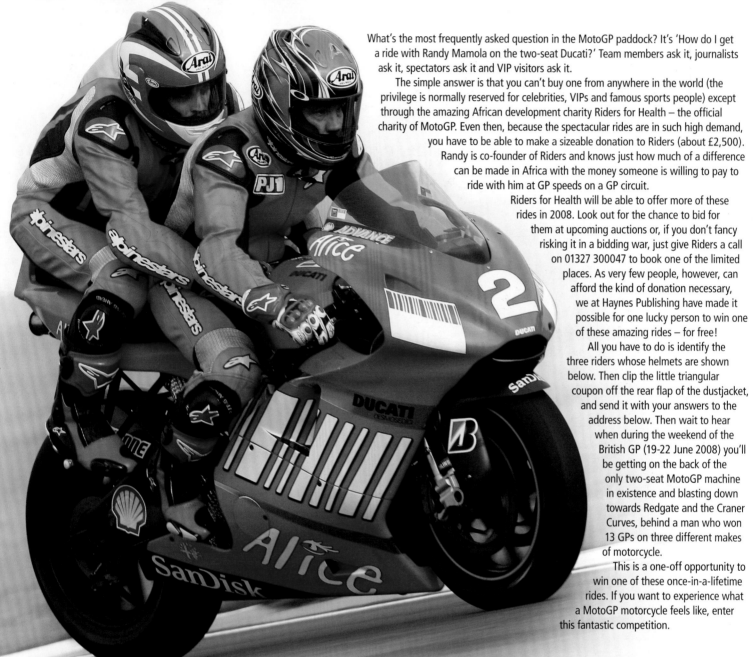

What's the most frequently asked question in the MotoGP paddock? It's 'How do I get a ride with Randy Mamola on the two-seat Ducati?' Team members ask it, journalists ask it, spectators ask it and VIP visitors ask it.

The simple answer is that you can't buy one from anywhere in the world (the privilege is normally reserved for celebrities, VIPs and famous sports people) except through the amazing African development charity Riders for Health – the official charity of MotoGP. Even then, because the spectacular rides are in such high demand, you have to be able to make a sizeable donation to Riders (about £2,500). Randy is co-founder of Riders and knows just how much of a difference can be made in Africa with the money someone is willing to pay to ride with him at GP speeds on a GP circuit.

Riders for Health will be able to offer more of these rides in 2008. Look out for the chance to bid for them at upcoming auctions or, if you don't fancy risking it in a bidding war, just give Riders a call on 01327 300047 to book one of the limited places. As very few people, however, can afford the kind of donation necessary, we at Haynes Publishing have made it possible for one lucky person to win one of these amazing rides – for free!

All you have to do is identify the three riders whose helmets are shown below. Then clip the little triangular coupon off the rear flap of the dustjacket, and send it with your answers to the address below. Then wait to hear when during the weekend of the British GP (19-22 June 2008) you'll be getting on the back of the only two-seat MotoGP machine in existence and blasting down towards Redgate and the Craner Curves, behind a man who won 13 GPs on three different makes of motorcycle.

This is a one-off opportunity to win one of these once-in-a-lifetime rides. If you want to experience what a MotoGP motorcycle feels like, enter this fantastic competition.

TO ENTER THIS FABULOUS COMPETITION, ALL YOU HAVE TO DO IS IDENTIFY THESE THREE RACERS

Write your answer on a postcard (or the back of a sealed envelope), stick on the coupon from the back flap of this book's dustjacket, add your name and address, and send to:

Ducati Two-Seater MotoGP Competition, Haynes Publishing (Books Division), Sparkford, Yeovil, Somerset BA22 7JJ

To find out more about Riders for Health and what is being achieved with motorcycles for healthcare delivery in Africa, read the article by CEO Barry Coleman (page 204) and visit

www.riders.org